Fundamentals of Production/Operations Management

F O U R T H   E D I T I O N

Fundamentals of Production/Operations Management

FOURTH EDITION

Harold E. Fearon
William A. Ruch
Department of Purchasing,
Transportation, Operations
Arizona State University

C. David Wieters
Department of Management
New Mexico State University

WEST PUBLISHING COMPANY
St. Paul • New York • Los Angeles • San Francisco

Copyediting: Carol Danielson

Composition: Parkwood Composition Services, Inc.

Cover Photo: Pete Turner, The Image Bank

COPYRIGHT ©1979, 1983, 1986 By WEST PUBLISHING COMPANY
COPYRIGHT ©1989 By WEST PUBLISHING COMPANY
50 W. Kellogg Boulevard
P.O. Box 64526
St. Paul, MN 55164-1003

All rights reserved
Printed in the United States of America
96 95 94 93 92 91 90 89   8 7 6 5 4 3 2 1
Library of Congress Cataloging-in-Publication Data

Fearon, Harold E.
  Fundamentals of production/operations management.

  Includes index.
  1. Production management. I. Ruch, William A.
II. Wieters, David C. III. Title.
TS155.F497 1988   658.5   88-20752
ISBN 0-314-47028-X

Contents

Figures, Exhibits, and Tables ... viii
Preface ... xi

CHAPTER 1
The Production Function ... 1

Products Equals Goods and Services ... 3
Why Study Production/Operations Management? ... 4
The Production Function ... 5
Production/Operations Management and Other Business Functions ... 8
History of Production/Operations Management ... 9
The Future of Production/Operations Management ... 12
Functions of Production/Operations Management ... 14
Types of Manufacturing ... 18
Types of Services ... 19
Goals of Production/Operations Management ... 21
Careers in Production/Operations Management ... 23
Key Concepts ... 26
References ... 26
Discussion Questions ... 27

CHAPTER 2
Product Design and Development ... 29

Product Life Cycle ... 30
Product Strategy ... 32
Research and Development ... 34
Product Design ... 36
Designing Services ... 42
Product Description ... 42
Evaluating Research and Development ... 46
Key Concepts ... 49
References ... 49
Discussion Questions ... 49
Problems ... 51

CHAPTER 3
Location, Layout, Work Study, and Measurement — 53

- Facilities Location — 54
- Facilities Layout — 60
- Work Study — 70
- Work Measurement — 77
- Key Concepts — 82
- References — 82
- Discussion Questions — 83
- Problems — 84

CHAPTER 4
Forecasting, Planning, and Scheduling Production — 85

- Forecasting Demand — 85
- Planning for Production — 92
- Scheduling Production — 95
- PERT/CPM — 105
- Key Concepts — 109
- References — 109
- Discussion Questions — 110
- Problems — 111

CHAPTER 5
Purchasing/Materials Management — 113

- Objectives of Purchasing/Materials Management — 114
- Importance of the Purchasing Function — 117
- Organization of Purchasing/Materials Management — 123
- Purchasing Prerogatives — 128
- The Standard Purchasing System — 128
- Recognition of Need — 130
- Description of Need — 130
- Source Selection — 133
- Determining Price — 137
- Preparation of the Purchase Agreement — 140
- Follow-up and Expediting — 141
- Receipt and Inspection — 142
- Invoice Clearance and Payment — 142
- Maintenance of Records — 143
- Current and Future Developments — 143
- Key Concepts — 147
- References — 147
- Discussion Questions — 148

CHAPTER 6
Inventory Management   **149**

The Functions of Inventories	149
Economics of Inventory Management	151
Economic Order Quantity Model	154
Safety Stocks and Uncertainty	159
MRP and Inventory Management	163
Inventory in Repetitive Manufacturing or the Pursuit of Stockless Operations	166
Physical Care of Inventories	168
Key Concepts	170
References	170
Discussion Questions	170
Problems	171

CHAPTER 7
Quality Management   **173**

Product Quality	174
The Meaning of Quality	174
Total Quality Control	176
Factors Affecting Quality	179
Quality Costs	182
Statistical Quality Control	187
Organization for Quality Control	194
The Growing Importance of Quality	196
Key Concepts	196
References	197
Discussion Questions	197

GLOSSARY	201
INDEX	213

Figures, Exhibits, and Tables

Figures

1-1	The Production Function	6
1-2	A Typology of Services	20
2-1	Stages of the Product Life Cycle	31
2-2	Bill of Materials for a Yo-Yo	44
2-3	Bill of Materials for a Car Wash	44
2-4	Route Sheet for a Yo-Yo	45
2-5	Break-Even Time Model	47
3-1	Total Costs for Alternative Locations A, B, C, and D Compared to Volume	58
3-2	Matrix for Transportation Method of Linear Programming	60
3-3	Solution Matrix for Proposed Site A	60
3-4	Solution Matrix for Proposed Site B	61
3-5	Process Layout Showing Movement of Two Different Products	62
3-6	Product or Line Layout Showing Movement of Two Different Products	63
3-7	Layout by Process Versus Cellular Layout	64
3-8	Travel Chart Used in Layout Planning	66
3-9	Process Chart	73
3-10	Flow Diagram	74
3-11	Assembly Chart (Garden Hoe)	75
3-12	Multiple-Activity Chart	76
3-13	Operation Chart	78
3-14	Calculation of Standard Time	80
3-15	Calculation of a Performance Rating	81
4-1	Illustrations of Seasonal, Trend, Cycle, and Random Time-Series Fluctuation Cycles	88
4-2	Multiplicative Model for Trend and Seasonals	91
4-3	The Detailed Schedule	96
4-4	Frame Bill of Materials	98

4-5	MRP Time-Phased Inventory Records	99
4-6	Gantt Chart	103
4-7	PERT Network	107
5-1	Return-on-Assets Factors	121
5-2	Multidivision Organization Structure for Purchasing	125
5-3	Organization Structure for Materials Management	127
6-1	Inventory Levels over Time	155
6-2	Inventory Costs With and Without Quantity Discounts	156
6-3	Inventory Levels with Replenishment Spread over Time	158
6-4	Safety Stock Determination Based on Historical Demand	161
6-5	Contrast Between Uniform and Lumpy Demands on Inventory	162
6-6	Time-Phased Inventory Record	165
7-1	Behavioral and Technical Factors Affecting Quality	181
7-2	Quality-Cost Relationships	186
7-3	Sampling Errors	189
7-4	Operating-Characteristics Curve	190
7-5	Effect of Changing the Acceptance Number	191
7-6	Effect of Changing the Sample Size	192
7-7	P-Chart	194
7-8	$\bar{X}$ and R-Chart	195

Exhibits

4-1	Forecast Model Selection Criteria	87
4-2	Job-Shop Priority Scheduling Rules	102
7-1	Costs of Quality	184

Tables

1-1	Production Function for Selected Firms	2
1-2	Career Tracks in Production/Operations Management	24
3-1	Weighted Factors Analysis of Locations	57
4-1	Methods of Smoothing Random Variations	90
4-2	PERT Data on Activities: Precedence and Time Estimates	106
5-1	Cost of Materials—Value of Industry Shipments Ratios for Manufacturing Firms, 1985	118

Preface

Production/operations management is the art and science of producing things for consumption. The creation of manufactured goods and services—which we refer to collectively as products—is fundamental to the survival and success of any business organization. It follows, therefore, that the concepts of POM are fundamental to the education of business managers and students alike.

This book was written with the belief that an understanding of the managerial issues involved in production can help prepare both college students and business executives to cope with competitive pressures. The teachings of POM need not use a highly mathematical approach; such an approach tends to distance students and managers from the problems they generally face. Nor should the subject be limited to applications in manufacturing. For those who need them, advanced texts and specialized courses delve more deeply into that field. Our purpose is twofold: to impart a broad understanding of production/operations management for students majoring in other areas, and to build a solid foundation of knowledge for those who have chosen this field as their primary area of study.

In this edition, the fourth, we have added new developments, concepts, and ideas, and we have broadened the application of the material to treat the service sector more explicitly. We have tried to make the book more "teachable" for the instructor, more readable for the student, and more relevant to the problems that manufacturing and service organizations face today.

We are indebted to our colleagues in the academic and business communities who have provided constructive advice for this edition. We thank the faculty and graduate students in the Department of Purchasing, Transporation, Operations at Arizona State University and in the Department of Management at the University of New Mexico who provided help and support. And special thanks go to Judy Litt, Jackie Wilcock, and Carol Ketchum for facilitating the manuscript preparation. The authors take full responsibility for the book's content.

The Authors

Fundamentals of Production/Operations Management

FOURTH EDITION

CHAPTER 1

The Production Function

What products does your organization produce? If you work for an automobile manufacturer, the answer seems obvious: automobiles! With a little more thought, you might add trucks, motor homes, and spare parts. With even more thought, the list could get longer: warranties, financing services, leasing arrangements, and a variety of other intangible products.

Lesson One: Besides services, almost all organizations produce a mix of physical goods and an array of related services. Rare is the firm that claims only one output. Fast-food restaurants produce hamburgers, but they are judged also on the speed and friendliness with which they serve them. Even universities produce products. If you currently are a student, are you the product being produced—as raw material molded into a finished unit; or are you a customer buying a service called education? Either way you see yourself, the output of the university is an educated college graduate.

In simplest terms, production/operations management (POM) is the study of the conversion of inputs into outputs in any organization. It deals with manufactured goods and with services. It includes large and small firms, profit and nonprofit organizations. With some modifications it applies to all government functions, bureaus, and agencies. Table 1-1 provides a sampling of organizations from different industries and lists the inputs, demand, conversion process, and outputs for each. Each of these terms and their interrelationships are explored in greater depth in the remainder of this chapter.

This book describes the fundamentals of those areas that make up production/operations management. It discusses the importance of each area and

Table 1-1
Production Function for Selected Firms

Organization	Basic Inputs	Demand	Conversion	Products
Automobile manufacturer	Labor, capital, material, energy	Forecasts	Fabrication and assembly	Autos and other vehicles; services such as financing and warranties
Fast-food restaurant	Labor, capital, material, energy	Counter customer	Cooking and preparation	Sandwiches, fries, drinks; friendly, efficient service
Hospital	Labor, capital, material, energy	Ill or injured people	Health care	Healthy people
University	Labor, capital, material, energy	Applications for enrollment	Teaching and research	Graduates and new knowledge (articles, books, papers, etc.)
Bank	Labor, capital, material, energy	Customer requests	Financial analysis, decision making, record keeping	Loans, checking accounts, savings plans
City Parks and Recreation Department	Labor, capital, material, energy	Voter preferences, enrollments, visitations	Construction and maintenance of parks; operation of programs	Softball leagues special events, park facilities
Home builder	Labor, capital, material, energy	Customer order	Construction activities	Houses
Airline	Labor, capital, material, energy	Ticket sales, shipping requests	Aircraft scheduling, operation, and maintenance	Transported freight and passengers; friendly service

shows how the various functions fit together to create an effective, efficient production system. It provides the key elements of each subfunction but does not attempt to explore all the details and nuances of each area. In-depth discussions of the tools, techniques, and issues in POM can be found in more advanced texts, some of which are listed at the end of each chapter.

Products Equals Goods and Services

Production and operations management often is mistakenly associated only with manufactured goods. Indeed, today's instruction in POM traces its roots to college courses titled "Production Management," "Manufacturing Management," and "Factory Management." Yet the addition of the word *operations* signifies that many of the concepts originally developed in and for the factory apply equally well to service firms, not-for-profit organizations, and government agencies.

All nonmanufacturing organizations perform the same basic functions. They acquire inputs of people, materials, and equipment, convert them into outputs (in this case, services), and deliver them to their customers. This is true for banks, hospitals, public utilities, restaurants, counseling services, state parks, military bases, barber shops, bookstores, trucking firms, libraries, health clubs, and, of course, universities.

Each firm must respond to a demand or customer order in some form. In many firms, especially large manufacturers, products are produced to meet forecasts of anticipated customer needs. In other cases, notably most services, the firm must wait for the customer order before the product can be completed. Consider three examples: buying a bicycle, contracting for landscaping services, and using a hospital emergency room. The bicycle manufacturer determines the design, color, and other features of the unit, produces the bicycle months in advance, and then offers it for sale. The landscaping service, in spite of its title, deals with physical products that can be held in inventory until a customer order allows the trees and plants to be arranged at a particular site. The hospital emergency room must be prepared to respond quickly and effectively to any medical emergency that arises at any time.

The nature of the demands in these three situations is different. In one case, the customer must be present for the product to be completed. In the other two cases, the action can be done by phone or through an agent. Similar contrasts can be drawn among these three in terms of timing, control over the specifications of the product, and other aspects of demand. As we will see later in the book, these situations differ also in the relative mix and importance of POM areas such as quality, scheduling, and inventory control.

Up to this point and throughout the book, we use the term **product** to refer to a manufactured good or to a service. Bicycles, automobiles, furniture, food products, and books are all products. So too are checking accounts, haircuts, counseling sessions, health-club packages, sporting events, and career training programs. The term **product** is a more efficient way of saying the cumbersome phrase *goods and services*. More importantly, it helps us deal with manufacturing and service firms within the same framework.

With services accounting for a larger and larger portion of business activity, it is important that principles and practices proven beneficial in manufacturing be used to make the provision of services more effective and efficient. Scheduling patients in the hospital emergency room example can be accomplished using waiting-line methods (queueing theory) just as these methods are used to schedule jobs in a machine shop. Assigning costs to waiting patients is more difficult than for batches of materials, but it can be done. The challenges may be greater because of the less tangible nature of the services, but the potential rewards make the effort worthwhile.

Why Study Production/Operations Management?

The study of production/operations management has sometimes suffered from a bad reputation among college students. The operations part of any organization is neither as obvious nor as well understood as marketing, advertising, personnel, and finance. Operations management has been mistakenly believed to be a highly quantitive field that applies only to the running of factories. In part, this erroneous view of operations as a technical field rather than as a key part of the management of any firm accounts for the competitive problems the United States is experiencing in international product markets. In this text, the emphasis is on the **management** of operations. Well-managed organizations are more competitive than poorly managed ones.

The first reason to study POM, therefore, is to develop a level of expertise in operations management graduates. The success of all types of organizations depends on the knowledge and talent of its managers.

Second, many students find that the field of production/operations management can be more intriguing and exciting than their initial impressions led them to believe. Production is where the action is in most business firms. The operation and control of the production process—whether producing hamburgers, automobiles, or insurance policies—is demanding work, requiring talent, skill, and a desire to get the job done right and on time. The people who manage the direct work process derive great satisfaction from seeing the results of their efforts in terms of goods shipped and services delivered.

A third reason for studying production/operations management relates to the laws of supply and demand. At present, more opportunities than graduates exist in this field. As the need continues to grow in service industries for people who can plan, schedule, and control, the market for POM graduates will remain stable. In many universities, POM graduates receive more job offers at higher salaries than any of their peers.

Not everyone should become a POM major, but all business students should be aware of the nature of each of the major subfunctions of business. The fourth reason for studying POM, then, is to complete an education that would be seriously lacking without it. Knowledge of the special problems and issues in POM enhances the effectiveness of the accountant, the marketing manager, the financial analyst, or the personnel specialist. An integrated-systems approach based upon an understanding and appreciation of all business functions is the goal of every organization.

The Production Function

Every organization has a production function, just as it has a finance function and a marketing function. Finance is concerned with the acquisition and use of funds, while marketing is focused on selling and distributing the products and services. The production function is the third side of this triangle, for it uses the funds acquired by finance to buy raw materials, machines, and labor, and converts these into products and services that marketing can sell.

Inputs

Part of the production function concerns the acquisition of inputs, as illustrated in figure 1-1. Any product or service that is created requires some combination of materials, machines, and people. General Motors employs hundreds of thousands of people, ranging from unskilled or semiskilled workers to top executives. GM uses billions of dollars worth of plants, machines, and tools and purchases materials (steel, glass, fabric, plastic, etc.) at the rate of more than 100 million dollars a day to produce the millions of cars the world wants. One of their suppliers, Small Parts, Inc., employs about fifty workers and a dozen machines to make tiny metal parts out of strip steel. The two firms are vastly different in size and scope, yet each draws from the same basic categories of inputs to produce its unique outputs.

The list of inputs is almost endless. The people category includes unskilled, semiskilled, and skilled workers; clerical personnel; secretaries; technicians; supervisors; professionals (doctors, teachers, etc.); part-time students; supervisors; engineers; artists; accountants; and executives.

Similarly, materials and equipment come in all forms, sizes, and shapes. A critical part of the production function is the acquisition of the proper raw materials, tools, machines, and other supplies and equipment to permit the efficient and effective operation of the firm. The lack of even low-cost parts can idle hundreds of workers and their equipment.

Acquisition of capital inputs (land, buildings, and machinery) is generally done at high levels in the organization. A firm frequently enlists specialists in real estate, finance, law, and capital budgeting to work as a team to decide on locations and equipment for new facilities. Large motel chains, fast-food firms, and many retail houses illustrate this situation. Where these acquisitions are less frequent, a firm may designate key executives to act as an ad hoc committee to work with outside consultants in reaching a decision.

Acquisition of people is the primary responsibility of the personnel department. Recruiting, interviewing, testing, selecting, hiring, placing, evaluating, compensating, and terminating are subfunctions of this activity. The personnel department provides a service to the rest of the firm by arranging for the proper workers when and where they are needed. Trained personnel specialists can

6 Fundamentals of Production/Operations Management

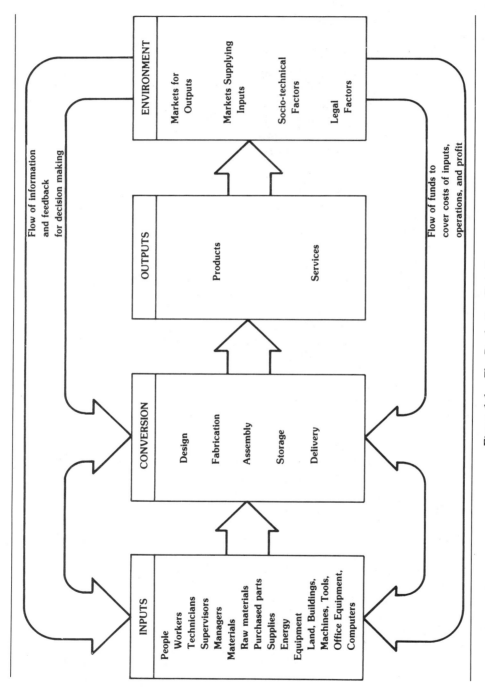

Figure 1-1. The Production Function

perform this task more effectively and efficiently than could each department duplicating these functions.

Both manufacturing firms and service organizations (including government) rely on purchasing managers to obtain material inputs, including raw materials, purchased parts, and supplies. Purchasing managers, skilled in the techniques of buying and knowledgeable about the products for which they are responsible, buy the proper raw materials for a hospital or a restaurant; this task is no less important than in a manufacturing firm.

The purchasing department staff may constitute a small percentage of the organization's personnel, yet, because of the dollars involved, it exerts a major influence on the profit-making ability of the firm. Chapter 5 examines this purchasing function in greater depth.

Conversion

The conversion process is the merging of time and place and the transformation of inputs to make them more usable and accessible to customers. The customers may be the final consumers, or they may be other business firms in the chain between natural resources and final users. Because decisions of time and place are handled primarily by the marketing and distribution functions of the firm, the emphasis in conversion is on form of the output—that is, the creation and production of goods and services.

A useful distinction can be made between the *technology* of transformation and the *methodology* of transformation. Technology refers to the scientific principles applied to convert inputs to outputs; often, this is unique within an industry. For example, the petroleum industry applies its technology—derived from chemistry, physics, hydraulics, and other sciences—to convert crude oil into gasoline, aviation fuel, asphalt, tar, paint, and many other salable products. No other industry uses exactly the same technology.

A dairy, on the other hand, begins with raw milk and produces whole milk, skim milk, butter, cheese, ice cream, and other products. The technology in a dairy is quite different from that of an oil company, yet the processes are similar enough to allow much of the same methodology to be applied. The problems of scheduling, controlling, storing, shipping, and generally *managing* the two processes are similar.

This text will concentrate on the methodology of transformation and will draw examples from specific technologies. Principles of scheduling can be discussed and then applied to either a machine shop or the receiving ward of a hospital. Techniques of inventory control apply equally well to inventories of fresh vegetables or auto parts. Although the examples vary, the reader is encouraged to apply the principles and techniques in each chapter to as many organizations or processes as possible. Laundries, libraries, fraternities, bicycle-repair shops, government bureaus, real estate agencies, car washes, liquor stores, banks, barber shops, medical offices, auto agencies, and even universities have transformation processes to which the tools and techniques of POM can be applied.

Outputs

It is easy to recognize that the output of an automobile manufacturer is automobiles, the output of a restaurant is meals, and the output of a university is graduates. Very few firms, however, produce only one output. As noted earlier, the auto manufacturer produces cars with an array of body styles, colors, and optional equipment. It also may produce trucks, industrial vehicles, refrigerators, and railroad engines. In addition to the physical products, the firm also may provide many services, such as repairs, delivery, setup, and financing.

Two outputs in the firm's array may complement or supplement each other to the firm's advantage. In other cases, outputs may conflict, to the detriment of profitability and effectiveness. For example, a firm that produces razor blades may benefit if it also produces razors, but a travel agency probably would not benefit from also selling TV sets.

When manufacturing a product, the firm begins with raw materials, feeds them through a conversion process, and ends up with a finished product ready to sell. In the decision-making process, however, the time sequence of the steps is reversed. The firm begins with the design of the output, forecasts sales, and then uses the specifications and projections it obtains to set up the conversion process and acquire inputs. Thus, the desired output is the goal from which all other decisions are derived.

Environment

Every business operates in an environment that provides markets for the products it produces, as well as markets from which the firm buys inputs. In addition, the environment provides sociotechnical and legal constraints and guidelines within which the firm must operate if it is to be law abiding, socially responsible, and successful.

To make the model complete, two feedback loops are necessary. First, the sale of goods and services produces the flow of dollars back to the firm so it can purchase additional inputs, pay operating costs, and generate profits for owners. Second, a constant flow of information from the environment to the firm allows management to employ new technology and respond to changing needs and desires of customers.

Production/Operations Management and Other Business Functions

The production/operations function of any business interacts closely with each of the other key functions of the organization. In concert, these functions—and their interactions—determine the success or failure of an organization. One company may be called a "marketing organization," another an "accounting firm"; yet each must integrate the functions of finance and accounting, human resources (personnel), marketing, and production/operations. Although often treated separately for purposes of analysis and study, the functions are merged into a total system in an organization; dividing lines between functions are not easy to see in the real world. It is important, therefore, not only to examine the production/operations function but to keep in mind critical interactions with other functions.

Production/operations employs the capital resources acquired by the finance function. It converts funds into equipment, tools, facilities, and inventories to produce products. The decision to replace an old machine with a new one is not solely a technical decision, nor is it solely a financial one; it is a combination of the two. The decision is made using capital budgeting analysis based on information concerning the capacity of the machine and its relationship to other phases of the production process. For example, the new machine may produce at a higher speed, but it may also require more maintenance, produce more scrap, or use more energy.

Accounting data are needed to make this equipment decision as well as most other decisions in the production/operations function. Inventory policies, for example, depend upon the value of the item in stock. The knotty problem of determining the value of the in-stock unit, either purchased or manufactured internally, depends on sound accounting principles applied through an accurate, timely management-information system to evaluate the effects of past production/operations decisions and to provide input to future decisions.

Production/operations cannot function without people. The human resources function is to recruit and train workers to fill positions within the production process according to the job design and skill assessments performed by work-study analysts. As changes—such as overtime, adding a shift, employing newer technologies, or redesigning the product—are made in the production process, they must be coordinated with the human resources function. To ensure a smooth transition as the change takes place, this coordination should occur during the planning phase.

The interaction between production/operations and the marketing function is both complex and critical. It is simplistic to say that marketing sells what production produces, or vice versa. Actually, marketing research gathers information that guides the design or redesign of products. A marketing forecast of sales potential must be integrated with a production forecast of capacity to provide a realistic production schedule. Marketing promotes and sells; production produces and delivers. If any link of that chain is weak, the entire organization suffers. Many cases can be found of firms with good production *and* good marketing functions that have failed because of a lack of coordination between the two.

History of Production/Operations Management

Production/operations management began when the first crude tool was produced. In the ensuing years, we have reached the point where nearly everything we touch is a manufactured or processed product. Improvement in *performing* manufacturing tasks has been a gradual, if not a consistent, trend. But the systematic *study* of production is a relatively recent phenomenon, confined mainly to the last two hundred years and concentrated in the last eighty.

We think of mass production as a twentieth-century concept, yet assembly lines were in use in the early fifteenth century. Venetian shipbuilders equipped their fighting galleys by towing them through a water channel between warehouses where the provisions and equipment were stored. They eventually reached a production level of equipping a ship every thirty-six minutes.

In the fifteenth century, no mass markets existed, nor were there advertising, distribution networks, or other support services. Measurement technology and manufacturing methods were not yet sufficiently precise to produce interchangeable parts. Mass production, therefore, was found only in rare, isolated instances; manufacturing at this time was performed predominantly by independent artisans.

Factories began to appear in the early eighteenth century in the textile industry. Later, factories were built to accommodate other types of manufacturing. In 1776, Adam Smith described, in *The Wealth of Nations,* the subdivision of labor employed in manufacturing straight pins. Later scholars, such as Charles Babbage, developed and refined Smith's theories of work organization. From 1700 to 1900, the industrial revolution flourished, and students of this field attempted to describe the new developments and provide theoretical foundations for existing practices. Not until the twentieth century were scholars able to develop theories based upon research and experimentation and then to implement them in business.

Frederick W. Taylor was one of the first people to study business using a scientific approach. In the early 1900s, business knowledge was not yet organized into principles. Taylor studied business by beginning with basics, experimenting and adding building blocks to form a cogent body of knowledge. Many of the principles of management he developed are still being taught and used today.

Other pioneering scholars such as Frank and Lillian Gilbreth advanced Taylor's work in their motion and time study. Industrialists like Henry Ford applied these principles to mass production and built empires from which flowed manufactured goods that many could afford.

The early twentieth century was a period of rapid growth and change in business. Factories were becoming more efficient, even though working conditions in many of them were not yet entirely humane. Upton Sinclair described the evils of this capitalistic system in his exposé of the meat-packing industry, *The Jungle.* The working conditions he described were horrifying, but rather than repelling people from capitalism, his writing led to government regulations (such as the Pure Food and Drug Act) and fueled the labor movement to develop powerful industrial unions to protect workers' rights. Before the middle of the twentieth century, human-relations research had begun to develop principles of effective utilization, rather than exploitation, of workers.

Many tools and techniques developed in the first half of this century have enhanced the efficiency and effectiveness of business organizations. In 1915, F. W. Harris developed the economic order quantity formula that now is a fundamental concept in inventory control. A decade later, several individuals, including H. F. Dodge, H. G. Romig, and W. A. Shewhart, applied probability theory to quality control and introduced the concept of assessing quality based on a random sample. Waiting-line theory was born, and work sampling was first applied. On other fronts, the first experiments in work-group behavior were laying foundations for human-relations and organization behavior theories.

The decade of the 1940s and World War II produced the most concentrated manufacturing effort yet known. Operations research (OR) teams found ways to better utilize severely limited resources to fill the greatly expanded needs caused by the war. When the war ended, the military outputs were changed, but the new OR techniques had found a permanent place in industry.

Perhaps the single most important technological advancement in the recent history of business is the computer. Computer applications in accounting, finance, marketing, and personnel abound, as they do in POM. The various tasks of scheduling and control always have been performed in business, but the computer now permits complex algorithms to be applied routinely in situations where judgment and guessing previously prevailed. Material requirements planning (MRP), a technique that determines when and how much material to order, is becoming an invaluable managerial tool, but it cannot be employed effectively without a computer because it involves a vast number of calculations.

Just-in-time (JIT) inventory systems, popularized in Japanese manufacturing firms, rely on computerized scheduling of raw materials to arrive just as they are needed in production, thus eliminating costly levels of inventory. (MRP, JIT, and other systems are described in more detail in chapters 4 and 6).

Recent developments in minicomputers are making it possible for many small manufacturing companies to take advantage of computer control techniques in manufacturing. In fact, the elements that constitute a minicomputer are becoming difficult to determine. Minicomputers originally were classified as small computer systems with limited storage capacity and functional capability; they often were used to support only a single application. With the explosive growth in computer technology, however, these so-called minicomputers have capacities and functions that equal or surpass the larger data-processing equipment of just a few years ago, and a wide assortment of manufacturing software support for the minicomputer user now is available.

The microprocessor—a computer on a chip—is another modern technological development that has far-reaching implications for the management of production systems. Microprocessors are designed to perform a single application but are inexpensive and can be preprogrammed to perform a wide variety of logic functions; consider, for example, the capabilities found in video games and hand-held calculators. The major difference between a microprocessor and a small computer is that there is limited ability to reprogram a microprocessor: All the programmed logic is predetermined and actually designed into the physical circuitry itself. Microprocessors are being developed to support new applications of industrial robots and many of the functions performed in computer-aided design and computer-aided manufacturing (CAD/CAM) systems.

As more and more elements of the production process become automated and computerized, operations managers have recognized the need to tie together these "islands of automation" into an integrated system to avoid problems of coordination and suboptimization. Computer-integrated manufacturing (CIM) is the new term for the systems that seek this objective. Still in its infancy, CIM promises to be the key link in advancing manufacturing into the flexible, responsive, efficient "factory of the future."

Technologies related to minicomputers and microprocessors also may affect production planning and control systems. These include magnetics (i.e., the magnetic stripe used on the back of bank cards); optical reading of numeric and alphabetic printed data; and light scanning or laser sensing devices like those used in supermarket checkout systems and department store point-of-sale terminals. In an operations environment, such devices may be used for data collection in receiving, storeroom, and shipping operations.

The Future of Production/Operations Management

Until recently, factories have become more efficient by employing mass-production technology that involved moving identical product units along a transfer line (as in the automobile assembly plant). The gains in efficiency were often offset by losses in flexibility. The factory of the past, for all of its advantages, could be characterized as rigid, inflexible, and unresponsive to rapid change. The factory of the future seeks to remove these disadvantages while retaining the cost efficiency of large-scale production.

Some describe the factory of the future as a design engineer working with a CAD system to design and test a product without having to build a prototype. Release of the design in this ideal environment would trigger the ordering of necessary materials and the programming of automated equipment from the design engineer's data. Flexible machines would produce one or many units of the product to the customer's order and quickly change over to produce other products. The CIM system would allow coordination of all aspects of ordering, processing, and distribution, with rapid response time to any changes.

Few factories have achieved this level of sophistication, but some are approaching it and many will achieve it in the near future. More engineers, technicians, and managers will displace production workers, and we will reach capital-to-labor ratios previously thought impossible.

Old services are being revamped and new ones are being created at a fantastic rate. The United States became a service economy in the early 1970s, when people began to have the money and leisure time to demand more services. This trend is bound to continue. Service firms will grow in absolute numbers, and the value of their output will grow as a percentage of the gross national product.

These new businesses provide services, primarily, but they still must convert inputs into outputs. They must make forecasts and purchase materials. Their activities must be planned, scheduled, and controlled. It may be more difficult to measure the quality of an intangible service than that of a manufactured item, but the quality is no less important. As services grow relative to manufactured goods, the emphasis of operations management will evolve into new applications of existing principles and the development of new techniques of measurement and control.

The similarities between manufacturing and service industries are closer than one might imagine. Just as the factory of the future will attempt to become more responsive while maintaining its efficiency through computerization and automation, we can see similar trends beginning to creep into service businesses. Fast-food restaurants, for example, are expanding their product lines (menus), becoming more flexible ("Have it your way"), adding more automated equipment such as soft drink–filling machines and automatic friers, while attempting to retain their cost effectiveness, quality of product, and level of service. With some creative thinking, we can imagine a totally automated fast-food facility in which the customer uses a debit card to place an order and watches as a hamburger and fries are prepared entirely by machines.

Although predicting the future is risky, another trend in operations management that is likely to continue in the foreseeable future is the increasing sophistication of technology in products and in the processes used to create them. Plastics and other synthetic substances have replaced many natural products such as leather and cotton. As a new basic product is created, existing industries change and new industries emerge. Oil companies become petrochemical firms, and electronics companies drop radios and televisions to produce medical instruments, calculators, and even watches. And we are standing on the threshold of an entirely new industry in biogenetics.

Just as bulldozers now substitute for a pick and shovel, lasers will be commonly employed in the future in such diverse industries as mining and medicine. Solar-powered equipment will alleviate demands and restraints on other energy-distribution networks. And the revolution that has begun in information processing, storage, and retrieval will cause many changes in communications within the business community. Evidence of this is the fact that cellular phones are now as common as pagers were a few years ago.

Another trend representing a challenge for the future is production of products on a worldwide scale. Many firms market their outputs in many countries, and, in some, the manufacturing process transcends national boundaries. Cotton grown in the United States is processed into printed cloth and cut into patterns; the pieces then are shipped to the other side of the globe (Taiwan, Korea, or Hong Kong), where they are sewn into shirts; finally, the shirts are transported back to the United States to be sold. Some of our "American" cars are assembled in one European country from parts made in half a dozen other countries. In some cases, we have seen entire product lines (radios and black-and-white TVs, for example) migrate to other countries where wage rates, natural resources, or some other factors permit sufficient manufacturing economies to outweigh increased transportation costs.

Services, too, are becoming international. Telephone service, credit cards, hotels, restaurants, and many other services can handle our needs in almost any part of the globe.

The trend toward increased internationalization will be enhanced by less expensive and faster transportation methods for physical goods and more efficient communication technologies for most services. The deterrents, however, include a lack of standardization of technologies, differences among common business practices, and conflicts among governments. In spite of these disadvantages, world trade is likely to increase in the future and carry with it greater challenges for operations management. When territorial boundaries are crossed, we enter new political and cultural ideologies and may find that our assumptions about designing jobs, scheduling work, and controlling operations must be replaced with new, creative solutions.

Functions of Production/Operations Management

The process of converting inputs into outputs requires certain functions to be performed. Some are design functions, which receive the most attention when the business is formed and at periodic intervals when major changes are made. Others are control functions, which must be performed continuously if an organization is to operate successfully.

Product Design and Development

Business organizations, research laboratories, and independent inventors are continuously developing new products. Yet few products are truly new. The Hula-Hoop, so successful in the 1950s, was a plastic adaptation of the cane hoops used by children in the late nineteenth century. The yo-yo traces its history to ancient Egypt, although many refinements have since been made in its design and materials. Most new products are variations and improvements on already-existing products.

Innovations in complete detail, ready for manufacture, seldom spring into the mind of an inventor. Usually an idea is developed, refined, and tested over many months before a working prototype is produced. The original idea may be creative, but the development of that idea into a marketable product requires a systematic, scientific study involving diligent work and attention to detail. Product specifications must be developed to assure that the item can be produced at a reasonable cost and be of the desired quality.

Most large organizations, and many small ones, have research and development departments that study new products and new processes to produce them. Few companies can afford to produce the same product in the same way, year after year; nor can they rely on copying the innovations of others.

In service industries, product development means determining the specifications of the service and how it is to be delivered. Services should be specified in terms of level of service, line of service, hours of availability, and many other, more detailed characteristics if the organization is to be competitive.

Facilities Location

The proper location for the organization's facilities can be a one-time decision when the business is formed, or it may be a frequently recurring question. The location decision may be critical to some firms and inconsequential to others. For example, the management of a small firm that makes garden tools for a major retailer may have to decide only on the original location, which may be anywhere within a 50-mile radius of the customer. A large fast-food chain, however, may be opening a new outlet every week, and the specific locations chosen for the outlets may be the most critical factor in determining their success.

The location decision must combine land and building costs, tax rates, distribution availability, customer access, growth potential, competitors' locations, suppliers' locations, energy sources, community acceptance, and a host of other factors. Depending on the importance and frequency of the decision, decision-making methods can range from simple rules of thumb and judgment to complex computer algorithms.

Capital Equipment

Included in capital equipment are the functions of determining the capital equipment needed, acquiring it at a reasonable cost, installing it, providing for both routine maintenance and emergency repair, and eventually replacing it. As with the location decision, capital-equipment decisions can be simple or complex. Large manufacturing firms succeed or fail on the basis of the management of their capital assets. Service firms often have minimal material inventories but huge investments in capital. One obvious example is a dentist's office; but airlines, trucking companies, and rental firms also fall into this category.

The small firm making only occasional capital acquisitions often can rely on the equipment supplier to provide much of the cost and performance analysis. For example, a lumber yard needing a forklift can get need assessments and competitive bids from two suppliers and then simply pick the best deal.

Facilities Layout

The layout of physical facilities has an important influence on the efficiency of a firm. Layout for a manufacturing plant should follow a logical sequence so that materials can flow smoothly through the process with minimal handling. For service functions, such as those performed by a bank teller, equipment and materials should be arranged to provide easy access and minimal delay. When several service functions interact, they should be arranged in sequence according to the main stream of customer flow through the process.

Unfortunately, many manufacturing and service operations are not laid out efficiently. This may be because they were never carefully laid out in the beginning, but it is more likely because the layout has grown inefficient as products and processes have changed. New machines have been added, old ones replaced, different products now are being produced, or space originally designated for material storage has been converted to office space for clerical workers.

Few layouts are perfect, yet it is difficult to determine when a layout is bad enough to justify the costs of disrupting production to move equipment and rearrange facilities.

Work Design and Measurement

Individual tasks within the production process must be designed to achieve goals of efficiency and cost. The higher the volume, the more critical the design. When even a few seconds of unnecessary activity are eliminated from routine, repetitive jobs with short cycle times, thousands of dollars can be saved.

Work design and measurement are necessary for worker control. The price of the output is largely a function of the labor and material it contains. If material usage, including scrap and waste, must be accurately measured and controlled, so, too, should the labor component. The problems associated with measuring labor efficiency are more difficult than with material, but they are surmountable.

Work design and measurement are not as widespread in services as in manufacturing, because services are less repetitive. Since services generally are more labor intensive, however, the need for more accurate labor measurement and control is critical, and the potential payoff is great.

Production Forecasting

Forecasting is necessary if a business firm is to anticipate the demand for its products. Sufficient time must be allowed to acquire inputs and transform them into outputs at the time and place needed. Forecasts can be based on analysis of past data, consideration of current events, and educated guesses about future developments.

Both simple and complex statistical techniques are available to help the decision maker form a reasonable and accurate prediction of needs. These forecasts then become the basis of the plans and schedules for the buying, manufacturing, and other activities of the firm.

Production Planning and Scheduling

To coordinate the many diverse yet dependent operations of an organization, a master plan of activities and a schedule of their timing are needed. Each operating unit should then derive from the master plan the information necessary to coordinate the activities for which it is responsible. Careful planning anticipates the needs for people, materials, and equipment so that sufficient lead time is available to make any changes that may be necessary.

Planning and scheduling are dynamic activities. No matter how carefully initial plans are formed, unanticipated events will occur and rescheduling will be necessary. Some activities may need to be expedited; others may need to be delayed. The planners and schedulers of the firm perform a juggling act with resources and available time in attempting to best utilize the firm's capacity to produce.

Purchasing/Materials Management

All organizations use materials. The material input may account for as much as 80 percent of the value of the output or for as little as 1 percent. The effort devoted to purchasing and materials management should reflect this relative importance; most firms place too little, rather than too much, emphasis on this activity.

The purchasing function includes researching, analyzing, and selecting vendors. Negotiation of contracts or other buying agreements are made to assure that the firm obtains the right quality, at the right time, in the right quantity, in the right place, and at the right price. The purchasing manager is responsible for vast amounts of the company's money, and failure to achieve any of these objectives will result in a less profitable operation.

Inventory Management

Once material is obtained, it must be stored—before it is processed, at intermediate stages in the process, and at the end of the process. These inventories—known as raw materials, work-in-process, and finished goods—represent a sizable portion of a firm's assets. Adequately controlled, the firm can be efficient. Inadequately controlled, the firm loses money through excess storage and handling costs, obsolescence, pilferage, breakage, and the opportunity costs of having too much or too little inventory on hand.

The solution to the problem is finding the balance between too much and too little inventory. Economic ordering and lot size formulas and techniques, as well as material requirements planning, aid the decision maker in achieving this balance.

Quality Control

Production planning and scheduling are responsible for the *quantity* and timing of production; quality control is responsible for its *quality*. No amount of inspection can make a bad product a good one. Quality must be designed and produced into the product. It is essential, however, that the company monitor the quality of incoming materials, goods-in-process, and finished items to assure that quality goals are being met or that necessary corrective action is taken.

In recent years, quality has become a major basis for competition, particularly in international markets. New research into the costs of poor quality to an organization have caused operations managers to raise the issue of quality to a higher priority. Rather than accepting low levels of quality as an inescapable fact, new approaches are being developed in the pursuit of quality improvement in materials, craftsmanship, processes, and systems.

Quality is no less important to service industries, although it may be more difficult to define and measure. Many advances are being made, but much work remains to be done on the application of existing principles and the development of new techniques to control the quality of services.

18 Fundamentals of Production/Operations Management

The functional areas outlined in this section form a plan for the remainder of the book. Chapter 2 deals with product design and development. The related functions of work design and location and the layout of facilities and equipment are combined in chapter 3. Forecasting, planning, and scheduling for production are the subjects of chapter 4. Chapter 5 details the fundamental principles and techniques of purchasing and materials management. Inventory control is the subject of chapter 6. And controlling the quality of output is addressed in chapter 7.

Before exploring each of these areas, however, several basic concepts of POM should be understood. The first of these is a classification format for manufacturing and service firms.

Types of Manufacturing

Manufacturing firms can be classified according to size, type of product, location and many other variables. A classification more useful to the study of POM concepts, however, is a subdivision based on the type of process employed.

Job-Shop Production

Job shop production is one type of manufacturing. Job shops do work on many different products in small lot sizes rather than manufacturing the same product continuously. In a print shop, for example, many different jobs go on at any one time. The press is set up to run one job; when that is completed, the press is set up to run the next job. In the meantime, the first job is routed to other areas, where it is folded, collated, stapled, trimmed, packaged, and shipped. Each work area in the job shop performs its function on each job as it arrives. When, for example, packaging jobs arrive in rapid succession from other work areas, a waiting line of jobs develops; at other times, when no jobs are ready to be packaged, the packaging facilities are idle. One of the major problems in a job shop is scheduling the work in the proper amount and sequence to balance the costs of idle time against the costs of having jobs waiting.

The resources in a job shop are general rather than specialized. Basic materials can be used in many different jobs with different specifications. Equipment should be adaptable to different uses. Similarly, the skills of the employees should be broad enough to allow them to work on any job within their area.

Repetitive Production

A second type of manufacturing is repetitive production, often associated with a moving assembly line. It involves high-volume production of discrete units such as automobiles, pencils, chairs, or bicycles. When the volume for one item is high enough, repetitive manufacture is more economical than the job-shop method. Specialized materials, equipment, and skills are employed to produce this one item and are not used on anything else.

The automobile industry is a good example of repetitive manufacturing. The lot size for a given model may be in the hundreds of thousands, and the production run will be almost one year. Specialized equipment is built to perform a task on this particular model, and workers are trained to be responsible for only one job. The critical problem in repetitive production is not daily scheduling, but setting up and balancing the jobs so the process will run smoothly and efficiently.

Intermittent Production

Repetitive production and job-shop production are extremes in manufacturing; the intermediate level between the extremes is intermittent production. Production runs in this type of manufacturing are longer than in a job shop but not as long as in repetitive production. Equipment is set up to run a job for several weeks and then is changed for a run of another product. The degree of specialization of the materials, equipment, and skills falls between the needs of the other two methods. Toy manufacturers, food processors, and some clothing manufacturers are examples of intermittent production.

Flow-Process Production

A fourth type of manufacturing is the flow-process method, characterized by the continuous flow required by production technology. The petroleum industry, for example, does not produce discrete units; it transforms crude oil into various end products through a process that rarely stops. Individual operations do not exist; the input gradually is converted to outputs. Because of these special characteristics, a strong emphasis is placed on design and planning. Once the process begins, replanning is seldom possible, so the process is carefully monitored and controlled to adhere to the original plan.

Project Production

Project production, the fifth category of manufacturing, is employed when only one very complex unit is being produced. Examples include building construction, shipbuilding, and missile programs. Since there is only one unit but myriad interrelated activities, the functions of planning and scheduling, quality control, and other POM functions assume a different meaning. Special techniques, such as PERT and CPM (see chapter 4), apply directly to the unique requirements in this type of manufacturing.

Types of Services

The above classification of production methods applies to manufacturing firms, but, to some extent, it can apply to services. For example, some aspects of food service resemble an assembly line in repetitive production (such as preparing identical plates for airline meals), while others more nearly resemble a job shop (as in preparing batches of salads or desserts in a restaurant). Similarly, a wedding banquet for 250 people could be considered a "project" and employ many of

Fundamentals of Production/Operations Management

CUSTOMER CONTACT

	Present	Not Present
Physical product	**PSEUDOMANUFACTURING** Food service Retailing Publishing Rentals	**PRODUCT DELIVERY** Mail-order catalogs Transportation/Shipping Stockbrokering Insurance
No physical product	**PERSONAL SERVICE** Counseling Health care Education Physical fitness	**ABSENTEE SERVICE** Lawn care Auto repair Security protection Custodial service

(TANGIBILITY on vertical axis)

Figure 1-2. A Typology of Services

the planning and scheduling techniques of project management. To the extent that a service firm approximates the characteristics and shares the problems of a given type of manufacturing firm, it probably can employ the problem-solving methodology already used in the other firms in that category.

A more useful classification of services, however, is based on a typology with two dimensions: (1) the degree to which a tangible product is produced as part of the service and (2) the requirement of the presence of the customer for the service to be delivered. Figure 1-2 depicts this typology.

At one extreme in the array of services, the firm produces a physical product (such as a hamburger) and delivers it to the customer. Moving along the tangibility continuum, we find a physical manifestation of the product, which is often treated as the product itself. An example is an insurance policy, which is a recording and description of the true service: payment in the event of some specified outcome. Further down the continuum is the instance of physical evidence that the service has been performed, such as a haircut, but, unlike the insurance policy, the haircut cannot be changed after it is delivered. Finally, at the end of the continuum are the "pure" services such as counseling, in which no physical product is evident.

The customer contact dimension is also a matter of degree. For haircuts and dental work, the customer must be present while the service is being performed. The middle range of this scale covers instances in which the customer is usually present or, at least, involved, as with most retailing and many financial services such as cashing a check or applying for a loan. At the far end are the "automatic" services such as having a paycheck deposited directly into a bank account, or contracting for a lawn-care service while you are at work.

Labels for the four major categories of services and examples of each kind are presented in figure 1-2. It should be noted, however, that some services are on the borderline between major categories, and some industries may span two or more categories. The entertainment industry, for example, covers the range from the production of compact discs and videotapes (pseudomanufacturing) to the production of Broadway plays (personal service). Similarly, utility companies (gas, electricity, and phones) have parts of their operations in all four categories.

Generally, the concepts of operations management apply most directly to the category of pseudomanufacturing. Adaptations of POM concepts can be made in many product delivery and absentee service firms, but the real challenge lies in adapting or developing new concepts, tools, and methods for the operations of firms producing personal services. Throughout this text, examples of services are used where applicable.

Goals of Production/Operations Management

To remain economically viable, a firm must convert inputs into outputs effectively and efficiently. It must be concerned with both the unit cost of its products and the contribution of its products to profit. In addition, the enlightened firm will look at various aspects of productivity and will always seek improvement. Each of these overlapping goals are defined and briefly discussed.

Effectiveness

Effectiveness is the degree to which the purpose of an organization is achieved. The purpose of a firm in the transportation industry is to move materials, people, or both; the more it moves, the more effective it is. Effectiveness requires eliminating unnecessary activities and outputs that fail to meet the quality standard. It is a combination, therefore, of how much and how well the output of the firm conforms to the purpose of the organization. Effectiveness can be measured by sales, market share, consumer opinion, and other global measures, as well as by comparing specific results to specific company objectives.

Efficiency

Efficiency refers to how fast the output is produced and how many resources are consumed. Efficiency generally relates to reducing waste—of time, effort, and materials. Greater efficiency can result through technical changes, such as better, faster machines; through managerial changes, such as better planning, scheduling, and control activities; or through behavioral changes in workers, such as working smarter or working harder. Improved efficiency means greater output for a given amount of resources, which leads to greater benefits for all concerned.

Unit Cost

One of the best "how are we doing?" measures available to a production manager is unit cost. If the production manager is doing a good job of controlling the quantity, quality, and price of the inputs and is carefully planning, scheduling, and controlling the process, those efforts will be reflected in a favorable unit cost. One must be wary, however, because many different accounting methods exist to determine unit cost. In making comparisons between firms or divisions or from year to year, one should use comparable accounting procedures.

Contribution to Profit

Because profit is one of the major objectives of the firm, contributions to profit should be recognized. When comparing one product line with another or one division with another, measures of unit cost, efficiency, or effectiveness may not be meaningful. Contribution to profit—the excess of revenue over costs—can determine whether a product line should be expanded or discontinued. Contribution to profit also can be a factor in decisions regarding new capital equipment, plant location, research and development activities, and other areas in which efficiency measures are incomplete or inappropriate.

Productivity

Perhaps the most often misunderstood objective of POM is productivity. Productivity frequently is used to mean output per hour, but it really means any ratio of output to input. The total productivity of the firm is the total of all outputs divided by the total of all inputs. However, this measure seldom is found because of the difficulty of identifying and measuring all these factors in some common unit of measurement. We usually deal with partial measures, such as labor productivity, capital productivity, or material productivity.

Productivity differs from efficiency in that efficiency seeks the maximum output from a *given* amount of resources. Productivity looks for the maximum *ratio* between the two and, thus, can involve a change in the output, the input, or both.

Productivity is critically important to individual business firms and to the economy as a whole. To remain profitable, a firm must maintain or improve its productivity. Improvements in a firm's productivity will lead to improved unit cost, profit, and return on investment. At the national level, improvements in productivity means less inflation, better use of natural resources, and a stronger position in the world market.

Responsiveness

Success in the world of fast-changing technology and intense international competition requires a rapid response rate. Firms must develop new products and get those products to market quickly. Being late in the market for a highly competitive new product might be much more costly to the manufacturing firm than even a significant overrun in research and development costs would be.

Efficiency, effectiveness, unit cost, and all the other criteria depend in part on the flexibility of the firm and its ability to respond quickly. For example, inventories can be greatly reduced without affecting customer service if the firm can restock its shelves in days instead of waiting weeks or months.

Environmental Responsibility

Every business firm operates within five environments: legal, social, economic, technological, and physical. The responsibility of the firm spans all of these. It is obligated to obey laws and regulations, operate in an ethical and socially responsible manner, and to help protect the physical environment upon which we all depend. Unfortunately, we read too often of a firm caught in the act of deceit, unfair trade practice, improper pricing policies, or suppression of technological advancements in the hope of protecting their competitive advantage. In the long run, however, illegal and unethical practices are costly for the firm and for individual managers within it. Firms that operate within high standards of ethical conduct prove that success can be achieved within the bounds of social responsibility.

Virtually every subfunction of operations management has implications for the environment and for the constituencies that the firm serves. Product design, for example, must consider safety features such as guards on power tools, regardless of whether they are required by law. Scheduling decisions can enhance or disrupt the personal lives of employees, and quality control decisions can affect the health and safety of both employees and customers.

Careers in Production/Operations Management

Positions in operations management span the organization from the lowest to the highest levels. Many opportunities are available for the college graduate, and it is possible to spend an entire career in various areas of the production/operations function while progressing from an entry-level position to upper management. Assignments in POM also provide a good background for entry into other areas of the organization.

The chart in Table 1-2 indicates some of the common position titles at the entry, department head, and division or corporate levels of the organization. One problem in compiling such a list is that different organizations use different terminology. For example, in one company the title "planner" may refer to a very senior position, while in another firm, it may be an entry-level job.

In the area of forecasting, planning, and scheduling, a junior planner or scheduler could be responsible for compiling the machine, material, and workforce schedules for one or more of the manufacturing departments. The department manager is responsible for organizing all schedules and forecasts into a realistic master production schedule and for seeing that the plans are being

Table 1-2
Career Tracks in Production/Operations Management

FUNCTION AND TITLE

Level	Forecasting, Planning, & Scheduling	Work Design, Location, & Layout	Purchasing	Inventory Control	Quality Control	Product Design & Development	Line
Division or corporate	VP (or Director), Planning	VP, Plant Engineering	VP, Materials Management VP, Purchasing		VP, Product Quality	VP, R & D	VP, Manufacturing
Department	Manager, Production Control	Manager, Industrial Engineering	Purchasing Manager	Inventory Manager	Quality-Control Manager	Manager, Product Development	Department Manager
Entry level	Scheduler/ Planner	Methods Analyst	Buyer	Inventory Control Specialist	Inspector	Product Engineer	Supervisor or Management Trainee

carried out and taking corrective action where necessary. Although the department head is responsible for these activities, this position involves more supervision of the people performing the activities than actually doing the day-to-day work. At the corporate level, the vice president of planning is concerned with a longer time span and more critical decisions, such as five-year forecasts, capacity additions, and major production changeovers.

Each of the other functions follows a similar pattern: entry-level jobs are more involved with *doing*, while upper-level jobs involve supervision of the activities and long-range planning. Methods analysts redesign jobs, buyers purchase materials, and inventory-control specialists make decisions about inventory levels, storage, and handling of materials.

Concern for professionalism within POM areas is reflected in the increased number of certification programs that have developed over the last decade. Organized mainly by professional associations, these programs establish criteria for knowledge, skill, and experience required to successfully perform the responsibilities of some POM jobs. Procedures then are developed to certify an individual as qualified; often the certification process requires individuals to pass a rigorous test and also may include education, experience, or other requirements. Although not required by law, certification can be a deciding factor for the firm when choosing among candidates for a POM position.

Many certification programs are now in operation, and more are being planned. For example, the American Production and Inventory Control Society (APICS) conducts a series of tests leading to the designation "Certified in Production and Inventory Management)," allowing Bill Jones, for instance, to write his name as William Jones, CPIM. The National Association of Purchasing Management (NAPM) awards a C.P.M. (Certified Purchasing Manager) designation based on educational and experiential requirements and test results. Through the American Society for Quality Control (ASQC), an individual can earn a CQE (Certified Quality Engineer), CQT (Certified Quality Technician), or CRE (Certified Reliability Engineer).

While the certification programs promote professionalism in specialized POM functions, the performance of the functions at the entry level often requires a close relationship between managers and engineers or other specialists. In the government, for example, management analysts and industrial engineers work jointly on problems of layout, equipment selection, and job design. Under the supervision of the manager of industrial engineering, each contributes special expertise to the problem.

While it is possible to take a straight track to the top, advancing from inspector to manager of quality control to vice president of product quality, diagonal tracks involving lateral transfers are more common. Many firms prefer—and some insist—that a corporate-level director have some experience in each of the areas under his or her control. A vice president of materials management, therefore, could have started as a scheduler, then worked as a senior buyer, and progressed through other positions in several related areas.

One track deserves special mention. In virtually every business, whether manufacturing or service, there is a manufacturing or operations department.

Beginning with the workers who create the product, the advancement track progresses through supervisor to department manager, plant manager, vice president of manufacturing, and president. These are the "line" positions, and in many organizations this is the shortest and surest route to the top. Automobile companies, for example, seldom have a top-level executive who has not had some line experience.

Service firms differ considerably from manufacturing firms (and from each other) in the way they organize these operations functions and the position titles they attach to them. These same functions must be performed, however, and the same general principles apply. An airline, for example, must carry an inventory of parts and supplies, and maintenance jobs must be carefully scheduled. In a hospital, purchasing obviously is a critical function; and, although job-design principles are being applied to health-care facilities, few have an industrial engineering department in their organization. Many POM positions in service industries are yet to be established, even though they are critically needed. Obviously, there is considerable opportunity for people to build careers in many service organizations.

Key Concepts

Products

The Production Function

Methodology/Technology of Transformation

Factory of the Future

Computer Integrated Manufacturing (CIM)

Job Shop

Repetitive Production

Types of Services

Effectiveness/Efficiency

Productivity

Responsiveness

Subfunctions of POM

References

Adam, Everett E., Jr., and Ebert, Ronald J. *Production and Operations Management.* 3rd ed. Englewood Cliffs, NJ: Prentice-Hall, 1986

Chase, Richard B., and Aquilano, Nicholas, J. *Production and Operations Management.* 4th ed. Homewood, IL: Richard D. Irwin, 1985.

Fitzsimmons, James A., and Sullivan, Robert S. *Service Operations Management.* New York: McGraw-Hill Book Company, 1982.

George, Clause S., Jr. *The History of Management Thought.* 2d ed. Englewood Cliffs, NJ: Prentice-Hall, 1972.

Hendrick, Thomas E., and Moore, Franklin G. *Production/Operations Management.* 9th ed. Homewood, IL: Richard D. Irwin, 1985.

Taylor, Frederick W. *The Principles of Scientific Management*. New York: Harper & Bros., 1911.

Discussion Questions

1. For each of the organizations listed below, (a) list the major inputs needed; (b) explain the nature of the conversion process; and (c) list the major outputs of goods, services, or both.

    a. Boeing Aircraft

    b. American Airlines

    c. Bechtel Construction Company

    d. The Village Delicatessen

    e. Sears

    f. U.S. Bureau of Engraving and Printing

2. List and explain three examples of real companies for each category of manufacturing: project, job shop, intermittent, repetitive, and flow process. Give two examples of companies that contain two or more of these categories within the same firm.

3. In what categories of the service typology (figure 1-2) would you place AT&T before divestiture? Give specific examples of different divisions such as Long Lines, Bell Labs, Western Electric, or the local repair service. Where would you place your local telephone company after divestiture? Where would you place long-distance competitors such as MCI?

4. Consider the ten functions of operations management discussed in this chapter. Lay them out in time sequence; that is, which functions must be (can be) performed before another is begun?

5. Is it possible for a business firm to be effective but not efficient? Efficient but not effective? Effective and efficient but not productive? Discuss.

6. "Students are processed (educated) in 'batches' (classes). In that respect, a university is a giant job shop."

    a. Indicate whether you agree or disagree with this statement. In what respects is a university similar or dissimilar to a print shop? Consider, for example, the sequence of operations and the sequence of courses as well as the scheduling of jobs and the scheduling of classes.

    b. In a typical job shop, each job takes a different amount of time. Describe the scheduling problems that would result if every class were a different number of weeks in length.

    c. Is the registration procedure at your university more like one of the other forms of production? Which one?

    d. What would be necessary in order to educate students using a repetitive type of production? Describe the process.

7. Use the model presented in figure 1-1 to compare and contrast these two firms: a manufacturer of doghouses and a dog-grooming service.
    a. What are the major differences in the types and relative amounts of inputs needed?
    b. How do the conversion processes differ? Is the customer involved in the conversion process?
    c. Are there differences in the flows of funds and/or information from the environment to the firms? Explain.
8. Why is mass production found only in the twentieth century?
9. Most large banks have a facility called the operations center. What is the purpose of this facility and what work is performed there?
10. What is the purpose of programs offering certification, for instance, as a CPIM or C.P.M.? What is the value to the person who is certified? How does this compare to licensing accountants, doctors, or lawyers?

CHAPTER

2

Product Design and Development

The purpose of any organization is to produce products that customers are willing to buy. But this task is not as easy as it seems. Not only are customer needs and preferences constantly changing, but competition and advancing technologies also continually make products obsolete. Most firms monitor shifting attitudes and demographics through market research and keep abreast of technological changes that might affect their industry. This information is fed into the firm's research and development activities to create new products or modifications of existing products to keep the firm competitive.

For example, not too many years ago the slide rule was a common product in a mature and stable market. Today, it is difficult to find a slide rule; they have been displaced by electronic hand-held calculators. Companies making slide rules either were forced out of business or they had to design and develop new products that matched some other consumer need. At the same time, new products caused new firms to flourish in a Darwinian-like battle between innovative companies and those still producing obsolete products. Similar circumstances have faced manufacturers of watches, cigarette lighters, computers, home appliances, and other products.

Remember, products include services as well as manufactured goods, and the same pressures for product innovation apply. Consumer attitudes toward physical fitness have changed, and consumers have more leisure time and more money to spend. Recent research has provided new knowledge linking diet and exercise to health and longevity. The result has been an explosion of new firms and new industries geared to take advantage of the opportunities. Innovative products abound in health clubs, diet foods, athletic equipment, and videotapes to help consumers develop their own fitness programs.

Few products are completely new; most "new" products are developments or refinements of existing products. And, contrary to what some might believe, new products seldom come from the mind of the eccentric inventor working in a garage. Most often they emerge from a corporate or government research laboratories after months or years of tedious work. Sometimes we can trace the history of a product and chronicle its development through a series of minor and major breakthroughs in technology or creativity.

For example, the first "washing machine" was a rock beside a stream. Later came the washboard, and, finally, the first crude machines consisting of a tub, an agitator, and a wringer. The major difference between the latter machine and the washer of today is the addition of automatic devices and electronics that enable the machine to perform preset functions. The modern washing machine has achieved the goal we have set for our "factory of the future"; it is fast, efficient, almost totally automatic, yet flexible and adaptable. In the future, we may see another major breakthrough in the method of washing clothes, such as the use of microwaves, sonar, lasers, or some technology not yet discovered.

Similarly, in services, major breakthroughs are interspersed with many minor refinements. The movie industry traces its origin to the Greek theater more than two thousand years ago. It then progressed through traveling shows, vaudeville acts, silent films, talkies, color movies, and videotape. In between were thousands of refinements that improved the quality of the sound and picture, as well as many developments in the artistry of motion-picture production.

Product Life Cycle

In the marketplace, most new products go through a product life cycle of five stages (figure 2-1):

1. **Introduction:** The product is brand new, high priced, and does not always work well. Furthermore, market awareness and acceptance of the product are minimal, with sales volume at a low level and growing very slowly. The only customers for the product at this point are the wealthy and the adventuresome.

2. **Growth:** The product is now accepted in the marketplace and is making rapid sales gains as a result of the combined effects of promotion, distribution, improved dependability, standardization, increased use, and lower selling prices. Customers buy the product with little prompting, but substantial profits gained by the innovating firm lure competition into the marketplace. The product begins to sell in much larger quantities as it becomes more commonly used.

3. **Maturity:** Now a number of competitors have entered the market. The rate of sales growth begins to slow because of the declining numbers of people

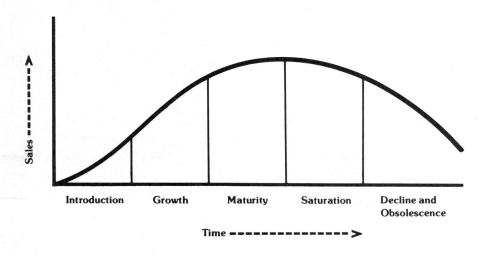

Figure 2-1. Stages of the Product Life Cycle

who still are unaware of the product. By now, the product has proved itself dependable in performance, and, because of increased competition, the product now is reasonably priced.

4. **Saturation:** At this stage, nearly everyone who wants the product has bought it. Sales thus level off at a rate determined by replacement demand plus sales resulting from population growth. Product promotion is very important in this stage, since the products of competitors differ very little, if at all. In our society, the markets for most automobiles, household appliances, and television sets have reached this stage.

5. **Decline and Obsolescence:** In the final stage, products are edged out of the market by better products or by substitutes that are entering the growth and maturity stages of their life cycles. This does not happen to all products; for example, scissors have been around for a long time, and newer products, such as electric scissors, have not replaced them. On the other hand, the slide rule had been at the saturation stage for a long time before it was driven from the marketplace by the electronic calculator.

One excellent illustration of the typical product life cycle is the Polaroid camera. Radically different from other cameras at the time it was introduced, the Polaroid initially was a very expensive toy for the rich. Compared to the Polaroid of today, these early models were crude, inconvenient to use, and often unreliable, yet the camera was successful enough to survive the introduction stage and experience rapid growth in the market. Technical refinements of the camera have made it more convenient to use, and patent protection has kept most direct competition at bay. Today, the Polaroid camera is a mature product, perhaps entering the saturation stage with competition coming from 35mm cameras and video cameras. If no further refinements are made, this product, too, will eventually fall into decline and obsolescence.

Product Strategy

Successful companies formulate strategies to guide their decisions and actions. Within an overall business strategy, a firm should have compatible strategies for marketing, finance, operations, and indeed, every part of the organization. From the set of strategies, it can then develop more specific goals and objectives, policies, and operating procedures.

Important in the set of strategies is the product strategy. The mission of the organization or the overall business strategy asks: "What kind of business are we in?" or "What is our basic purpose?" Only after these questions are satisfactorily answered can the product strategy be developed.

For example, if a company stated that its basic purpose was to produce oil, then the researchers in the firm would not direct their attention toward other sources of energy such as solar or nuclear power. They could, however, seek new uses for oil and develop new products using oil as a primary ingredient. The same is true in services. Recent deregulation in the banking industry has caused many banks to redefine themselves as "total service financial institutions" and to quickly develop new products to serve their customers' financial needs.

The product strategy guides the firm in the development of new products, modification of existing products, and the elimination of old products that no longer fit with the company's mission. A product strategy contains several dimensions.

First, the firm must decide what part of the market to compete in by establishing the *level* of product. The level connotes a certain market segment and usually a price range. Depending on the product involved, the level may imply certain features, capacity, or performance characteristics. For example, a manufacturer of dinnerware may chose to compete at the low end of the market, with the least expensive china for everyday use and not try to compete with the fine-china firms of the world. To use a service example, a barbershop may choose the market for basic barbering services at reasonable prices or cater to consumers wanting expensive styling and conditioning treatments. Rare is the firm that can compete at all levels.

The second dimension of a product strategy is product *line*. Some firms achieve a competitive advantage by offering a limited line of products and providing better products, faster delivery, or some other feature to make up for the lack of depth. Fast-food restaurants, convenience markets, and many small manufacturers are examples. On the other hand, some firms strive to offer a complete array of products to their customers. Contrary to the strategy of the convenience market, some traditional grocery stores have added departments for sporting goods, lawn-care products, appliances, pharmaceuticals, eyeglasses, and even a branch bank to attract customers who want one-stop shopping. Interestingly, both strategies are successful.

The third dimension of product strategy is product *availability*. Some manufactured items are available almost anywhere, while others can be purchased only through company-owned or franchise outlets such as Radio Shack. Some manufacturers limit the geographic region in which their products are sold. Until recently, Coors beer was available only west of the Mississippi. For services, availability takes on different meanings. Number of outlets, hours of operation, and delivery or house-call policy determine when and where the service is available.

A complete product strategy will consider, at a minimum, the level, line, and availability of products to be offered by the firm. In addition, however, the strategy should incorporate other factors relevant to the firm such as resources available, supplier relationships, marketing and distribution channels, market segments served, and company image and reputation. Products that do not fit in the product line with respect to these factors are candidates for abandonment; new products that do fit are candidates for development.

The Bic Pen Corporation is an interesting example of a product strategy. The company was formed to produce the original Bic pen, which combined the design of the common lead pencil with the technology of the ballpoint pen. The first Bic pen was the same color, the same size, and the same configuration as the pencil, but it had a ballpoint cartridge in a plastic casing. As the product became successful, the company introduced different points and ink colors while staying with its original philosophy of producing a high-quality, inexpensive product with a high market volume that permitted economies of mass production.

Later, Bic produced a felt-tip pen, but the pen was not introduced into the marketplace quickly enough. Gillette had researched and developed the new Flair pen, patterned after the early fountain pens, and the Flair was a great success. Bic's version, the Banana, was fashioned after the successful "stick" version of its pens, but the design and timing in the market led to its downfall.

Bic learned from this experience and entered the market with an entirely new product, the Bic lighter. Like the pen, the lighter was a reliable, inexpensive, disposable, high-volume, mass-produced item using plastic and metal as its primary materials. Bic could produce the lighter using the same technology, the same knowledge, and often the same marketing channels. The Bic lighter was a huge success; Gillette's version, the Cricket, could not catch up.

Bic's next major product introduction was a disaster. For reasons that were related more to corporate finance than to following a consistent product strategy, Bic began to market pantyhose produced by a French subsidiary under the name "Fannyhose." The differences in technology of the process, market, marketing channels, and competition were too much for Bic to overcome.

But Bic was too strong a company to let one product lead to its downfall. It swallowed its losses and returned to the product strategy that had spelled success by introducing the Bic disposable shaver, another highly successful product. Today, Bic continues its research and development into new or modified products that fit with the strategy and philosophy of the company.

Research and Development

Research and development (R&D) refers to those investigative activities leading to the discovery of new knowledge (research) and the translation of this new knowledge into marketable products (development). R&D has taken us from 78-rpm phonograph records (that shattered when dropped) to 45-rpm records, LP albums, cassette tapes, and compact discs. Digital tape is still in the R&D lab but is about to emerge.

Not every firm engages in R&D activities. Some buy research results through patent rights or some other form, and others simply copy products that have already reached the market. In some industries, however, it is essential to spend considerable amounts of money on R&D to maintain a competitive position. In those businesses, R&D efforts can be applied in a number of ways.

New products. New products usually are brought into existence for one of three basic reasons:

1. **To fill a gap in an existing product line.** For example, a home-appliance producer may decide to manufacture a home air conditioner to make its line of home appliances more complete.

2. **To supplement an already complete product line.** For example, a house-paint manufacturer may decide to produce paintbrushes to supplement an already complete line of home paints.

3. **To capitalize on a potential market opportunity not related to existing product lines.** For example, a full-line manufacturer of plastic toys may see a potentially strong market for plastic sports equipment. This reason for introducing new products carries the most risk, since the company may be getting involved with markets and production processes about which it knows very little. Additional skills in product design, development, production, and marketing may be required to make the product successful.

One method of entering new product areas is to undertake a full-blown R&D effort of gathering new knowledge and translating this knowledge into the desired products. Although this type of effort has resulted in the manufacture of products such as the polio vaccine, television, and the jet engine, its high cost and associated risks normally limit such activity to the larger firms. On the other hand, the payoff to the firm making such a breakthrough through its own R&D efforts can be impressive.

Another way a firm can enter a new product area is to buy the R&D efforts of other firms. This often is done by marketing finished products under the buying company's own label. For example, a manufacturer and marketer of drafting supplies, such as rulers, triangles, and templates, may round out its product line by purchasing mechanical drawing instruments (which it does not produce) from a manufacturer in Germany and marketing them under its own label. The private product lines or brands of most large retailers are good examples of this practice. Although this practice tends to minimize R&D costs and risks, it also reduces the possibility of the substantial profits that often result from breakthroughs due to internal R&D activities.

Still another way a firm can enter a new product area is to merge with a firm that already has product lines in that area. The acquired firm has the skills necessary to produce and market the new product or product line. Mergers, however, do not always produce the anticipated results. Often a merger will cause new organizational problems that adversely affect the new company's operations.

Modification of existing products. One reason for modifying an existing product is to improve its customer appeal. This can be accomplished by (1) reshaping the product to conform to current styling trends; (2) adding new features that will set the product uniquely apart, as was the intent when the remote-control channel selector was added to the color television product package; or (3) giving the product a new package that will produce a new look or image.

Another reason for modifying an existing product is to reduce its production costs. One of the best ways to reduce production costs is to redesign the product so that the cost of its materials is reduced. For example, a product often can be modified, without changing its functional performance, so that its production will require less material, less expensive material (such as the substitution of plastic for metal), or both. Furthermore, material costs and assembly costs often can be greatly reduced if the product is modified to include the use of standard parts and components.

New uses for existing products. Exploration of new uses for an existing product is often another objective of a firm's R&D efforts. R&D efforts are aimed at discovering ways that an existing product, or a slightly modified version of it, can be adapted to new markets. For example, a manufacturer of an industrial-grade liquid floor cleaner might take this same cleaner, dilute it, and market it as a liquid floor cleaner for households. This type of R&D activity allows a firm to satisfy a greater number of customers within the realm of its existing products.

New packaging. Changing the packaging of an existing product involves changes in the size, shape, layout, or other external characteristics without affecting the product's purpose. Packaging changes often have the effect of creating a "new" product by giving regular customers, or customers in new markets, the existing product in a new form or in a quantity that is more satisfactory. For example, packaging frozen vegetables in 1-pound packages instead of 10-ounce packages greatly improved sales to large-family consumers; the ten-ounce package contained too little product for such families, but two such packages contained too much.

By offering attractive packages, a firm often can compete more effectively. A better box, wrapper, label, can, or bottle may even enable a relatively small and unknown firm to market successfully against established competitors.

Creating a model. The immediate outcome of a successful R&D effort is the creation of a model or prototype of the product. For a manufactured item, this may be a physical model, while in services it may be a detailed set of specifications with a demonstration or "dress rehearsal" of the service to be performed. One reason for creating a prototype is to assure that the ideas upon which the product is based are feasible. A second reason is to help management visualize how the product will look and perform. Although these initial models may be changed before final production, they provide the basis for decisions regarding final product specifications, facilities design, and materials required.

Product Design

Taking a model and modifying its design into a product that can be produced and marketed profitably requires information input from a number of areas within the firm as well as from the marketplace. Factors such as alternative material costs, use of standard parts and components, results of product tests, and inputs from market research, all must be considered. Once this needed information is gathered and properly analyzed, the specifications of the final product can be determined.

Material

Often the product designer can choose from several different materials. For example, automobile hoods can be made out of aluminum, steel, or fiberglass. In choosing from available material alternatives, the designer must consider (1) the performance requirements of the product, (2) the relative costs of the alternative materials, (3) the relative processing costs associated with the alternative materials, (4) the effect of each material on the appearance of the final product, and (5) the relative availability of each material.

When two or more of the alternatives can produce the required performance, the lowest-priced alternative does not automatically win out. It may be that the highest-priced material costs less to process. Thus, the highest-priced alternative may be the most desirable alternative when *total* production costs are considered. For example, aircraft producers save a substantial sum of money by using higher-priced bronze rather than steel extrusions in aircraft elevator and rudder counterweights. Even though bronze is higher priced than steel, the savings in machining time more than offsets the increase in material costs.

A material alternative also may be desirable from the standpoint of performance, cost, and appearance but may be obtainable from only one supplier. In this case, a material decision is also a supplier decision, and the firm should carefully evaluate the reliability of the supplier's ability to meet desired future quantity requirements and delivery schedules. At a minimum, this decision calls for a thorough investigation of the supplier's available plant capacity, financial strength, and labor situation.

Value Analysis/Value Engineering

Value analysis/value engineering (VA/VE) involves an organized, systematic study of every element of cost in a part, material, or product to ensure that it fulfills its function at the lowest total cost. VA/VE is the study of function and value. *Function* refers to the job that the material, part, or product performs. For example, the function of a ballpoint pen may be to write. *Value* is defined as the lowest end cost at which the function may be accomplished at the time and place required and with the quality required. For example, if the only function of a ballpoint pen were to write, the least expensive pen probably would do the job. If, on the other hand, the pen must fulfill an additional function, such as indicating status, then perhaps a more expensive, gold-filled pen would be required.

Although it may sound technical, VA/VE actually is a straightforward, basic approach designed to reduce material and production costs while ensuring that the product still fulfills its intended function in a satisfactory manner. A VA/VE study cannot be done effectively unless the function of the product is first determined—that is, "to write" or "to connote status." Once the function of the product has been determined, the remainder of the study involves asking and objectively answering a number of basic questions about the particular item. Most companies develop a checklist to systematize this activity. In some cases, these checklists consist of hundreds of questions, such as

1. Would a less costly design work as well?
2. Can a standard item be used?
3. Can the product's weight be reduced?
4. Can a less expensive material do the job?
5. Can the costs of packaging be reduced?
6. Is the capacity of the item greater than required?

By answering such questions thoughtfully, analysts generally will arrive at alternatives. If the answer to a particular question is not entirely satisfactory, this becomes the starting point for a more detailed investigation. The use of a well-developed checklist of questions focuses attention on those factors that may further reduce production costs.

The cost savings attributed to VA/VE efforts have been impressive. For example, one firm that had been using a specially designed screw costing 15¢ each found a way to make the screw for 1.5¢, resulting in an annual savings of $20,000. In another instance, a gasket costing $4.15 each when made in-house was found to cost 15¢ when purchased from an outside supplier.

Standardization

Standardization is the process of establishing agreement upon uniform identifications for certain characteristics of quality, design, performance, quantity, and service. A uniform identification that generally is agreed upon is called a *standard*. For example, if a person in the United States buys an electric appliance such as a toaster, the buyer knows that this toaster will operate on the same voltage available from the electrical outlets at home. Why? Because in the United States the voltage in homes has been standardized at 110 volts. Likewise, when you buy a light bulb, you know that the bulb will screw into your sockets at home because light-bulb sockets in the United States are standard. Just think of the problems that would exist if each typewriter manufacturer's typewriter keyboard were arranged in a different configuration!

Standards do not exist for consumer products alone. They also exist for a wide variety of items used in manufacturing, such as nuts, bolts, screws, and electric motors. Without these standards, there could be no assembly line, since there would be no interchangeable parts. The lack of standards also would complicate repair services greatly. Many of the items we use on a daily basis would cost more to buy and maintain.

There are several reasons for incorporating, whenever possible, standard parts and components into the design of a product. The use of standard items in a company's products permits the company, as a whole, to purchase fewer items in larger quantities at lower prices. If fewer items are purchased, then fewer items need to be processed and stocked. This has the immediate effect of lowering purchasing, receiving, inspection, and accounts-payable costs. In addition, stocking fewer items makes controlling inventories and production easier and less costly, and it greatly simplifies assembly operations. Furthermore, since suppliers generally stock standard items in their inventories, deliveries can be made more quickly, allowing the firm to maintain lower inventory levels, which, in turn, result in another substantial saving. Thus, lower prices, lower processing costs, lower inventory costs, and lower scheduling costs are all reasons why a firm uses standard parts and components in the design of its products. As a result, a product can be brought to market at a lower total cost.

Modular Design

Modular design refers to designing products with separate sections or modules. When an item fails, the whole module (of which the item is a part) is removed and replaced with a new module. The module that has failed either can be repaired at a central facility (which is usually less costly than on-site repair), or it can be discarded. For example, if a transistor in a television set fails, the whole printed-circuit board (of which the transistor is a part) is removed and replaced.

The basic reason why industries, such as electronics, have turned to modular design has been the high cost of repair labor, which has made breakdowns associated with conventional forms of design extremely expensive. Under the modular design concept, the on-site time it takes to repair a complicated piece of electronic equipment is greatly reduced. If the replaced module is worth repairing, the repair work then can be accomplished at a central facility utilizing less expensive labor.

Modular design also is gaining rapid acceptance in the home-building industry. In this case, the impetus behind modular design is the high cost of construction labor. Under the modular design concept, standard house components (such as the bathroom) can be mass produced at a central facility with less expensive assembly labor. The components then are transported to the building site and put together, requiring only a fraction of the time and expensive labor associated with conventional construction methods.

Computer-aided Design (CAD)

Computer-aided design (CAD) is a complex and imaginative new tool that is revolutionizing product design. CAD first was used in the aerospace industry and soon was adopted by the automobile industry to help deal with the engineering and design nightmare of downsizing the entire fleet of America's gas-guzzling cars. Today, because of the declining prices of computer equipment and the increased capabilities of computer software, CAD techniques commonly are used in many other industries as well.

Basically, CAD consists of a computer that draws pictures, on a television screen or cathode-ray tube (CRT), of what the engineer has designed. The sophisticated CAD software is able to draw lines between points, creating a three-dimensional drawing that can be rotated to show all sides of the design. As a result, CAD greatly speeds up the normally slow and laborious work of drafting.

CAD is an especially effective way to design and analyze products because the computer communicates with the designer directly through pictures. By looking at these pictures, the designer is able to absorb and interpret the informational content of the design much faster than if he or she were looking at an array of numbers or words and then trying to translate them into mental pictures. Furthermore, if the necessary programming has been done, the designer can analyze and test the things designed by subjecting them to electronically simulated temperature changes, mechanical stresses, or other potential problems the product is likely to encounter in its real-world application. For example, color graphics can be used to show heat or stress points of a design in red and cool points in blue, thus enabling the engineer to understand more easily the design's temperature fields.

Such on-screen testing and analysis can save huge amounts of time and money associated with the more traditional way of designing a product—that is, building a prototype, testing it, modifying the design, and retesting the prototype. Products designed using a CAD system are more likely to work properly when built, since many of the problems associated with a new or modified product can be removed before the product leaves the design stage.

Market Research Inputs

Thus far in our discussion, all the inputs to the product design process have come from within the firm. But because the success of a product ultimately is determined by consumers, they also should be allowed to express opinions about the product's design. This important information is gathered through market research.

In the initial stage of a product's development, market information concerning the product's salability normally is gathered through the use of a questionnaire. The questionnaire is a list of carefully phrased questions to be used to guide a series of personal interviews with potential customers or to elicit information in a mailing to specially selected potential customers.

Information collected should indicate the size (quantity) of a potential market over time for alternative product characteristics (designs, packages, quality, and reliability levels, as well as any other selected operating features) and alternate prices. The survey also should provide valuable information concerning the activities of major competitors, styling trends, and predictable seasonal variations in sales, if they exist.

Information gathered this way can be extremely useful in guiding a product through its final design and development stages. Without such information, it would be difficult to differentiate between products that only seem to be a good idea from those that have sound market potential. For example, consider the individual who decided he had the greatest idea in the world for packaging and marketing unprocessed wheat bran. He packaged his product in a rustic brown paper bag with an eye-catching sea-gull logo printed on the front. A recipe incorporating bran was printed on the back of the bag, and a copy of a copyrighted bran recipe was included inside. Our entrepreneur also decided to price his product far below his competitors in order to gain immediate market acceptance. The whole idea seemed so good that the fellow proceeded, without conducting even the most basic market research, to buy 20,000 printed bags, enough bran to fill them, and enough master cartons to ship them. The initial investment was $10,000.

When sales did not pick up as rapidly as expected—in fact, they never even got off the ground—the bran man decided to conduct a survey to find the problem. The results indicated that the bag idea, although quaint and seemingly clever, was unattractive to retailers because the bags couldn't be stacked on the shelf the way conventional cereal boxes could. Furthermore, since unprocessed bran was a slow-moving item regardless of its price, most retailers were reluctant to give the product any shelf space to start with. To make matters even worse, the master cartons were the wrong size; when the allocated shelf space was completely filled, there still were some bags of bran left in the carton, which then had to be put in inventory in the storeroom. Conclusion: The idea was a loser to start with. Cost of the market survey: less than $100. Had this individual conducted the survey *before* taking action, he would have saved himself $9,900 and a lot of grief.

Resources

The resources of a firm, including its facilities and equipment, the skills of its personnel, and its financial strength, have an important impact on the final design of each product that will be manufactured. The closer the production requirements of a product match the capabilities of a firm's existing equipment and personnel resources, the more efficient will be the manufacturing process. On the other hand, the less the production requirements of a product match the firm's resources, the less efficient the product will be to manufacture. For example, if a firm currently produces products on an assembly line, it probably would not be in the company's best interest to initiate a new product requiring much custom work at individual work stations. Such a move probably would be inefficient because the workers would have to learn new skills, new equipment would have to be purchased, material handling patterns would have to be altered, and inventories would have to be adjusted.

The design of a product should not be approved nor the decision made to produce it until the firm objectively examines its financial condition to ensure that it has the necessary dollar resources to see the product through to the point where it begins to return a profit. For a major new product (especially one requiring substantial investments in new equipment and facilities), this often takes a long time, since buildings may have to be built, equipment purchased and installed, and raw materials and parts purchased. In addition, the actual production of a brand-new product initially proceeds slowly because it usually takes time to work the "bugs" out of a new production system. Each of these activities takes time and is costly. But no money is coming in from the new product's sales to help offset these costs. To make matters worse, when the product finally does hit the market, initial sales normally are slow until market acceptance for the product is gained. Thus, if a firm doesn't have the financial resources (cash or credit) to offset these initial costs, the company may go out of business before the product ever has a chance to realize its long-term potential.

Testing

Before a product is placed into production, prototypes of the product should be tested sufficiently to ensure that the final product will perform its intended function. This is the stage of product design at which steel-belted tires run over boards full of nails, and wristwatches are thrown into cement mixers or worn by football players during practice. The main concerns here are quality and reliability as they relate to the product's intended function.

Another important factor in product testing is consumer safety. Product recalls are expensive, both in terms of the cost of the recall and the damaging effect on a company's image. A good example is the product-recall problem Firestone Tire and Rubber Company faced with certain models of its steel-belted radial tires. One major goal of product testing should be to preclude such product-use problems and recalls.

Pilot Production Run

After all the information concerning materials, VA/VE, standardization, market research, company resources, and product testing have been incorporated into the product design, a complete set of tentative specifications is drafted, and the product is put through a pilot production run. For a manufactured product, the pilot run involves the manufacture of a small quantity of a new product under simulated normal-production conditions. For services, the pilot may involve a trial run of the process using other employees or even real customers as "guinea pigs."

In either case, the purpose is to test the product and the process to remove any defects or inefficiencies that are revealed. Once this stage is completed, the product design becomes definite, and product specifications can be finalized.

Designing Services

Throughout this discussion, the term *product* has referred to both manufactured items and services. It may be helpful, however, to use a service example to illustrate specifically how the concepts apply.

Years ago, innovative entrepreneurs borrowed ideas from the automobile assembly line to create the automatic car wash. At first a novelty, the car wash is now in the saturation stage of the product life cycle, where it is likely to stay until some radical new technology displaces it. The earliest car washes used rough brushes that scrubbed the car, but continued research and development has developed a variety of better cleaning equipment as well as more effective detergents, spray waxes, vinyl dressings, and other products.

Most car washes today offer a menu of options for the customer. Like the product line in a manufacturing business, the car wash offers a line of services including wash, spray wax, floor-mat cleaning, dressings for tires and vinyl roofs, and perhaps other special features as the car passes down the line. Often, several of these options are packaged as "sets" with special reduced prices. Larger car washes may have separate facilities for waxing, interior cleaning, and detailing.

Like manufacturing, services use materials, and the components of the service (such as the elements of the car wash) are subject to value analysis/value engineering, standardization, and modular design. Although CAD systems exist expressly for the design of physical products, services may also employ computer simulations or other sophisticated tools in their design. Certainly market research plays a major role in the development and refinement of services that meet the needs of customers, and the service firm must consider its resources in the selection of products to offer. Many car washes sell accessories for automobiles, but few go so far as to offer maintenance or repair for cars.

Finally, the service must be tested and perhaps subjected to a pilot run before it is open to the public. Each of the components of the car wash, such as the spray wax, should be tested on different paints and exterior surfaces and under different temperature and weather conditions. In the pilot run, each combination of services (wash, wax, etc.) should be tested on several cars to assure that the modules that work well separately do not work together to form an incompatible combination that turns the finish on your new Corvette into a sticky mess.

Product Description

After a product design is established, much supporting work must be done before finished products can be produced. Material must be ordered, employees trained, and all production activities scheduled. Control systems for quantity, quality, time, and cost must be in place. None of these activities could begin to occur with any degree of coordination without the entire product being completely, clearly, and accurately described with a set of product specifications, a bill of materials, and a route sheet.

Product Specifications

Product specifications refer to the detailed description of the product. For a manufactured item, the description usually includes a list of the product's measurable characteristics (dimensions, weight, volume, and tolerances), the different parts and components that go into the product, and a detailed set of directions for assembling the unit. For a complicated product such as an aircraft, teams of experts develop thousands of pages of descriptions and blueprints showing every part, dimension, material, and method of assembly. But even simple products may require detailed descriptions. The U.S. government specification for a mousetrap, for example, contains more than 120,000 words and many pages of supporting documents.

Service specifications normally include a list of resources needed such as material, tools and equipment, and labor, as well as a detailed set of directions for delivering the service and a list of measurable characteristics that determine satisfactory performance. In many services, the product specifications are even more important than they are for a manufactured item. For example, if a customer is buying a lawn mower, he or she can examine the product, check its specifications visually, test the item, and then make a decision to purchase. But if the customer is buying a lawn-care service, he or she must trust the written product specification to make the purchase decision. In this case, as with many services, the product is created, produced, and delivered simultaneously. There is no way to examine the service before it is performed.

Bill of Materials

In addition to clear, complete, and accurate product specifications, a bill of materials (B/M), usually developed by the designer from the product specifications, lists all the components, including the quantities of each, required to produce one unit of the finished product. For example, the bill of materials for a bicycle would specify the two pedals, two handle grips, and one seat (among other things). An example of the bill of materials for the manufacture of a yo-yo is illustrated in figure 2-2 and for a car wash in figure 2-3. (A more detailed and complex bill of materials is shown in chapter 4).

An important function of the bill of materials is to permit a production schedule to be "exploded" into a list of required raw materials. *Exploding* means that the quantity of finished product in the production schedule is multiplied by the quantities of components in the bill of materials. For example, if 2,000 yo-yos are scheduled for production next month, we will need 4,000 wooden discs,

	Product Description	
	Yo-Yo	
Part or Material Number	Part Description	Quantity per Assembly
2010	Wooden Disc	2
2011	Connecting Pin	1
2012	3 Feet of String	1
2013	Glue	.04 oz
2014	Paint	.1 oz
2015	Cardboard Box	1

Figure 2-2. Bill of Materials for a Yo-Yo

	Product Description	
	Car Wash	
Material Number	Material Description	Quantity Per Unit (Washing One Car)
3010	Detergent	3 oz.
3011	White-wall Cleaner	1 oz.
3012	Water	12 gals.
3013	Hot Wax	4 oz.

Figure 2-3. Bill of Materials for a Car Wash

2,000 connecting pins, 2,000 strings, 80 ounces of glue, 200 ounces of paint, and 2,000 cardboard boxes.

After computing the total number of each component needed for production, the purchasing department can then check the firm's inventory to see if any of the parts currently are in stock. Purchasing then will buy those materials

Product Description Yo-Yo

Operation Number	Dept. Number	Machine Number	Operation Description	Setup Time (Minutes)	Per Piece Time (Minutes)
1	13	383	Paint wooden discs	1.3	.015
2	8	211	Connect discs with connecting pin	.75	.02
3	6	101	Attach string	.5	.01
4	7		Inspect		
5	21	622	Package	1.0	.015

Figure 2-4. Route Sheet for a Yo-Yo

needed to complete the production schedule. For example, if 4,000 wooden discs are needed and 1,500 units are in stock, purchasing must acquire an additional 2,500 discs to fulfill the requirement.

For services, it is important that some unit of service be agreed upon and that the bill of materials be expressed in these terms. For carpet cleaning, 1 square yard is a frequently used unit, while in roofing the common unit of measure is 100 square feet. In many service industries, the unit is a transaction (such as in a bank) or a customer served (as in a restaurant). In the car wash example, the unit is one car; so a forecast of 500 cars for the coming week could be multiplied by the bill of materials to determine the needed amount of detergent, wax, and other materials.

Other Supporting Documents

Certain situations might require the employment of other supporting documents to communicate the product specifications to purchasing, scheduling, quality control, production control, and other units within the organization as well as to the sales force and to the customer. Blueprints, models, pictures, route sheets, and assembly diagrams are applicable to manufactured products. Services may require written descriptions, diagrams, samples, demonstrations, or even videotapes of the service being performed.

An example of a route sheet for the manufacture of yo-yos is figure 2-4. It lists the sequence of production operations necessary to make the finished product, including inspection and assembly operations. The route sheet contains a separate entry for each operation performed on a different machine or in a different work center. As an aid in production planning and scheduling, the route sheet almost always includes the standard times allowed for setting up each operation and for producing each piece after the setup has been approved. Additional examples of a route sheet and other production documents are given in chapter 3.

Evaluating Research and Development

Of all the areas of the business firm, research and development has always been considered the most difficult to evaluate because of the uncertain links from research activities to research results and because of the time involved. A researcher or design engineer may work on a project for months or years, only to find that the resulting product is not salable. Even if the product seems promising, the value of the engineer's work may not be known for several years.

For these reasons, many firms engage in R&D based on faith and fear; they have faith that their efforts will produce usable products, and they are afraid *not* to have an R&D department for competitive reasons. The size of the R&D budget differs considerably among industries, but often the decision is made to devote a given percentage of sales to R&D, under the logic that as the firm gets larger its R&D effort should grow in proportion.

Traditional measures of R&D effectiveness have focused on two factors: control of projects underway and final results. Most R&D projects start as proposals that are approved for funding. As the project unfolds, it is monitored for time and cost relative to the budget and schedule contained in the proposal. If possible, the project will contain milestone events that mark the accomplishment of each phase of the project. At such times, the project often undergoes an intense evaluation, and a decision is then made to continue, change, or abandon the project.

Upon completion, the projects should produce measurable results in the form of new products, process improvements, or patents for new discoveries. These results can be evaluated along with other outcomes, such as papers presented at scientific meetings or reports published in scholarly or trade journals.

Break-Even Time

Recently, Hewlett Packard, a major manufacturer of computers and electronic equipment, developed a concise way of evaluating its R&D efforts from initial idea to the time the idea becomes a successful product in the marketplace. This model, called Break-Even Time, is not a remedy for all R&D evaluation problems, but it combines in a single measure the time and costs of development with the profit from the sale of the product.

An example will illustrate the R&D process at Hewlett Packard and help explain the Break-Even Time (BET) diagram in figure 2-5. A new product, such as the Hewlett Packard plotter, begins as an idea in phase 1, when the idea is explored and a decision is made to develop the idea as a laboratory project (phase 2) into a workable product. In phase 3, the prototype is further developed so that it can be manufactured efficiently, and it is then released to the manufacturing division for production.

Chapter 2 Product Design and Development 47

Figure 2-5. Break-Even Time Model

At this point, the graph indicates that the majority of development costs have been expended, but the product has not yet been manufactured or sold. As it enters this next stage (phase 4), the product will incur manufacturing costs such as setup, material, labor, and overhead, to produce the initial stock of the item. As these units are sold (at a profit) the total profit attributable to this product begins to accumulate. Eventually, if the product is successful in the market, it will earn enough profit to cover all of its development costs. At this point, the new product has truly reached break-even for the company.

The primary objective in this analysis is to minimize the break-even time, defined as the time from the beginning of exploration of the idea until the product that stemmed from that idea has earned enough profit to cover all of its development costs. A second objective is to minimize break-even after release (BEAR), the time from the beginning of manufacturing until profits cover development costs.

At first, the emphasis in this standard of measurement seems to be on time—on doing things rapidly; and, indeed, part of it is. In the fast-changing electronics markets, a new product that is late in the market will lose a lot of profit to the competition. John Young, the president of Hewlett Packard has said that a project that is six months late is far worse than a project with a 50 percent overrun in development costs.

But very rapid development of new products will not be beneficial in the long run if the development work is not done well. Problems in the manufacturing stage could slow down the time the product takes to reach the market, and hidden defects in the design could eat away the profits in warranty costs. If, on the other hand, development is very effective at removing all bugs before release to manufacturing, the startup time can be reduced and some manufacturing problems eliminated, thus allowing the product to reach the market and begin earning more profit sooner. On the graph, the operating profit line climbs at a steeper slope and reaches break-even sooner.

The break-even-time model helps us focus on the critical factors in research and development:

1. Maximize the effectiveness of development activities in creating salable products
2. Minimize the time required to develop an idea
3. Keep development costs under control
4. Coordinate the relationship between development and manufacturing
5. Develop products that are cost effective to manufacture
6. Develop products that will return a good profit.

Research and development may always be the riskiest part of any business firm, but doing these activities a little better than the competition will enhance one's chances for business survival and even success.

Key Concepts

Product Life Cycle

Product Strategy

Product Level

Product Line

Research and Development

Value Analysis

Modular Design

Computer-Aided Design (CAD)

Service Design

Product Specifications

Bill of Materials

Route Sheet

Break-Even Time

References

Albrecht, Karl, and Zemke, Ron. *Service America!* Homewood, Ill: Dow Jones-Irwin, 1985.

Groover, J. D., and Zimmers, E. W., Jr. *CAD/CAM: Computer Aided Design and Manufacturing.* Englewood Cliffs, NJ: Prentice-Hall, 1984.

Haas, Elizabeth A. "Breakthrough Manufacturing." *Harvard Business Review.* 65 (March–April 1987): 75–81.

Hayes, R. H., and Wheelwright, S. "The Dynamics of Process-Product Life Cycles." *Harvard Business Review.* 59 (March–April 1979): 127–136.

Hayes, R. H., and Wheelwright, S. *Restoring Our Competitive Edge: Competing Through Manufacturing.* New York: John Wiley & Sons, 1984.

Takeuchi, Hirotaka, and Nonaka, Ikujiro, "The New Product Development Game." *Harvard Business Review.* 64 (January–February, 1986): 137–146.

Discussion Questions

1. A list of manufactured products is given below. Describe the progression of each product through the product life cycle, ending at the point where you think the product is today. Include in your discussion how long the progression took, the entry or exit of competitors at various stages, product price changes from stage to stage, and other factors relevant to the product life cycle.

    a. Automobile

    b. Television

c. Compact disc

   d. Duplicating machine

   e. Personal computer

2. In the same manner as question 1, above, discuss the life cycle of the following services:

   a. College education

   b. Golf course

   c. Automatic bank teller

   d. Convenience market

   e. Home-security system

3. Under deregulation, banks have been able to offer many new products that combine services previously offered only by other financial institutions and to develop some new products that have never been offered previously by any financial institutions. Describe several new products developed by banks in the last five years. Suggest at least one new product that banks might develop in the future.

4. Outline the elements of Bic Pen Corporation's product strategy. Name several current or new products that would fit the strategy.

5. One application of R&D is modification of existing products. Select a product (manufactured item or service) and suggest how it might be modified to better fit your needs as a customer.

6. Standardization exists for many, but not all, products in the United States. Give several examples of a lack of standardization that (a) was created because of independent development by different companies, or (b) was created purposely for competitive reasons.

7. Although some products are standardized in the United States, they are not necessarily standardized across international boundaries. Give examples of this lack of standardization. What problems does this create, and how are the problems resolved?

8. Select a product such as a disposable cigarette lighter and discuss how the product should be tested and under what conditions it should be tested before it is released for sale throughout the United States.

9. Suppose you are planning to develop a new "same-day" document-delivery service in your hometown.

   a. Write a detailed description of this product.

   b. Explain how you would do market research on the product.

   c. Should you do a pilot run of the product and, if so, how would you do it?

10. For the Break-Even Time model, make two lists of factors: one for those that would reduce break even time and another for those that would extend it.

Problems

1. The owner of the car wash forecasts that 500 cars will be washed this week. Currently in stock he has

Detergent	400 oz.
White wall cleaner	0
Hot wax	1,000 oz.

   How much of each item should the car wash owner order to be able to meet the needs for this week's production?

2. Use the information from figure 2-4 to determine the total amount of labor for setup and production of one batch of 2,000 yo-yos. Would the same amount of labor be required if the yo-yos were produced in four batches of 500 each?

CHAPTER
3
Location, Layout, Work Study, and Measurement

Suppose you wanted to start your own small business. In addition to developing a marketing plan and arranging financing, you would have to develop an overall business strategy and decide what products you want to produce, as we discussed in chapter 2.

This chapter continues the discussion of the design functions necessary to set up an effective and efficient production system. Later, chapter 4 will cover the forecasting, planning, and scheduling of production within the facility, and chapter 5 will deal with the complexities of acquiring the raw materials, parts, and supplies needed. Chapters 6 and 7 will focus on the control activities for managing the materials in inventory and controlling the quality of the process.

Necessary design functions covered in this chapter include finding a proper location for the facilities, deciding on the best layout of the work flow within the facility, studying the work to determine the best methods, and measuring the work to establish time standards for planning and control.

Although these functions must be performed at the startup stage of a new business to avoid chaos, it is equally important for existing businesses to re-evaluate their operations periodically to maintain an effective system in the face of changing product lines, growth of the firm, and the many changes in the environment over time. As a business firm evolves, it usually finds that locations, layouts, or process designs that worked well in the past have become obsolete with the addition of new products, new equipment, and different demands by customers. For some firms, such as high-technology manufacturers and multi-location retailers, these decisions must be made very frequently, sometimes monthly or even weekly. For other firms in basic industries such as steel or mining, years may pass before the firm feels the need to reevaluate.

To develop and sustain a competitive and profitable operation, managers of new and existing businesses must consider the following four factors:

1. **Location.** The regional, community, and specific site factors involved in selecting an original, replacement, or additional location for a manufacturing, warehouse, office, or service facility;
2. **Layout.** The arrangement of machines, equipment, materials handling, aisles, service areas, storage areas, work stations, and customer areas within the facility;
3. **Work study.** The design of work procedures to establish the process and methods to perform specific jobs within the process efficiently; and
4. **Work measurement.** The analysis of work to establish time standards or estimates of the amount of labor needed to perform a task.

Facilities Location

An improper location for a manufacturing firm usually results in increased production and distribution costs, placing an otherwise efficiently managed company at a competitive disadvantage. The location of service facilities is critical because proximity to the customer and a convenient location may be the major factor in determining the success of the enterprise. The location decision takes on added significance because that choice, once made and implemented, cannot be changed without considerable cost.

Sequence of Location Choices

The facilities location decision involves three phases: (1) the region or general area, (2) the particular community within the region selected, and (3) the specific site within the community.

Regional factors requiring serious consideration include the following:

1. **Proximity to markets.** Distance increases transit time and costs and thereby affects the service provided.
2. **Relationship to other facilities.** A multilocation firm may select a region for an additional facility based primarily on the best coverage of the market territory it serves.
3. **Access to materials and vendors.** This determines transport times and costs for materials, supplies, tools, equipment, and components supplied by vendors.
4. **Transportation and communication facilities.** Prompt, regular, dependable, low-cost shipment and communication services are essential. De-

pending upon the volume, frequency, and cost of movements, the company may prefer rail, truck, air, or barge carriers, or some combination of these.

5. **Concentration of skilled labor and the overall labor supply.** The objective is to develop and maintain an effective work force with minimum recruiting and training costs. Favorable regional wage rate differentials are a strong positive factor in situations where labor cost represents a major part of a firm's total operating cost.

6. **Competition.** In some industries, locations as far from competitors as possible provide the best advantage, while in other industries, similar firms tend to cluster in an area to their mutual advantage.

7. **Climate.** Climate may be a major factor in attracting the desired labor supply. A mild climate generally is preferable; its influence is evident in the rapid growth of the Sunbelt states in both manufacturing industries and population.

Factors that affect the location decision at the community level include the following:

1. **Labor supply.** This should be sufficient to provide the number of people and skills to be employed in both new and existing facilities.

2. **Managerial preferences.** Many plants are located in the community where the founder lived when the firm was established.

3. **Community facilities and living conditions.** Schools, churches, medical facilities, shopping facilities, recreational and cultural opportunities, available housing, and municipal services (such as water, power, sewer, garbage, and police and fire protection) are important in recruiting an adequate work force.

4. **Laws and taxes.** These may restrict or support a firm's operation.

5. **Availability of suitable sites.** The desirable locations already may be occupied.

6. **Attitudes.** The community, labor groups, and other business firms may have cooperative attitudes or be resistant to any change.

7. **Inducements.** The community may make financial or tax inducements to attract the organization.

The following specific site location factors within a community should be considered:

1. Size must be adequate for present needs and sufficient for future expansion.
2. Topography, drainage, and soil conditions of the plot should be suitable and permit reasonable construction costs.

3. Land costs, plus total development costs, should be realistic.
4. Utilities, such as electricity, gas, water, and sewers, should be available on a dependable basis at a reasonable cost.
5. Transportation facilities, such as roads, rail sidings, and airports, should facilitate the efficient and low-cost receipt and distribution of the materials and the necessary travel of key personnel.
6. Provision for waste disposal and environmental considerations should minimize restrictive legislation, control costs, and prevent loss of public support.
7. Amenities, such as parking, access to public transportation, lunch facilities and other factors must be available or be provided by the firm.
8. Type of locale, such as central city, industrial park, suburban or rural area, has both advantages and disadvantages. Major traffic intersections, shopping malls, or other types of locations may be a part of the location strategy for some organizations.

Location Decision Making

Some firms, such as convenience stores, fast-food restaurants, motel chains, and gasoline distributors, locate new facilities frequently. In these companies, departments of experts in the field of location-analysis methods and real estate are continually working on location projects. Depending on the firm, they may make decisions at the department level or make recommendations to higher levels of management for a final decision.

In other firms, where the decision to locate or relocate is made infrequently, the typical procedure is to establish a committee, gather data, perhaps hire specialized consultants, meet with representatives from possible sites, and eventually present a recommendation to top management for a decision. When General Motors decided to locate its new facility in Tennessee, the press followed the process over years of study because of the impact this decision would have on some small community.

Analysis Methods

A variety of approaches, methods, and quantitive tools are available to make the location decision. Several of the more important methods are reviewed here.

Weighted Factor Method. One way to make the location decision is to assign weights to the regional, community, and site factors considered important. Each alternative site is evaluated on each factor, evaluations are multiplied by the weights, and the weighted evaluations are totaled for each site to provide insights into the location decision.

Table 3-1 provides an example of this method. Notice that, for this firm, the industrial park emerged as the best located overall, even though each of the other sites was better on one of the criteria.

Table 3-1
Weighted Factor Analysis of Locations

FACTORS (weights)

SITES	Land Cost (.40)	Possible Expansion (.10)	Transportation Availability (.30)	Amenities (.20)	Total Weighted Factor
Industrial Park					
Evaluation	8	5	8	8	
Weighted	3.2	0.5	2.4	1.6	7.7
Rural					
Evaluation	10	10	4	1	
Weighted	4.0	1.0	1.2	0.2	6.4
Central City					
Evaluation	2	0	10	6	
Weighted	0.8	0.0	3.0	1.2	5.0
Suburban					
Evaluation	6	5	6	10	
Weighted	2.4	0.5	1.8	2.0	6.7

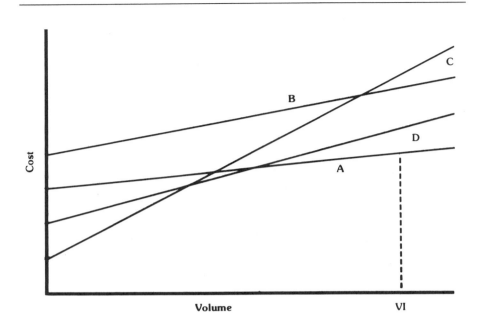

Figure 3-1. Total Costs for Alternative Locations A, B, C, and D Compared to Volume

Break-Even Analysis. Another approach is to make a location break-even analysis. First, relevant fixed and variable costs are determined for each proposed location. Next, the total cost curves for each alternative are plotted on a single graph (figure 3-1). Then, based on forecasted level of activity, the alternative location with the lowest total cost is selected.

In this example, projected volume of VI would lead to the selection of site A. In general, site A is best for high volumes, D for intermediate levels, and C for low volumes. Site B would never be chosen by this method, because it is never the low-cost alternative.

Simulation. Sometimes the location selected determines the type of facility that can be built, which, in turn, affects the operating costs and perhaps the revenues for the facility. One way to handle the complicated interactions of site costs, facility costs, and impact on the firm is to simulate the operation of this alternative for time to see the likely results.

A large motel chain built a simulation model to do just that. Some of its locations are in rural areas where two major interstate highways intersect. A facility here would require larger dining facilities (since there were few alternatives for the traveler) but no banquet facilities for local club meetings. The demand is almost exclusively from travelers staying only one night, and this has implications for the configuration of the rooms, staffing of employees, registration procedures, and many other factors. By contrast, small-town locations and downtown metropolitan locations would differ considerably on these factors.

For each proposed location, the type of facility was plugged into the simulation, along with specific data on the cost of the land, traffic rates on the highways, number of nearby competing facilities, and other relevant data. The computer then simulated the operation of the facility for several years, and projected revenues, costs, profits, and other data with distributions on the degree of risk involved. At this point, the decision makers can adjust input data (such as more or fewer rooms in the facility) and make successive runs of the simulation until they are satisfied with the combination of factors for that project and make a decision.

Linear Programming. A special form of linear programming known as the transportation method is especially useful for the firm that has multiple plants serving multiple warehouses. When deciding to locate a new plant or a new warehouse, this quantitative tool will evaluate each proposed site in terms of its impact on the cost of the entire system, particularly the transportation and distribution costs. The analysis provides the optimal distribution of products from plants to warehouses, including the proposed facility.

As an example, one firm has manufacturing plants in Chicago, Los Angeles, and Phoenix. These plants supply distribution centers in regional locations which, in turn, supply retail outlets throughout the country. An additional distribution center is needed and two sites, A and B, have been proposed. The matrix in figure 3-2 shows the three plants with their production capacities and the demand from the four distribution centers, including the new one. The numbers in the upper left corner of each cell represent the transportation costs of shipping from a plant to a distribution center.

Each proposed location is plugged into the last column of the matrix with its appropriate transportation costs, and the allocation problem is solved to yield the optimal distribution of products from the plants to the regional centers. (Solution techniques are explained in most operations-research texts and are available in many computer programs.)

Figures 3-3 and 3-4 are the solution matrices for the two proposed sites. Site A would receive 100 units of product from Chicago and 600 units from Los Angeles to fill its demand of 700 units. The low-cost solution for site B would involve shipping all 700 units from the Phoenix plant and making necessary adjustments in other shipping schedules to assure that supply from the plants meets demand from the distribution centers. With site B, total shipping costs for the system would be $3,000 less. This is then factored in with the other costs for the two proposed sites, and a final decision is made.

Figure 3-2

PLANTS	DISTRIBUTION CENTERS				CAPACITIES
	I	II	III	New	
Chicago	8	10	15		1000
Los Angeles	12	7	4		1500
Phoenix	14	10	8		1200
DEMAND	900	1300	800	700	

Figure 3-2. Matrix For Transportation Method of Linear Programming

Figure 3-3

PLANTS	DISTRIBUTION CENTERS				CAPACITIES
	I	II	III	A	
Chicago	8 900	10	5	4 100	1000
Los Angeles	12	7 100	4 800	6 600	1500
Phoenix	14	10 1200	8	10	1200
DEMAND	900	1300	800	700	3700

TOTAL COST = $27,100

Figure 3-3. Solution Matrix For Proposed Site A

Facilities Layout

Facilities layout is the overall arrangement of machines, personnel, materials handling, service facilities, and aisles required to facilitate efficient operation of the production system.

Several specific objectives of good facilities layout include the following:

DISTRIBUTION CENTERS

PLANTS	I	II	III	B	CAPACITIES
Chicago	8 900	10 100	15	6	1000
Los Angeles	12	7 700	4 800	10	1500
Phoenix	14	10 500	8	4 700	1200
DEMAND	900	1300	800	700	3700

TOTAL COST = $24,100

Figure 3-4. Solution Matrix For Proposed Site B

1. Minimizing materials handling and plant transportation requirements. This reduces the costs and time to move materials through the production process and reduces work-in-process inventories.
2. Maximize the return on the fixed investment in facilities by minimizing the amount of floor space required. Floor congestion and production bottlenecks should be eliminated.
3. Utilizing labor efficiently and effectively by minimizing the distance and time to obtain materials, tools, and supplies; by facilitating maintenance and housecleaning; and by facilitating production supervision and use of support personnel.
4. Reducing the hazards affecting employees and products. Provision of adequate exhaust ducts, guard rails, and operating clearances makes the job safer.
5. Providing for a smooth, logical flow of customers through the process where applicable.
6. Providing flexibility for expansion caused by growth, new products, and new processes.

The net effect should be to increase efficiency, reduce costs, and improve employee and customer satisfaction.

Regardless of how effective the original layout is, changes are inevitable. Changes in demand, the introduction of new products, product-design changes, obsolescence of processes or equipment, changes in safety and personnel needs, and changes made to reduce costs may prompt a new layout.

Figure 3-5. **Process Layout Showing Movement of Two Different Products**

Manufacturing Layout

Four basic layout patterns are used in manufacturing operations:

1. Process layout
2. Product or line layout
3. Fixed-position layout
4. Group or cellular layout

A *process layout,* which is used in the job-shop or intermittent-production system, groups similar equipment together. For example, all drilling equipment would be in one area, all grinding equipment would be in another work center, and all milling equipment in still another. Figure 3-5 presents a graphic representation of a process layout. The variable-path nature of materials handling in process layouts eliminates much of the savings possible from the use of chutes, conveyors, or transfer machines.

The process layout is used where volume is low, several products are made, and processing flexibility is desired. General-purpose, low-cost machines generally are used. If one machine breaks down, the work usually can be shifted to other, similar machines. Because equipment in a process layout does not depend on a given sequence, machines that produce excessive noise, vibration, fumes, or heat can be located in isolated areas. Since the work normally is paced by the employee rather than by the machines, individual incentive-pay systems can be used.

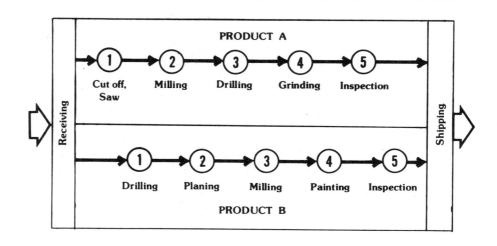

Figure 3-6. Product or Line Layout Showing Movement of Two Different Products

There are several disadvantages to the process layout: more complex planning and control because of routing, scheduling and cost-accounting requirements; costlier materials handling; larger work-in-process inventories; increased storage and floor area requirements; increased costs for more skilled labor; more frequent inspection requirements; and more extensive supervision requirements.

A *product* or *line layout* arranges the equipment according to the progressive steps by which the product is made. Product layout is used in the repetitive production system, in which the number of end products is small, the parts are highly standardized and interchangeable, and the volume is large. Figure 3-6 presents a graphic representation of a product or line layout.

Product or line layout permits the use of costly, specialized, high-volume equipment; materials handling is simplified by means of transfer machines or conveyors; both production control and job training are easier; less inspection is required; there is less work-in-process; smaller aisles are required; and the floor area is more productive.

Disadvantages of the product or line layout include the higher initial equipment investment; greater vulnerability to work stoppage; the highly repetitive nature of the work; and the inflexibility that makes it more costly when changes are made because of product redesign.

With a *fixed-position layout*, the product remains in one position because of its bulk or weight, and the workers, materials, and tools move to it. This layout normally is used in making items such as locomotives, ships, or large printing presses in project production.

A *group* or *cellular layout* is indicated when a product is manufactured by means of group technology; that is, equipment and operations that have a

Figure 3-7. Layout by Process Versus Cellular Layout

common sequence for a family of parts or products are grouped together. This permits economic production of very small lots, thereby minimizing work-in-process inventories, space requirements, and production leadtimes. In layout by process, machines are grouped by type, and parts travel long distances between steps. By applying group technology with a cellular layout—that is, by combining several steps within an independent machining cell—production lead time can be reduced, and less space is required. Figure 3-7 shows the differences between process layout and cellular layout.

Other types of layout include marketing, storage, yard, and office. A *marketing layout* is arranged primarily to facilitate the sale of products, such as in a supermarket. A *storage layout* is designed to fill an inventory and stock-keeping function, providing effective use of storage facilities and materials-handling equipment. A *yard layout* is used for outside storage, thereby reducing the need for inside facility requirements. An *office layout* facilitates the work of clerical and administrative employees. In addition, many flow process operations, such as in an oil refinery, are laid out according to the technology of the process.

Service Layout

Service organizations, such as banks, insurance companies, hospitals, restaurants, and offices, face many of the same layout problems as manufacturing organizations. The primary difference is that their facilities exist to bring customers together with the organization's services. The layouts provide easy automobile entrance into parking areas from which sidewalks and well-marked entrances guide the customer into the service facility. Receiving or holding areas, cash registers, service counters, and employee work stations frequently are part of a service layout.

Service layouts receive and serve the customer or process physical materials. A hospital, for example, may have a product or line layout for preparing serving trays; a process layout for various medical technologies, such as laboratory tests, radiology, and surgery; and a fixed-position layout within an operating room or intensive-care facility.

Restaurants also could have mixed layouts. For example, a buffet line represents a product layout, and a seated dining area represents a fixed-position layout. The kitchen itself, with its freezers, grills, ovens, dessert areas, and salad areas, represents a process layout.

In office automation and clerical applications, the primary considerations are the location and movement of people, paperwork, and equipment.

Layout Cost Comparisons

As volume increases, the cost advantage moves successively from fixed-position layout, to process layout, to product layout. For this reason, many companies strive for high-volume operations to permit use of product layout in a repetitive production system.

In actual practice, most firms use a combination of layouts. For example, machining operations, even in large-volume operations such as those in the automobile industry, frequently are performed with a process layout. Automobile assembly operations, on the other hand, normally use a product or line-layout pattern.

Layout Analysis

The layout analyst frequently starts the manufacturing layout by locating the receiving and shipping departments, which are influenced by the location of rail

From	To							
	A	B	C	D	E	F	G	Total
A		40		15				55
B			50	10		22		82
C		5		55	15		5	80
D					55	15		70
E	15		10			25		50
F		5					30	35
G	10			15				25

Figure 3-8. Travel Chart Used in Layout Planning

lines, highways, and existing or potential dock facilities. Then the analyst must determine the size and shape of the other departments.

For process layouts, the primary consideration is minimizing materials-handling costs. A travel chart (figure 3-8) tabulates the frequency of loads between each of the departments. Multiplying the distance between each department by the number of loads moved provides a means of weighting the materials-handling cost. Loads below the diagonal line indicate undesirable backtracking. By rearranging the relative positions of the departments to obtain the greatest total weighting just above the diagonal line, the analyst develops various solutions before reaching the most satisfactory one.

For product layouts, balance is the key criterion. Each step in the process should provide equal capacity so that material flow will be uninterrupted. With line-assembly operations, workers should be assigned to each successive set of work stations so there will be a minimum of idle time in the assembly line. This process is called *line balancing*.

Within the actual production department, the analyst must provide adequate floor space for the worker-machine interface, plus space for necessary incoming and outgoing materials and access for maintenance service. Floor loads, ceiling heights, special plant utilities, dangerous operations, environmental problems (light, temperature, humidity, noise, vibration, and dirt), and safety (aisle widths and machine clearances) also must be considered.

Stockrooms, tool cribs, inspection stations, drinking fountains, and restrooms should be located to minimize the travel time for employees who will be using them. Locker rooms and washrooms should be located near where employees enter and leave the facility.

Layouts for service industries in which the customer is not present (such as offices) follow the same guidelines, except that the flow of material may be reports, documents, or other forms of information. When the customer is a part of the process, as in retail stores and personal services, generally the flow of the customer is plotted first to maximize efficiency and convenience, and then the equipment, materials, and service operators are placed in positions to support the primary customer flow.

Process charts and flow diagrams help determine the most effective patterns. Often, the actual placement of equipment, materials, work stations, counters, and other components is decided after experimentally placing templates or three-dimensional scale models in position on a floor plan.

Materials Handling

Materials handling frequently is considered the twin of facilities layout because the type of materials-handling equipment utilized influences the plant layout, and vice versa.

Materials-handling equipment is classified as either fixed-path or varied-path equipment. Fixed-path equipment (conveyors, chutes, cranes, and hoists) is relatively inflexible and handles material in large volume, normally in a continuous flow. Varied-path equipment (forklift trucks and four-wheel trucks) is flexible and normally handles materials in lots. Fixed-path equipment occupies space constantly, while varied-path equipment occupies space only intermittently.

Where variability is not required, there is a tendency to use fixed-path equipment for several reasons: (1) lower initial cost, (2) lower operating cost (no operator is required), (3) less supervision required, and (4) less space required.

A recent trend in some facilities is to use automated materials-handling systems. Automatic storage and retrieval systems (AS/RS) place pallet loads within very large storage racks by means of automated stacking cranes. A computer locates an empty rack cell, directs the stacking crane to place the pallet within the rack, and then records the pallet's location for inventory purposes and automatic retrieval when desired. Robotic carriers automatically convey loads between the rack area and specified delivery areas by using wires installed in the floor to guide the carriers to their destination. These systems do not require operating personnel, and it is even possible to operate in total darkness.

Data Needed for Layout Planning

The layout analyst requires certain types of information. For example, the bill of materials (B/M) specifies the kinds of materials and parts required to make a unit of product (see chapter 2). This, coupled with the forecasted demand for end products and spare parts, helps determine the scale of operations. In addition, the analyst must know the sequence of operations for processing and assembling parts into the end product. A master route sheet helps in making these determinations. With information concerning the products, product mix, market demand, and work standards, the analyst can determine the number and kinds of machines and tooling systems required and can proceed to make an effective layout.

Equipment Types and Their Selection

Equipment affects labor requirements, quality control, production capacity, and job design. Selection of equipment is based primarily on the product design, product volume, quality requirements, and cost considerations.

Firms must determine whether a specific type of work requires general-purpose machines or special-purpose machines. General-purpose machines—lathes or drill presses, for example—are capable of handling a variety of jobs. On the other hand, special-purpose machines, such as an automated transfer line, usually are faster and more efficient, but changing these complex systems to handle different product designs is difficult and costly.

General-purpose machines are less costly then special-purpose machines, have a broad range of job applications, are relatively simple to maintain, and have less obsolescence. On the other hand, they usually have slower operating rates, are less productive, have less consistent quality, and involve large work-in-process inventories. Special-purpose machines are extremely costly and normally are used only for high-volume production.

Numerical-control (N/C) machines are the most costly general-purpose machines, but they are faster and more efficient than other general-purpose machines. Such machines are preprogrammed, by means of alphanumeric instructions on punched paper tape or magnetic tape, to perform a cycle of operations repetitively. Since production is almost automatic, labor costs are reduced because a single operator often can operate several machines at the same time. Quality is improved and is more consistent. Tooling costs and lead time requirements also are reduced considerably. The primary disadvantages of N/C machines are their higher initial cost, the need for specially trained programmers, and higher maintenance costs.

Automated batch manufacturing systems (ABMS) or transfer machines are superior to N/C machines when large volumes are involved. Parts are attached to a conveying system and carried through a system of individual machines that transform the parts into finished units. All product handling is eliminated, except in the first and last operations. In one early installation, 42 machines were connected to perform 530 operations required to machine engine blocks. The ABMS reduced time from nine hours per block to less than 15 minutes.

Computer-aided manufacturing (CAM) is a sophisticated extension of direct numerical control of machine tools, robots, and inspection machines. Ideally, CAM interfaces with computer-aided design (see chapter 2). Data bases developed by CAD are used to manufacture tooling, program tooling for N/C machines, and program inspection machines in the development of CAM applications. In the future, information may pass directly from CAD to CAM via the data base with minimal use of engineering drawings. The CAD/CAM linkage greatly shortens the time between design and production. For example, in designing and making hydraulic tubing for aircraft, one manufacturer reduced the work force from twelve to three persons; time from release of the drawing to finished product was reduced from six weeks to eighteen minutes.

Industrial robots are increasingly used for highly repetitive manual jobs. The robots are computer controlled and usually are programmed initially by being hand guided through the required operation. Their greatest disadvantage is the initial cost; however, their operating costs usually are low, and they are easy to reprogram for other jobs.

Equipment in many service firms is following the same trends as in manufacturing. Restaurants and bars use automatic dispensing equipment, and the use of mini- or microcomputers in office applications make many of the tedious operations automatic.

Maintenance

Maintenance operations include all efforts to keep production facilities and equipment in proper operating condition. The four types of maintenance operations are (1) breakdown repair, (2) millwright (people who move and install equipment) activities and minor construction, (3) preventive maintenance, and (4) custodial services. Breakdown and millwright are called irregular maintenance because the demands for such services occur at irregular intervals and impose variable loads on the maintenance department. Preventive and custodial may be called regular or periodic maintenance for they may be performed on a set schedule.

Much attention has been given to the proper relationship of breakdown repair to preventive maintenance. Breakdown repair is a special problem because breakdowns are random, creating peaks and valleys in the work load. Queuing theory and Monte Carlo simulation (two specialized operation research techniques) are methods of analyzing breakdown waiting lines and distributions to determine personnel and scheduling requirements. In any case, the uneven maintenance work load may cause the maintenance department to operate inefficiently. However, in the interest of maximizing performance of the manufacturing departments, the firm may decide to accept some inefficiencies in the operation of the maintenance department.

Preventive maintenance (PM) is performed before the equipment breaks down so that it continues to operate satisfactorily and reduces the likelihood of breakdown. Its primary advantages are that it enables maintenance crews to schedule their time evenly, tends to minimize equipment breakdowns, and may be scheduled to avoid work stoppages. PM schedules may be based on calendar time or equipment usage time. To function successfully, a good PM program depends upon records, which include a maintenance history for each piece of equipment. These permit analysis of breakdown frequency and causes, thereby providing a basis for improving the PM procedure.

Two modifications of a PM program designed to reduce costs are group replacement and standby equipment. Group replacement applies to a large group of identical components, such as light bulbs. Analysis based on failure-probability distribution may justify replacing components after a certain time, along with units that already have failed, rather than replacing the units individually as they fail. In standby equipment analysis, the minimum total cost between the costs of lost service due to out-of-service machines versus the costs of keeping extra machines on hand to avoid a shutdown is sought.

In the past, maintenance was not a high priority for a service firm. But as service firms become more automated and use more sophisticated equipment, they are subject to the same dependencies on maintenance as manufacturing firms. American Express, for example, depends heavily on the proper functioning of its computer equipment for the rapid and accurate processing of customer information. Even minor breakdowns for very short periods can be extremely costly.

Maintenance of computers and other office equipment may be done by the firm's employees, by the company that sold the equipment to the firm, or by an independent maintenance contractor. Some estimates say that 1 percent of the purchase cost is spent monthly in maintenance. With the amount of electronic equipment now used in industry, and with the great need for maintenance, electronic-equipment and office-systems maintenance has become a service industry in itself.

Energy Management

Energy is one of the major purchased resources most firms use. Since the oil crunch of the early 1970s, the high costs of oil and petroleum derivatives have focused much more attention on energy management. Energy sources such as coal, nuclear power, hydrogenated electricity, wood, the sun, geothermal heat, shale oil, and wind are possible energy alternatives. Government programs and tax incentives now encourage investments in energy-conserving devices and materials, such as more efficient motors or insulating materials.

Many firms now have formal energy-management programs (EMP). Such programs start with an audit to determine an organization's current energy utilization. The gross energy audit measures total energy consumption and identifies the types of energy used. A detailed energy audit determines how much of each type of energy is being used and where (i.e., which process, operations, or machines).

Energy-management programs seek improvements through several types of conservation methods: (1) process changes, (2) product changes, (3) materials conservation, (4) heat-recovery applications, (5) improved equipment controls, (6) housekeeping practices, and (7) facilities design and insulation. Through these programs, many firms actually have reduced their energy requirements even in the face of organization growth.

Work Study

In the broadest sense, every organization is concerned with providing goods or offering services while utilizing men and women, machines, materials, and facilities as resources. All operating units should be concerned with performing their work more effectively, efficiently, and economically. Work study is an effective way to coordinate and use available resources. Work study means finding the most effective way of doing a job. It involves analyzing present and preferred work systems to develop an optimal transformation of resources into desired products.

The competitive pressures on today's manager greatly increase the need for work study. Specifically, work analysis should result in greater productivity through improved methods that normally permit an increased output with the same or less effort. Additional benefits often include reduction in worker fatigue, improved workplace layout, better product design, more efficient materials handling, and increased safety.

Work study is best applicable to large-scale repetitive manufacturing operations with standardized products and materials. In automobile manufacturing, for example, where millions of essentially identical units will be produced, work is studied in great detail to eliminate any wasted motion, to make the job easier to perform, and to find the right sequence of operations for maximum efficiency. Volume justifies the time and effort taken in work study.

But work study is finding more and more applications in the office and in a variety of service operations. Bank tellers, for example, can provide better, quicker service if their job has been studied to determine the proper equipment, layout of the work station, arrangement of materials, and procedures for each type of transaction. Although less routine than a job on an auto assembly line, the teller's job can be standardized for most typical transactions and the unusual cases handled as exceptions. Financial institutions, insurance companies, and even health-care facilities are finding that work study is not limited to manufactured products.

Those who perform work studies should be creative, questioning people who love efficiency and abhor waste. It has been claimed that work study is 80 percent attitude and 20 percent knowledge. The person who is continually trying to find faster, more effective ways of doing things or who manages to do several tasks at once is a good candidate for a work-study position. Given the proper skills and management support, that individual can pay company back in cost savings that equal many times his or her salary.

Work study can be applied in three separate phases:

1. Analysis of the initial design of the product and the process;
2. Periodic reviews of an existing method to see if further improvements can be made;
3. Special studies to resolve problems or to incorporate changes made to the product or process.

An organization's work is accomplished by a series of interdependent operations performed by individuals at work stations. Depending on the process, the tasks may be connected in a line (as in auto assembly) or separate but linked (as in the claims-processing department of an insurance company). The job of the work study analyst is to break down the work into its necessary elements, analyze each element to make it as efficient as possible, and combine the elements into a process that effectively produces the desired product. Key among the tools and techniques available are work-study charts.

Work-Study Charts

Charts using special symbols and formats enable the analyst to describe existing operations and processes and make changes on paper before real work is modified. Besides being useful analysis tools, charts aid in communicating proposed changes to management, employees, and others. The most commonly used charts are (1) process charts, (2) flow diagrams, (3) assembly charts, (4) multiple-activity charts, and (5) operation charts.

The American Society of Mechanical Engineers (ASME) has established a set of five symbols that are now standard in constructing process charts:

1. A large circle ◯ denotes an *operation*.
2. An arrow ➪ or denotes the *transportation* or movement of worker or material over three feet.
3. A square ☐ denotes an *inspection* for quality or quantity.
4. A large letter D denotes a *delay*.
5. An inverted triangle ▽ indicates *storage*.

In a process chart (figure 3-9), chronological steps of the process are listed following the worker, the product, or, in some cases, the customer. Time, distance, or other relevant descriptive information may be included also. It is then possible to summarize the data to determine how much time is spent in operations, inspections, transporting, storage, necessary delays (such as waiting for glue to dry) or unnecessary delays (such as waiting in line for processing).

Analysis of the process can proceed using questions such as the following:

1. **Can unnecessary work be eliminated?** Could a transportation be eliminated, for example, by performing two operations at the same work station?
2. **Can operations or elements be combined?** In one instance, a manufacturer of wood products found that he could move the product to the next work station while the finish on the product was drying; thus he combined the elements of transport and delay.
3. **Can the sequence of operations be changed?** Sometimes simply asking the question leads to new creative solutions such as attaching the wheels to a toy as an early step in the assembly process so the unit is easier to transport to successive work stations.

Advanced texts and work-study manuals contain long lists of questions such as these to help guide the thinking and stimulate the creativity of the work-study analyst.

Present Method ☒ ; Proposed Method ☐
Subject charted: *Manufacture mounting bracket*
Begins: *Receiving Department*
Ends: *Finished Stores Department*

Date *Dec. 3, 1988*
Charted by *J. Jones*
Page *1* of *1*

Step	Symbol	Distance	Time	Description
1	⇨	40'	15 min	Received from delivery truck
2	☐	–	5 min	Inspected
3	⇨	40'	5 min	To raw material stores
4	▽	–		In raw material stores
5	⇨	60'	10 min	Truck to cut-off saws
6	D			Wait at saws
7	○		30 min	Cut to size
8	D			Wait for truck
9	⇨	60'	5 min	Truck to drills
10	○		5 min	Drill 2 holes
11	⇨	120'	10 min	Truck to assembly
12	D			Wait for assembly
13	○		10 min	Assembly
14	☐		2 min	Inspect assembly
15	⇨	60'	5 min	Truck to finished stores
16	▽			In finished stores inventory

Figure 3-9. Process Chart

74 Fundamentals of Production/Operations Management

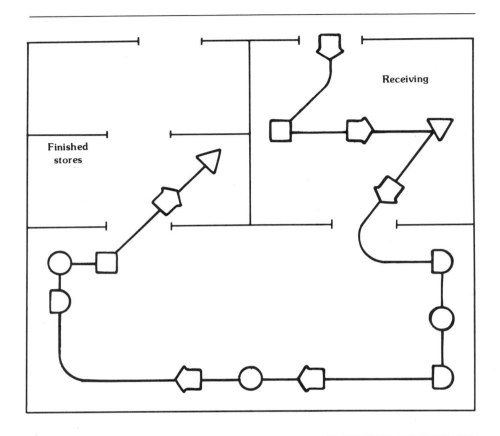

Figure 3-10. Flow Diagram

A flow diagram (figure 3-10) uses the ASME symbols connected by arrows on a floor plan of the facility to depict the flow of the product as it is completed. With this tool, one or several products can be traced to predict problems that could arise with material handling, bottleneck operations, or needed layout changes. Flow diagrams have become frequently used in service businesses to track the flow of customers through a facility. Although customers in a grocery store may be free to choose their own route, patients in a hospital may be charted as they progress through laboratories and other facilities to give the analyst insights into developing a more efficient system.

An assembly chart (figure 3-11) focuses on the subassemblies of components and the final assembly of those components into a finished product. Combined with the bill of materials and route sheet (see examples in chapters 2 and 6), the assembly chart gives a good picture of the elements of the product and the sequence of production. The assembly chart also may be called a

Chapter 3 Location, Layout, Work Study, and Measurement 75

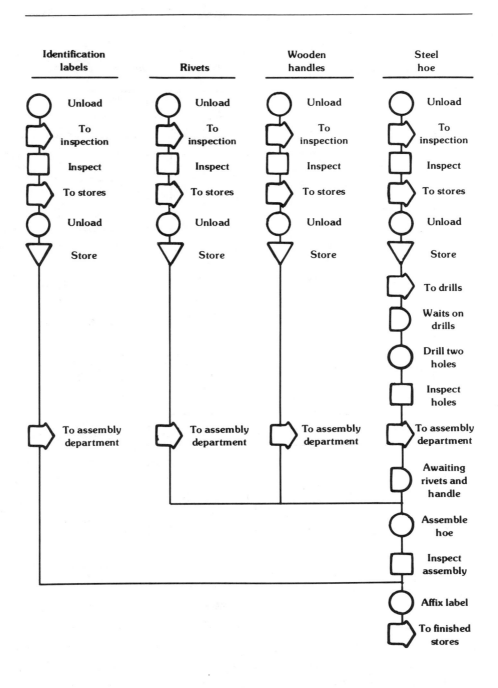

Figure 3-11. Assembly Chart (Garden Hoe)

76 Fundamentals of Production/Operations Management

Subject: **_Operating Two Printing Machines_**			Date **_Dec. 3, 1988_**			
Present ☒ ; Proposed ☐			Department: **_Printing_**		Charted by **_V.M.R._**	
	Operator		Machine #1		Machine #2	
	Activity	Time*	Activity	Time*	Activity	Time*
1	Unload #2	1½	Running	7	Necessary Idle	
2	Load #2	1½				
3	Walk to #1	1				
4	Idle	2			Running	7
5						
6	Unload #1	1½	Necessary Idle	3		
7						
8	Load #1	1½				
9	Walk to #2	1				
10	Unload #2	1½	Running	7	Necessary Idle	3
11						
12	Load #2	1½				
13	Walk to #1	1			Running	7
14						

Figure 3-12. Multiple-Activity Chart

"gozinto" chart (we will not try to convince you that the chart was developed by an Italian scientist named Vito Gozinto). Although seldom used in services, an assembly chart for a hamburger is known to exist.

When one worker can operate two or more semiautomatic machines such as a turret lathe or a copy machine, a multiple-activity chart (figure 3-12) plots activities against a time scale to determine the cycle time and calculate worker and machine utilization. In the example, both printing machines are operating at 100 percent capacity because the only idle time is that which is necessary for loading and unloading. The operator, however, is idle two minutes in every ten-minute cycle, for a utilization rate of 80 percent. This idle time may be acceptable, or it may be put to use to complete additional duties, such as quality-control checks, which could be performed while both machines are running.

The operation chart (figure 3-13) also may be called a left-hand/right-hand chart or a "simo" chart (for "simultaneous motion"). The most detailed of the charting techniques, the operations chart depicts every motion of both hands of the operator during the work cycle. Because it is so detailed and difficult to construct, it is used only for manipulative operations with very short cycle times and very high volumes.

Although the chart in Figure 3-13 uses the ASME symbols, other variations are available. Frank and Lillian Gilbreth, pioneers in the field of work study and time-and-motion analysis, used countless feet of film of workers to devise a set of standard motions they called Therbligs. Each of the seventeen fundamental Therbligs—such as reach, grasp, and release—has a precise definition, a standard time, and a symbol with a color code to permit detailed analysis of existing jobs or the design of new jobs, using the Therbligs as building blocks and applying the principles developed in their lifelong study of work.

Together, these charts and the principles of work study form the basic "tool box" for the work-study analyst.

Work Measurement

Work measurement often is misunderstood because the time-study analyst may be perceived as trying to achieve a speedup of work to squeeze every ounce of work out of the employee. This image holds true especially when the analyst approaches the worker with a stopwatch in hand! Actually, work measurement does for the labor resource what material control does for the material in the process. Specifically, it attempts to determine the standard time, defined as the time required for a normal worker with normal skill and effort, to perform a task over an extended period, with allowances made for breaks, personal time, fatigue, and working conditions.

Knowing the standard time allows production planners and others in the organization to have the information needed to

1. Schedule the amount of labor needed to complete a job;
2. Determine the amount of additional labor needed because of nonproductive time;
3. Calculate the amount of labor per unit of product to determine pricing and other decisions;
4. Evaluate proposed work improvements by comparing before and after standard times.

78 Fundamentals of Production/Operations Management

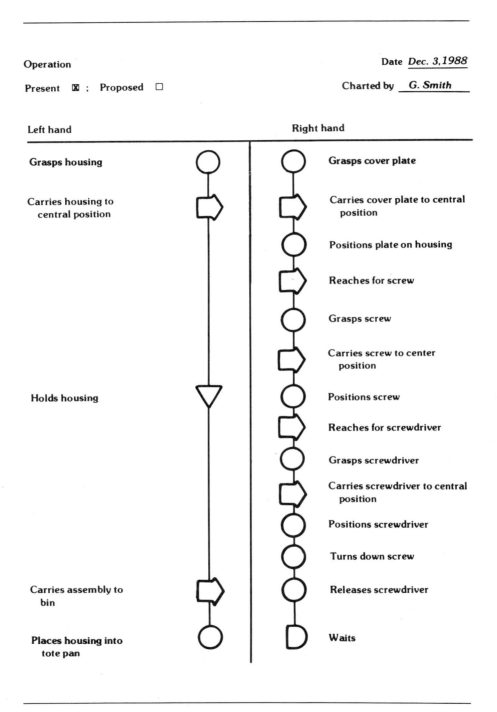

Figure 3-13. Operation Chart

Several methods are used to establish work standards:

1. Estimates based on historical data;
2. Stopwatch time studies;
3. Predetermined time-and-motion study
4. Work sampling

Estimates Based on Historical Data

Estimating the standard time for a job is the easiest method to use but also the least precise. It involves making an educated guess of the time needed to perform a job before the job is done. Formal analysis would use past data from similar jobs in a statistical model to project a reasonably accurate estimate. Informally, an experienced operator can use judgment to compare the current job to others that have been done in the past.

Often, this is the most reasonable and cost-effective method to use (and the method you use most often to estimate the time to do a job, travel to a meeting, or write a term project). In a job shop, for example, a machinist must drill a hole in each end of a shaft in a batch of twenty units. If other methods of time study were used, the batch would be completed before the standard time was established and the information would then be useless for planning purposes. The machinist just uses experience in drilling a hole in this type of metal and estimates that it will take three minutes per piece or about one hour for the entire job. The estimate will be accurate enough for this purpose, but if we had dozens of machinists drilling millions of holes in millions of shafts, we would use a more detailed method of analysis.

Stopwatch Time Study

A direct time study applies to visible work that is routine and repetitive (as opposed to mental work). Operating a machine or assembling identical units of product are examples of work that can be observed in which the operator performs the same motions over and over again. A skilled time-study analyst can observe the job, time the operator with a stopwatch through repeated cycles, and analyze the data to arrive at a standard time.

Since the standard will later be applied to all operators performing this job, the standard should be set for a normal worker, not an exceptionally fast or skilled one. To meet this objective, the analyst first selects a typical worker for the study and then applies a judgmental rating factor to the study. Just as you could judge whether a person was dealing cards at an exceptionally fast or slow rate, the analyst is trained to judge the rate or efficiency of the operator being observed.

Finally, since the time standard will be applied to work over the course of the day, week, or month, allowances must be made for worker fatigue, personal time, and interference such as breakdowns, shortage of material, or machine reloading.

SUMMARY OF WORK STUDY DATA

Operator: Mary Alice

Working Conditions: Standard

A.	Cycle time (from time study)	18.7 minutes per report
B.	Rating (by analyst)	90%
C.	Normalized time (A x B)	16.83 minutes per report

D. Allowances
    Fatigue   5%
    Personal   5%
    Delay   5%

    Total 15%

E. Allowance Factor $\frac{1}{1-\%}$ 1.176

F. Standard Time (C x E)   19.8 minutes per report

Standard:
    19.8 minutes per report
    0.33 hours per report
    3.03 reports per hour
    0.05 reports per minute

Figure 3-14. Calculation of Standard Time

The example in figure 3-14 will illustrate how the work standard is determined. Mary Alice, a good worker in the copy department, is assigned the task of checking, duplicating, and mailing reports received from a government agency. The analyst timed Mary Alice under normal operating conditions for thirty consecutive reports and averaged the time at 18.7 minutes per report. Having judged Mary Alice as working at 90 percent of normal, the analyst multiplies the cycle time by the rating to get a normalized cycle time of 16.83 minutes per report. Allowances in this study are factored in using a formula to assure that 15 percent of the final standard time is allotted to allowances. The result is a time standard of 19.8 minutes per report, which can be applied to any operator performing this job.

Application of the standard is illustrated in figure 3-15. Jane, another worker in the department, worked forty hours and produced 131 reports. Application

---

APPLICATION OF STANDARD TIME

Jane worked a forty-hour week and completed 131 reports. What is her performance rating?

Method #1: TIME. How long should it have taken a worker to complete 131 reports?

    Actual time   =   40 hours
    Standard time   =   131 x 0.33 = 42.23 hours

    Performance   =   standard/actual = 42.23/40 = 108%

Method #2: UNITS. How many units should a worker complete in 40 hours?

    Actual units   =   131 reports
    Standard units   =   40 x 3.03 = 121.2 reports

    Performance   =   actual/standard = 131/121.2 = 108%

Figure 3-15. Calculation of a Performance Rating

of the time standard tells if she is working below standard and needs counseling, retraining, or a reprimand; working at standard and deserves a compliment; or working well above standard and deserves a reward. Although the supervisor should look at the data from several operators over a longer period of time to determine the normal variability in the work, it appears from the analysis in the example that Jane is doing very well and may receive a bonus for her superior work.

Predetermined Time-and-Motion Study

Predetermined time standards are used as building blocks to determine the standard time for a complete job. Elements of work are studied to establish a standard time, and the time for the job is simply the sum of the times of the elements in it.

At a gross level of analysis, the owner of a housecleaning service may establish time standards for units of work, in this case the time needed to clean a bedroom, bathroom, kitchen, den, or other units of the house. Then, when planning the time needed or the price to charge for a job, the owner needs to know the number and type of rooms the house contains. From that preliminary estimate, adjustments may then be made for special cleaning problems such as wood floors, patio doors, or teenagers' bedrooms.

At a detailed level of analysis, Therbligs or similar systems for analyzing hand movements can be used to describe every movement required to perform a given task. Since every Therblig has an associated time standard, the time for the task is the sum of the times of the motions involved. Allowances are then added to establish the time standard for the complete job. Since this method requires a skilled analyst and a great deal of time, it is applicable to jobs with short cycle times and high volumes.

Work Sampling

For work that is routine but not strictly repetitive, work sampling may be used to establish a standard. The analyst observes the worker at random times throughout the day for a period of days or weeks, recording from each observation what type of work the operator is doing. For example, a forklift driver may be traveling loaded or unloaded, may be loading or unloading, may be servicing the truck, may be taking personal time, or may be performing some other activity. Using the principles of probability theory, the analyst can determine the percentage of time in each category and begin to establish the amount of time needed to perform nonrepetitive activities to accomplish a given amount of work such as unloading a truck or picking parts from a warehouse to fill an order.

Because of the nature of the jobs, work sampling often can be applied to clerical work and to jobs in many service firms more effectively than other methods for establishing time standards.

Regardless of the method used, establishment of time standards is necessary if the work of the organization is to be planned, scheduled, and controlled in an effective and efficient operating system.

Key Concepts

Location Factors

Weighted Factor Analysis

Transportation Method of Linear Programming

Process Layout

Product Layout

Work-Study Charts

Process Chart Symbols

Standard Time

Stopwatch Time Study

Work Sampling

Cellular Layout

References

Barnes, Ralph M. *Motion and Time Study: Design and Measurement of Work.* 7th ed. New York: John Wiley & Sons, 1980.

Greene, T. J., and Sadowski, Randall P. "A Review of Cellular Manufacturing Assumptions, Advantages, and Design Techniques." *Journal of Operations Management* 4 (February 1984): 85–97.

Hyer, N. L., and Wemmerlov, Urban. "Group Technology and Productivity." *Harvard Business Review* 62 (July–August 1984): 140–149.

Schmenner, Roger W. *Making Business Location Decisions.* Englewood Cliffs, New Jersey: Prentice-Hall, 1982.

Voss, C. A. *Managing New Manufacturing Technologies. Operations Management Association Monograph No. 1.* East Lansing, Michigan: Michigan State University, 1986.

Discussion Questions

1. Many cities and towns have an "automobile row," where car dealers are located side by side for several blocks. What are the advantages and disadvantages of a car dealer locating beside a competitor? What types of firms try to locate *away* from their competitors?

2. Name a type of firm for which each of the following factors would be the most critical location criterion:

   A. Closeness to raw materials
   B. Land cost
   C. Available skilled labor supply
   D. Climate

3. A manufacturer of kitchen cabinets chose a location just outside city limits on county land. List the advantages and disadvantages of this location compared to a nearby location just inside city limits.

4. A toy manufacturer makes wooden pull toys, stuffed animals, and a series of board games in small lot sizes. Discuss the advantages of a cellular or group layout as compared to a process layout for this company.

5. If you were assigned to do a layout for a grocery store and you knew that most customers traveled through the store from left to right, where would you place frozen foods, canned goods, produce, meat, dairy foods, and other items? Why?

6. If a time standard is set too tight (that is, if there are not enough allowances or if the rating is too severe), what problems would this cause? What problems would occur if the standard is too loose?

7. In applying a time standard, do you divide actual work by the standard, or do you divide the standard by the actual work? Explain.

8. Work sampling can be used to help establish a time standard for nonrepetitive work, but it can also be used as a tool for identifying inefficient work. Explain how this might be done.

Problems

1. In the example of the transportation method of linear programming, suppose we had to ship 100 units from the Chicago plant to a new location, site B. Make the necessary adjustments in the other cells to ensure that the rows and columns have the proper totals, and then calculate the new total cost for this alternative.

2. If the cycle time for an operation is eight minutes, the rating is 110 percent, and allowances total 20 percent, what is the standard time?

3. Choose a task that is familiar to you, such as changing a tire, preparing a meal, or performing an activity at work, and construct a process chart describing the present method including all operations, transportations, inspections, and delays. Analyze the job and make suggestions for improvement. Construct a chart for the improved method.

4. In the multiple-activity chart example, add a third machine for the worker to operate, and chart the worker and three machines through two complete cycles. Calculate the machine and operator utilization. What are the advantages and disadvantages of three machines compared to two machines?

CHAPTER

4

Forecasting, Planning, and Scheduling Production

So far, we have explored how a product is designed and what steps are necessary to get both the product and physical facility ready for actual production. This chapter discusses how the demand for a product is determined and then, based upon this demand, how the actual production is planned and the required resources scheduled.

These three activities are closely tied together in a hierarchical arrangement, with forecasting at the top, followed by planning, and then scheduling. This means that if the demand forecast changes, the production plan probably will have to be adjusted, and the scheduling of resources also must be altered to reflect the new plan.

Forecasting Demand

The basis for all business activity is a forecast of demand, which indicates that the venture will be profitable. Perfect forecasts, however, are rare. Realizing this, the forecaster must make an effort to develop forecasts that represent the best estimates of future demand. The five basic steps to be reviewed are (1) determining the forecasting objective, (2) selecting a model, (3) assessing the proposed model, (4) applying the model that passes initial assessment, and (5) monitoring the performance of the model to determine the justification of continued use of the selected model.

Determining the Objective

The forecaster actually must forecast *two* types of demand—internal and external.

Internal, or dependent, demand is derived from or contingent on the demand for some other product or item. Raw materials, components, and subassemblies are examples of items subject to internal demand; that is, they are dependent upon the demand for the final product. The paper used in printing this text is dependent upon the demand for this and other texts to be printed. This paper raw material faces only an internal demand as specified by a detailed component list of materials required to manufacture various books (the bill of materials, see chapter 2).

Since the bill of materials for a product indicates, in detail, the requirements for items facing internal demands, the forecaster also must be concerned with external demands. External demands, which are unrelated to the demands for other items produced by the firm, also are known as independent demands. Items that have independent or external demands usually are end products or items used for maintenance and repair purposes. Using the previous example, the forecaster must determine the demands for the various books to be published by the firm. The demand for products that have an external or independent demand must be forecast.

Once the items to be forecast have been selected, a decision must be made about the time period of the forecast. This is done by establishing the forecast horizon, which depends upon many variables. As the horizon is pushed out, confidence in the accuracy of the forecast drops, and the forecasting methodologies become more costly to develop and utilize. Selection of the forecast horizon must consider the product's life cycle, the manufacturing cycle, the firm's ability to gather the necessary production resources, and the cost of developing a forecasting model. The product-life-cycle concept maintains that a product goes through predictable stages: introduction, growth, saturation or maturity, and then decline. Different forecasting models are appropriate depending on the current stage of a product. An industry may experience a manufacturing cycle that requires new models or major new-product introductions at reasonably consistent intervals. Such cycles that exceed annual seasonal patterns will tend to extend the forecast horizon. The forecast horizon must provide adequate visibility into the future for informed decision making as it pertains to plant expansion or contraction and, on a day-to-day basis, sufficient visibility in terms of the purchase of materials and the design of an efficient production plan.

Selecting the Model

Before discussing the actual types of forecasting models, let us consider the criteria for selecting a model. These criteria are listed in exhibit 4-1.

Once decisions concerning each of the criteria have been made, the actual model that best fits this set of decisions may be chosen.

Methods of forecasting. Three general categories of forecasting methods exist—judgmental, intrinsic, and extrinsic. Each differs in terms of the kinds of data utilized and the settings in which each is most effective.

Exhibit 4-1

Forecast Model Selection Criteria

1. Who will use the forecast, and what are their information needs?
2. What are the relevance and availability of historical data?
3. What degree of accuracy is desired?
4. What time period (horizon) is to be forecast?
5. How much time is available for making the analysis and forecast?
6. What is the cost/benefit (value) of the forecast to the company?

Judgmental methods, or qualitative rather than quantitative methods, rely on expert opinions regarding the future. Two examples of judgmental forecasting techniques are the Delphi technique and market-survey techniques.

The Delphi technique utilizes several experts in the area to be forecast. Instead of bringing these experts together and perhaps having their reputations influence one another, the employing firm does not reveal the identities of the experts to each other. The forecasts of these experts are summarized and fed back to each contributor, and their individual revisions are solicited in light of the anonymous views of the group. After several revisions, it is hoped that a consensus can be reached based on the shared expertise. This technique applies where quantitative data are unavailable and judgments of knowledgeable persons can be obtained economically.

Market surveys attempt to measure customer intentions by collecting a sample of opinions. The sample may consist of forecasts by sales personnel, stated intentions of key customers, or a representative consumer panel. Key customers may be especially effective for some industrial suppliers who might have sales concentrated among a small number of accounts. Consumer panels often provide an economical measure of a new consumer-product market. Consumer-opinion surveys, while expensive, are particularly relevant where the firm has no historical experience—for example, when it is introducing a new product.

Intrinsic models, or time-series models, extrapolate historical data patterns into the future. The type of intrinsic model used depends on the historical pattern of the forecast variable (e.g., sales units). Time-series data can be plotted on graph paper and analyzed for the four basic components of variation. These components are (1) seasonal, (2) trend, (3) cycle, and (4) the residual, unexplainable component, or random "noise." Graphic illustration of these influences is shown in figure 4-1.

In the fourth, and simplest case, there are no apparent cycles, seasons, or trends. The goal is to smooth out the random noise so that production levels

88 Fundamentals of Production/Operations Management

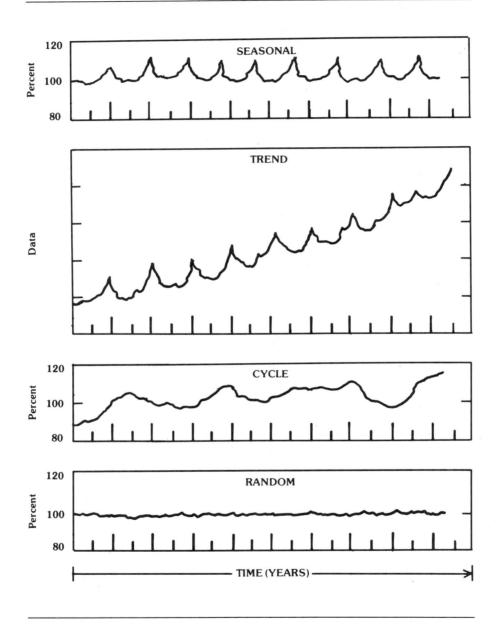

Figure 4-1. Illustrations of Seasonal, Trend, Cycle, and Random Time-Series Fluctuation Cycles

and staffing are not changed in response to transient conditions. Simple models, such as moving averages, weighted-average models, and exponential smoothing techniques, apply in this case.

A simple moving average merely sums the data for the most recent months and divides by the number of months. Take a three-month moving average, for example, where the sales were: January, 1,200 units; February, 1,300 units; and March, 1,100 units. The three-month average is 1,200 units, and this would be the forecast for April. Now April has come and gone. April's sales were 1,150 units. To compute the new three-month average, the oldest month is dropped (January's 1,200 units), and the newest demand is added (April's 1,150 units) to get (1,300 + 1,100 + 1,150) ÷ 3 = 1,183.3 or 1,183 units.

A simple weighted average works in much the same way. The three-month moving average really applied a weight of one-third to each of the months. In our previous example, we would get the same answer if we added ⅓ × 1,300 plus ⅓ × 1,100 plus ⅓ × 1,150. The advantage of a weighted-average approach is that it allows different emphasis on different pieces of data. For example, we might want to place more importance on last month than on the month before. In the case of retail sales, we might want to place more emphasis on Thursday through Saturday sales and less on Monday through Wednesday sales. The weighted-average approach allows this flexibility.

A final variation is simple exponential smoothing. In this case, we apply a weight, alpha, to the most recent demand. Although alpha can be any value between 0 and 1, typical values are between .1 and .3. The balance of the weight (1-alpha) is placed on the previously exponentially smoothed average. An equivalent approach is to apply the weight, alpha, to the forecast error of the previous period. These two approaches are represented by the following formulas.

$$SF_{t+1} = \alpha(A_t) + (1-\alpha)(SF_t) \text{ or } SF_{t+1} = SF_t + \alpha(A_t - SF_t)$$

Where: SF_t is the smoothed forecast for period t
SF_{t+1} is the smoothed forecast one period in the future
A_t is the actual demand in period t
α is the weighting constant alpha

The three methods—moving average, weighted average, and exponential smoothing—are illustrated in table 4-1. Check to see if you can compute the averages illustrated in table 4-1. Note that the exponential-smoothing model consists of two multiplications and one addition. The moving-average method consists of one addition per month and a division. The weighted-average method consist of one multiplication and one addition per month. The relative efficiency of exponential smoothing is one of its advantages; it also requires the storage of less data.

When a trend is clearly present, the simple moving-average models and exponential smoothing lag behind actual demand and therefore do not perform very well. Trends can be handled by making a trend adjustment to the simple

Table 4-1

Methods of Smoothing Random Variations

Month	Demand	3 Month (Moving Average)	3 Month (Weighted Average[a])	Exponential Smoothing[b]
January	1,200	—	—	1,200 (assumed base)
February	1,300	—	—	.1(1,300) + .9(1,200) = 1,210
March	1,100	1,200	1,183.33	.1(1,100) + .9(1,210) = 1,199
April	1,150	1,183.33	1,158.33	.1(1,150) + .9(1,199) = 1,194

[a]Weight 1 = 1/6; weight 2 = 2/6; weight 3 = 3/6
[b]Alpha = .1: The values are the smoothed average for the associated month. The average, therefore, for April (1194)—would be the forecast for May.

exponential-smoothing model. An alternate method is to use linear regression to determine the slope (trend) of the historical data. This method finds the straight line that minimizes the squared errors, as measured by the vertical distance between the historical points and the trend line. Extending this trend line into the future provides a forecast of the expected average sales or other forecast variables. Random variations about these forecast points are to be expected. Also, standard statistical measures are available to evaluate whether or not the trend is statistically significant. If the trend is not significant, then the simple moving average or similar models would be more appropriate. Finally, to be valid, regression models require a significant number of data points and should not be extrapolated into the distant future.

Another matter of concern to the operations manager is the seasonal component. Time-series models handle this by deseasonalizing the data. One approach is the multiplicative model, where a trend line is computed. The trend could be zero, in which case the line represents the average level. Next, each data point is divided by the point on the trend line for the corresponding observed data at that point in time. This tells us what percentage the demand is of the trend line. For example, if the data point is 120 percent of the trend line, then the actual demand can be found by 1.20 × point on the trend line. If we compute these percentages for several years, we can average the percentage for January, February, and so on or for quarter 1, quarter 2, and so on; then these seasonal percentages can be used to forecast the future. First, find the trend point for the future period, and then multiply that value by the seasonal percentage to get the desired forecast. This approach is illustrated in figure 4-2.

The influence of a cyclical factor on time-series models will not be discussed here, but one example would be the demand for yo-yos, where the product falls in and out of favor regularly over long time periods.

Figure 4-2. Multiplicative Model for Trend and Seasonals

Extrinsic models attempt to forecast desired variables, such as sales, based on variables outside the system. These models are referred to as causal models because they hypothesize a cause-and-effect relationship between the independent and the dependent (forecasted) variables. The statistical techniques of correlation analysis and regression analysis are the primary means for specifying these relationships. An example of a causal model in forecasting would be a model relating housing permits to lumber sales. By statistical analysis of historical data, it may be found that lumber sales are highly correlated to housing permits and lag behind the permits by two months. Such a model is of great value to the lumber producer, since the number of housing permits issued is easily obtained, and the fact that it provides a two-months' warning of changes in demand is very useful.

Assessing the Model

Now the forecaster must reexamine the model to see whether it adequately describes the forecasting situation under the real constraints of time and cost. The model usually is assessed by using historical data to make forecasts for periods in which the level of activity is known. Then, by comparing the model's forecasts with the known outcome, the forecaster can determine the model's predictive ability. If the resulting forecasts are either positively or negatively biased to an unacceptable degree or the magnitude of the errors is excessive, the forecaster must return to the selection step in an effort to reformulate the existing model or choose a different one.

The magnitude of the forecast errors is often measured by the mean absolute deviation (MAD). The MAD is computed by taking the actual demand minus the forecast for a set of historical data. The absolute values (ignore minus signs) of these errors are summed and divided by the number of values to arrive at the average, the MAD. The procedure is easier than computing the standard deviation of the errors and serves the same purpose. Within other constraints, the model that provides a smaller MAD is preferred to one with a larger MAD. Bias in a forecasting model may be evaluated by computing the running sum of the forecast errors (RSFE).

Consider a model that consistently provides forecasts on the low side. The error (actual minus forecast) would be consistently a positive value, and, hence, the RSFE would become a bigger positive value each period. The same would be true if the model consistently provided forecasts on the high side, except the RSFE would become a bigger negative number. An unbiased forecasting model would tend to overforecast about as often as it would underforecast; therefore, the errors would tend to cancel each other out, resulting in a small RSFE. The MAD and the RSFE are useful measures of a forecasting model's performance.

Applying the Model

Here the acceptable model is put to work in a real forecasting situation. When the model is first put into action, previous forecasting methodologies typically are continued as backup. By continuing to use the old method, the forecaster has the forecast from the previous technique to use in evaluating the new model.

Evaluating the Model

Because forecasting methodologies are adaptable to computer applications, it is tempting to give the computer total forecasting responsibility. Although safeguards may be built into the computer model to recognize when the forecast exceeds some set of reasonable limits, the human touch is required to make a good evaluation of any model.

Forecast evaluation is a continuing process that requires the forecaster to monitor the validity of each new forecast. Only through judgment can one recognize external variables that cause fundamental changes in the forecast variable.

Planning for Production

Once the future levels of demand for the firm's products have been forecast, the manager must plan the production. At this stage, the manager is concerned with only the broadest level of plant activity rather than with the more detailed scheduling needed to carry out the day-to-day operations. The broad, overall decisions required usually are referred to as aggregate planning, a practice that relates specifically to programming resources over an established time horizon.

Concept of Aggregate Planning

The goal of aggregate planning is to use a representative measure of productive activity and market demand to simplify the selection of an operating strategy that deals effectively with seasonal or cyclical variations in market demand. Management must find a strategy that balances the costs of hiring and firing, carrying inventories, having idle facilities, using subcontractors, or losing sales.

Three basic inputs are needed to make aggregate planning decisions. The first is the development of a single, overall measure of production. This is relatively easy for a one-product firm. Firms that produce many diverse products, however, need a measure that represents the product mix and operating processes, so that labor and equipment capabilities will be fairly represented. For example, cases of soft drink for a bottling plant, tons for a steel mill, cars for an automobile assembly plant, or equivalent machine hours for a job shop may serve as representative measures. The second requirement is forecasting the selected measure of output with some reasonable degree of accuracy over the planning period. These forecasts represent the market's demands on the firm's capacity in each of the planning periods. The final input needed is a determination of the costs associated with each of the resources that will be combined in a strategy for meeting the market demand.

Operating strategies fall along a continuum from level production (the same number of units produced each period) to a variable-production approach (number of units produced matches the number the market demands). The level-production plan leads to storing inventories during slow sales periods so the product will be available when the demand increases above the firm's steady production rate. This approach utilizes plant and equipment effectively and maintains a stable work force at the expense of warehouse space, dollars in stocks, and related costs of inventory. In some cases, the firm can "store" the market demand by a back-order strategy; this method makes the customer wait longer during the peak season than in the off season. If the market permits this strategy, the firm can produce at a steady rate and still not require excessive inventories. An organization may not have the option of an inventory strategy—for example, those service industries or firms that provide a highly perishable product. In this case, varying production rates can be achieved by hiring and firing, overtime, or subcontracting the excess demand to other firms. In between these two extreme strategies are any number of combinations using some level of inventory, some overtime and hiring or firing, some back ordering, and some level of subcontracting. Finding a good balance is the challenge.

Making the Aggregate Plan

The aggregate plan should establish the employment levels, production rates, inventory levels, back-order levels, and magnitude of subcontracting for each period over the planning horizon. The various techniques for solving aggregate planning problems involve varying levels of cost and sophistication in their development and implementation. These techniques include graphing, mathematical programming, heuristic decision rules, search techniques, and simulation.

Graphical methods plot the chosen aggregate measure (e.g., tons, units, hours) against production periods over the planning horizon. Cumulative data are plotted, providing a year-to-date graph of market demand. On this same graph, various production plans can be tested against constraints imposed by management. Such constraints might include upper limits on inventory, hiring and firing, or back orders. A cumulative graph of production provides the year-to-date available units for sale at any given time over the planning horizon. An inventory balance exists whenever the point on the cumulative production graph is above the corresponding point (same time in the year) on the cumulative market-demand graph. Similarly, if, at a specified point, the cumulative market graph is above the cumulative production graph, this is a back-order situation, since fewer units have been supplied to date, by production than desired by the market. Changes in the slope of the cumulative production graph signify changes in the production rate and imply changes in the labor force and possibly in hiring and firing. This graphical trial-and-error technique does not guarantee an optimal solution, but it does provide a quick visual method of evaluating possible alternative manufacturing plans.

Another trial-and-error approach to aggregate planning employs the power of computer spreadsheets. The "what-if" capabilities of spread sheets retain the ability of the graphical approach to test many possible plans in a reasonable period of time. Moreover, a computerized spread sheet permits fast and accurate economic analysis of various proposed strategies on dimensions of direct labor, inventory, back orders, overtime, and subcontracting costs.

Mathematical programming methods provide optimal solutions within the constraints and assumptions of the models. Linear, quadratic, and goal-programming algorithms are some of the techniques available to optimize a cost or profit objective function subject to one or more resource constraints—for example, inventory of $1,000,000 or less. While more sophisticated, these methods are more costly to develop and use than the graphical approach.

Heuristic decision rules require systematic evaluations of various cost functions at a selected number of trial points. An attempt is made to minimize the cost function, but heuristic methods do not test for minimums over the entire range of the function. It is possible, therefore, to state only that the best minimum has been found, based on that set of decision rules. These models may be less costly to construct and implement than programming models, but they do not assure an optimal solution.

Heuristic decision rules or programming models may be designed into search techniques that will evaluate an objective function at many different points, as variables are manipulated. Such models can deal with some of the weaknesses of the heuristic and programming models but not without significant costs of development and computer time. Optimal solutions are still not guaranteed.

Regardless of the method used, an aggregate plan is the outcome of the analysis. This aggregate plan is stated in the selected broad measure of production and is not suitable for the detailed scheduling of labor and work centers.

Translating the aggregate plan into the manufacture of specific products on specific dates is the task of master scheduling.

Scheduling Production

Once the aggregate plan has been developed according to the planned resources available and the market demand, the disaggregating process begins and leads to the specific production plan. The goal is to establish a realistic master production schedule from which detailed shop loadings and job-order sequences are derived. The disaggregation process and its trial-and-error nature are illustrated in figure 4-3.

The Master Schedule

The master schedule states the desired quantities to be produced by end product or product group. It also indicates when the "end items" are to be available. The guiding principle for setting a master schedule is to make it realistic. A common error in practice is to schedule excessive production quantities, even though it is not remotely possible to achieve the schedule.

Difficulties can occur when the product mix differs from the typical mix assumed in the aggregate plan. The organization may not be able to adhere to the aggregate plan without using expensive strategies such as excessive hiring and firing or massive inventory buildup during slack periods. The assignment of specific products to be made in specific periods brings with it the need to check the demands on the productive resources of the organization. This rough-cut capacity planning focuses on key resources that might bottleneck the flow of work through the organization. The master production schedule should be modified until a feasible schedule is obtained, that is, one that does not exceed planned capacity in the facility. The master production schedule is the basis for planning the detailed requirements for assemblies, parts, and raw materials that make the final product. This planning process is very complex when many different products, parts, and materials are involved. Such environments often use the materials-requirements planning approach to perform the detailed computations.

Materials Requirements Planning (MRP)

Materials-requirement planning was originally viewed as an inventory system because the approach specified order quantities and the timing of the orders. MRP has since taken on a larger role that includes short- and medium-range corporatewide planning as well as the setting and maintenance of work priorities in the factory. MRP uses three data bases to perform its functions: the master production schedule, the bill of materials file, and the inventory status file.

To illustrate the way MRP translates the master production schedule into detailed, time-phased material plans, we will develop a bill of materials (B/M) for a mass-produced picture frame. This product will be considered one of many

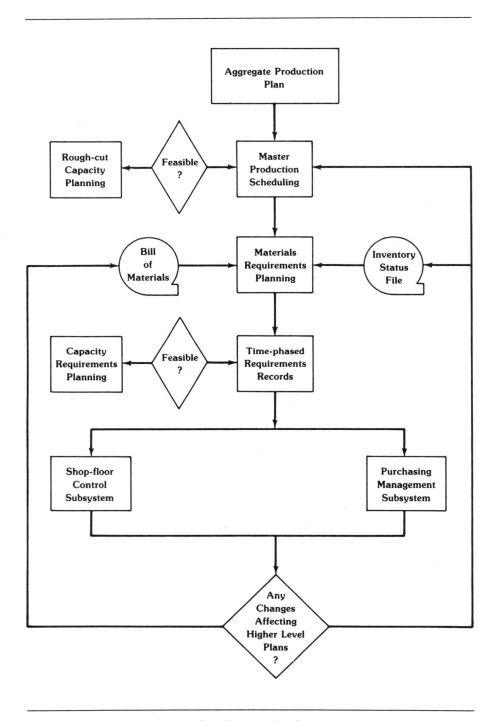

Figure 4-3. The Detailed Schedule

variations. Possible variations derive from choices of three sizes, five colors, seven frame materials, and ten mats. These choices lead to 1,050 unique end products made from less than seventy-five parts and twenty-five raw materials. A bill of materials for one of these products is shown in figure 4-4 in two formats: a structure tree B/M format, and in an indented B/M format.

Inventory status must be maintained on each unique inventory item. Such information as the quantity on hand and on order must be accurately recorded along with precise storage locations of the material. Each inventory item will have a lot-sizing rule to guide how much to order when a shortage is anticipated. Furthermore, the data base will contain the planned lead times required to purchase or make each of the inventory items. We now have the data that MRP uses to develop detailed material plans for several weeks, months, or years into the future. How far we plan into the future is called the planning horizon. The planning horizon is determined by the product that takes the longest time to build. In our simplified example, we will plan only five periods into the future.

The MRP planning process begins with the master production schedule for the end items. These end items are the highest level of the bill of materials, level 0 by convention. The master production schedule identifies the gross requirements for these items and, if appropriate, any independent (direct customer) demand for lower-level components (e.g., replacement parts). The procedure is to try to satisfy the gross requirements from inventory before building more of a product or its parts. Items that are on hand can be used for this purpose and so can on-order material that is expected to arrive in time to meet a specific gross requirement. Once all the on-hand and on-order material has been used to reduce the gross requirements, the remaining requirements are called net requirements. This is the *netting* process.

The projection of a negative balance indicates a net requirement and the need to plan a receipt of the product or material. Since each item is associated with a planned lead time, we must start a planned order earlier than its due date. The start time is the date of the planned order release for that inventory item. This process is often called time phasing or offsetting.

The bill of materials for this item is used to identify all the parts and materials that must be on hand at the time the planned order is released. This linking of requirements from one item or parent to a lower-level component is called *exploding* requirements from the planned order releases of the parent to the gross requirements of the components. Note that the bill of materials provides the recipe. If the planned order release for Part No. 101401, unpainted 10 × 14 frame, is 200 units in period 1, then the gross requirements for Part No. 100001, 10-inch sides, is 400 in period 1 because we need two of these components for each Part No. 101401. Figure 4-5 illustrates these steps, starting with a master production schedule for 100 units of the 10 × 14 picture frame, Part No. 10141101, due in week 3, 50 units due in week 4, and a final batch of 75 units due in week 5. The on-hand inventory for each item is indicated in a box before the first time period. The on-hand line represents projected inventory at the end of the associated period. When the projected balance becomes negative, the negative number is the trigger that caused MRP to plan a receipt which then modified

98 Fundamentals of Production/Operations Management

Level	Part No.	Description	Quantity per Parent
0	10141101	10 × 14 Frame-White-Pine-White	no parent
1	101411xx	10 × 14 Frame-White-Pine	1 each
2	000001xx	White Antique Stain	2 ounces
2	101401xx	10 × 14 Frame-xxxxx-Pine	1 each
3	100001xx	10 inch Mitered Pine Sides	2 each
3	001401xx	14 inch Mitered Pine Top/Bottoms	2 each
3	08010001	Staples	8 each
1	10140001	10 × 14 Glass	1 each
2	20280001	20 × 28 Plate Glass	¼ sheet
1	10140001	10 × 14 White Mat	1 each
2	20280001	20 × 28 White Mat Board	¼ sheet
1	10400003	10 × 14 Paper Backing	1 each
2	20280003	20 × 28 Paper Backing Sheets	¼ sheet
1	10140009	10 × 14 Wire Hanging Packet	1 each

Bill of Materials Showing Indented Format

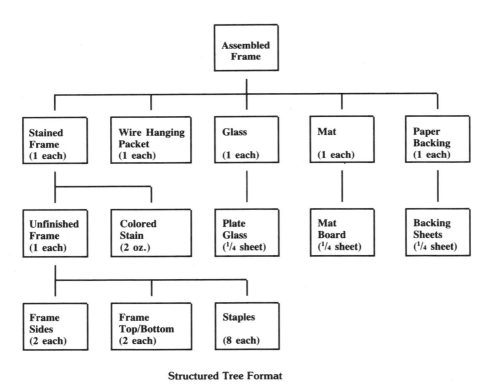

Structured Tree Format

Figure 4-4. Frame Bill of Materials

PART NO. 10141101 10×14 Frame, White, Pine, White		Period				
		1	2	3	4	5
GROSS REQUIREMENTS	from MPS			100	50	75
ON ORDER						
PROJECTED ON-HAND BALANCE	80	80	80	−20* 80	30	−45 35
NET REQUIREMENTS				20		45
PLANNED ORDER RECEIPTS				100		100
PLANNED ORDER RELEASES			100		100	

PLANNED LEAD TIME = 1 Week   ORDER QUANTITY = 100 units

* NOTE: A negative projected on-hand balance triggers a planned order receipt which in turn causes the balance to be adjusted.

PART NO. 101411xx 10×14 Frame, White Pine		Period				
		1	2	3	4	5
GROSS REQUIREMENTS	from Part # 10141101		100		100	
ON ORDER						
PROJECTED ON-HAND BALANCE	0	0	−100 0	0	−100 0	0
NET REQUIREMENTS			100		100	
PLANNED ORDER RECEIPTS			100		100	
PLANNED ORDER RELEASES		100		100		

PLANNED LEAD TIME = 1 Week   ORDER QUANTITY = Lot-for-Lot

Figure 4-5. MRP Time-Phased Inventory Records

the project on-hand balance. Order quantities and planned lead times are indicated below each time-phased inventory record in figure 4-5. The lot-for-lot order quantity means that one should order only enough to meet the net requirements for one period at a time.

PART NO. 101401xx 10 × 14 Frame, Unfinished, Pine		Period				
		1	2	3	4	5
GROSS REQUIREMENTS	from Part # 101411xx	100		100		
ON ORDER		100				
PROJECTED ON-HAND BALANCE	0	0	0	−100 0	0	0
NET REQUIREMENTS				100		
PLANNED ORDER RECEIPTS				100		
PLANNED ORDER RELEASES		100				

PLANNED LEAD TIME = 2 Weeks   ORDER QUANTITY = Lot-for-Lot

PART NO. 0000001 White Antique Stain		Period				
		1	2	3	4	5
GROSS REQUIREMENTS	from Part # 101411xx	200				
ON ORDER		800				
PROJECTED ON-HAND BALANCE	100	700	700	700	700	700
NET REQUIREMENTS						
PLANNED ORDER RECEIPTS						
PLANNED ORDER RELEASES						

PLANNED LEAD TIME = 2 Weeks   ORDER QUANTITY = 800 ounces

Figure 4-5. MRP Time-Phased Inventory Records (continued)

The power of MRP comes from the improved timing of the correct quantities of materials to support production and the timely updating of job priorities, (i.e., planned order releases and on-order due dates). Any changes in plans because of customer wishes, manufacturing problems or opportunities, or supplier problems can be effectively evaluated using the MRP time-phased records and exception messages provided by MRP systems. Finally, the detailed material plans permit careful analysis of work loads in various work centers in comparison to their capacity. This load analysis is the function of capacity requirements planning.

Capacity Requirements Planning

CRP is concerned with the loading of specific jobs onto various work centers for specific periods of time. By combining MRP data on the timing of units needed with standard data on manufacturing processes, one can identify the machine hours and labor hours required by a work center to meet the master schedule. There are two general approaches to loading: (1) infinite loading and (2) finite loading.

Infinite loading assumes that each work center has sufficient capacity to produce whatever it is assigned, using standard manufacturing processes. This approach has the main advantage of being simple. When a plant has more-than-ample capacity, it may be valid to assume that no resource will be strained to capacity. Here infinite loading is both simple and effective. But, regardless of its short-term validity, infinite loading is useful for long-term capacity planning. Because infinite loading assumes use of the primary method of manufacturing and no limit in capacity, it gives a good picture of what capacity the plant should have in the future.

Finite loading does not assume that enough capacity will be available in all work centers and does not restrict itself to the primary method of manufacture. The elimination of these two assumptions makes the analysis much more complicated and time consuming. In essence, when a bottleneck is encountered, the load is shifted to secondary methods in work centers with available capacity, or the load is shifted to different time slots. Allowing loads to be shifted in these ways opens up for consideration thousands of possible schedules. The large number of alternatives makes this problem impressive even when large-scale computers are available. Techniques such as linear programming, simulation, and heuristic rules have been applied to solve this problem. The advantage of finite loading is that it indicates what can be produced in the short term—that is, what is realistic given current conditions.

Sequencing Jobs

The loading of work centers for a block of time does not specify the order in which the individual jobs are to be processed. Often this sequencing is left to the foreman, or a central planning group may specify the sequence based on sophisticated computerized analysis. In either event, some of the common goals are (1) maximum flow through the shop, (2) minimum number of late orders, (3) minimum average lateness, (4) minimum variance from due dates, and (5) minimum cost.

One way to sequence jobs is to use a priority rule. There are many such rules, each with its own unique performance characteristics. One popular priority

---

Exhibit 4-2

Job-Shop Priority Scheduling Rules

FCFS   First come, first served—priority based upon time of arrival at the work center or place in line.

SOT   Shortest operation time—process the quickest jobs first. This rule maximizes mean flow rate but tends to delay excessively the important large jobs.

FISFS   First in system, first served—this differs from FCFS, where the priority can change at each work center. For example, air travelers flying standby have priority based on when they started the journey, not necessarily when they arrived at an intermediate stop.

LCFS   Last come, first served—this is a convenience rule, that is, do the job on the top of the stack first.

Critical Ratio   This is the ratio of time remaining to work time remaining. This is a popular dynamic rule in which a job with a ratio >1 is ahead of schedule, ratio of 1 is on schedule and a ratio <1 needs to be expedited.

---

rule is the shortest-operation-time job first (SOT). This rule is effective with respect to minimizing the average flow time through the shop. Its major weakness is that long jobs continually may be "bumped" to last and thereby delayed excessively. Since long jobs may be the most important jobs, it might make sense to use another priority rule, one called longest-operation-time first (LOT). The performance characteristics of this rule are the opposite of SOT. The choice of a priority rule depends upon what is important to the organization; obviously, no rule will achieve all the possible desirable goals.

Other common priority rules are summarized in exhibit 4-2. First come, first served (FCFS) is an easily defended rule as far as customers are concerned. The various slack rules consider how much time there is between a reference time, for example, time of arrival at a work center, and the due date. Some rules divide this by a measure of the amount of work that still remains to be done, such as the remaining processing time or the number of operations remaining. Such ratios give a measure of urgency for each job.

Development of Detailed Schedules

When all the aforementioned decisions and revisions have been made, detailed schedules finally will be prepared. Detailed schedules take the job and flow sequences established at the last stage and overlay them on a time scale, which

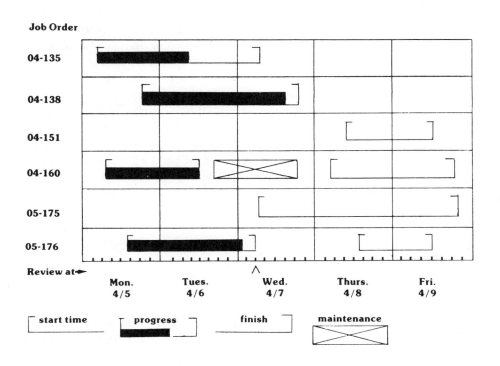

Figure 4-6. Gantt Chart

is divided into periods appropriate for the manufacturing setting, extending over the entire planning period. Job shops may require daily scales, while an assembly line might use weekly or longer time frames. Gantt charts are particularly useful in blocking out plans and providing quick and easy visual presentation. Figure 4-6 illustrates a set of work orders scheduled using the common Gantt chart symbols. By updating progress on the chart, one can see at a glance the jobs that are behind schedule, on time, and ahead of schedule, as well as the jobs coming up in the near future. Such a chart facilitates the coordination of setups, maintenance, and scheduling of labor crews.

After scheduling conflicts have been resolved, specific start and finish dates are assigned to jobs. These start and finish dates may be set by working back from the due date on a job (backward scheduling) or by starting a job as early as possible (forward scheduling.) Backward scheduling reduces inventory and maintains flexibility on schedule changes as long as possible, at the risk of having more late jobs than with a forward-scheduling approach. In either case, when the start date is reached on a dispatch list, work orders are released to the manufacturing facility, and processing commences.

Progress Control/Shop-Floor Control

Progress control, the final stage in the scheduling process, involves constant monitoring of the jobs as they pass through the facility in an attempt to detect and to resolve problems that may arise. One method of detecting problems or bottlenecks in the flow of jobs is through input/output (I/O) control charts. I/O control monitors planned work input and output against actual input and output by work center. If backlogs arise, the I/O table focuses attention on the work center causing the problem. The importance of bottlenecks has been stressed by the concepts and philosophies advanced by Creative Output, Inc. and Eliyahu Goldratt, co-founder of the company. The bottlenecks determine the flow through the factory and to the customer who pays for the product. If the flow is constrained, then profit is reduced. Therefore, everything should be done to fully utilize the bottleneck facility. Here fewer and shorter setup times are very beneficial. Avoiding delays caused by lack of material or labor or by breakdowns is very important to overall capacity. Do not be distracted from this goal by pressures to appear efficient in non-bottleneck work centers, especially if such actions are not supportive of the bottlenecks. Extra setups or other changes in non-bottleneck operations should be considered if they reduce delays at the key bottleneck work centers.

Another approach to shop-floor control is the pull system of the Just-in-Time (JIT) philosophy. Under conditions of a level load on the factory, we can consider using a simple card system, called kanban (or its equivalent) to authorize production. In essence, we produce only when a customer comes to us and makes a withdrawal from our stock. If the withdrawal is from finished goods, then final assembly may make a standard (small, ideally equal to one) replacement lot. The authorization to assemble will lead to withdrawals of parts, which in turn authorizes production of replacement parts. This process repeats back through the system until it reaches the suppliers of raw materials. The kanban approach applies to a repetitive manufacturing environment when a reasonably stable flow and simple sequencing rules can be maintained.

In any system, a job can fall behind schedule. Expediting can get a late job back on schedule by reducing the time spent waiting for jobs ahead of it. This works when some of the jobs ahead of the late one can be delayed. Lot splitting and lap scheduling can speed a job through a facility. By splitting a lot into two or more smaller lots, the first split lot moves on through the system as soon as it finishes an operation. By lap scheduling we transfer part of a lot to the next operation before completing the entire batch. Both lot splitting and lap scheduling reduce normal delays in the system for rush jobs. Alternate routings, using other machines or processes, can be used to temporarily deal with a bottleneck and keep jobs on schedule. If the schedule cannot be maintained, then feedback to the scheduling process may lead to a revised master schedule.

Managing the shop floor requires constant revision of plans. This necessitates accurate and current feedback data on the status of in-process jobs.

PERT/CPM

The program evaluation and review technique (PERT) and the critical path method (CPM) are widely recognized and successfully applied techniques that require special attention. These similar methodologies belong to a special set of operations-research techniques known as network models. They are particularly applicable to the management of unique projects that have a broad scope.

PERT and CPM are so similar that it is unnecessary to attempt to distinguish one from the other. PERT originally was developed by the U.S. Navy Special Projects Office and Lockheed Aircraft Corporation in cooperation with the consulting firm of Booz, Allen, and Hamilton. It was introduced in 1958 in an effort to reduce the original time forecast for the development of the Polaris ballistic missile and is credited with reducing the time span by several years. CPM was developed in 1957 to help with the scheduling of maintenance in chemical plants. Next to PERT, CPM is the second most widely used system for planning and controlling large projects. Both techniques have been applied to such projects as startups and shutdowns of production facilities; installations of major new equipment, such as computer systems and assembly lines; construction of subdivisions, shopping centers, skyscrapers, dams, and power stations; and virtually all government development contracts.

As a planning tool, PERT allows the manager to plan a project well in advance and estimate its expected completion time and date. This early planning identifies possible bottlenecks and indicates which activities may require modification. For controlling the project, PERT permits the manager to compare the actual and planned progress of each activity. This procedure identifies those activities that are behind schedule and that ultimately may delay the overall project completion date.

PERT Network Analysis

The PERT analysis proceeds chronologically through the following steps:

1. Identification of activities required by the project
2. Identification of the precedence relationships among the activities (i.e., which activities must be completed before others can begin)
3. Determination of the expected time requirements for each activity
4. Development of the network diagram of activities (arrows) and events or nodes (circles)
5. Determination of the earliest and latest feasible event times (an event is the beginning or end of an activity)
6. Identification of the critical path

Steps 1 through 3 require extensive data gathering from people knowledgeable about the various activities of the project. Because their expert opinions

Table 4-2

PERT Data on Activities: Precedence and Time Estimates

ACTIVITY Code	Description	TIME Optimistic	TIME Most Likely	TIME Pessimistic	TIME Expected*	Precedence Relationships
A	Acquire Equipment	20 days	25 days	36 days	26 days	None
B	Clear Floor Space	2	5	8	5	None
C	Mark Floor Location	1	3	11	4	B
D	Inspect Equipment	1	1	7	2	A
E	Store Installation Materials	1	1	1	1	B
F	Install Equipment	5	10	27	12	C,D,E
G	Test & Debug Equip.	3	7	23	9	F

*Expected Time $= \dfrac{t(\text{optimistic}) + 4 \times t(\text{most likely}) + t(\text{pessimistic})}{6}$

form the basis for the PERT analysis, they represent a critical input to the planning. It is important to solicit the full and honest cooperation of these people, who, in many cases, will be the same people responsible for the successful implementation of the project plans.

Network diagramming. The network must relate the activities so that each arrow representing an activity does not begin before all necessary preceding requirements have been completed. Furthermore, each activity should be described uniquely by its starting and ending event nodes. The latter requirement leads to the use of "dummy" activities, those that require zero time but permit the unique identification of activities. The network representing a simplified equipment installation is developed in table 4-2 and figure 4-7.

In table 4-2, three times are provided by the experts: optimistic, most likely, and pessimistic. Since the actual distribution of times may be skewed instead of symmetrical, it may be difficult for the experts to estimate directly the mean (expected) time. In PERT, the expected time is computed as a weighted average of the three time estimates. Traditionally, the optimistic and pessimistic estimates are given a weight of one, and the most likely is given a weight of four. The computed expected time is the estimate used in evaluating the PERT network.

The precedence requirements in table 4-2 resulted in the network in figure 4-7. Check the network to assure yourself that you understand how the precedence relationships are incorporated into the diagram. For example, notice that

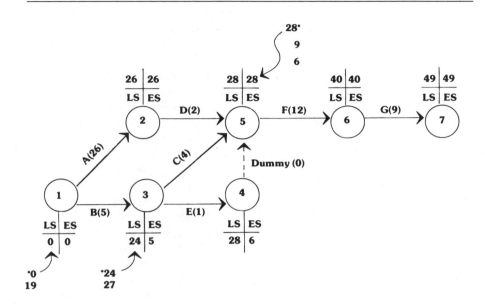

* Indicates the selected values when more than one path is relevant to the computation of LS (latest start time) or ES (earliest start time).

Figure 4-7. PERT Network

activities C and E cannot begin until activity B has been completed. Event 3 marks the completion of activity B and the beginning of activities C and E. The dummy activity is required to uniquely identify activity E; otherwise, both activities C and E would begin at node 3 and end at node 5.

Determining earliest and latest event times. The earliest possible event times are computed first in what is termed the "forward pass." Starting with the first node, we set the earliest event time to 0. We call this the early start time (ES). To compute the ES for node 2, we add the time from node 1 to 2, or 26 days to the ES(1), which was 0. Next we compute ES(3) = 0 + 5, or 5 days. This says that day 5 is the earliest we can expect to have progressed as far as event 3. Similarly, ES(4) = ES(3) + expected time for activity E, which numerically means that ES(4) = 5 + 1 or 6 days from the start date. Event 5 is more complicated because there are several paths leading to that node: path 1-2-5, path 1-3-5, and path 1-3-4-5. We must find the longest of these three paths since all the associated activities must be completed before event 5 is reached and activity F can begin. To find the longest path, we merely have to check each of the arrows (activities) leading into node 5. Therefore, for activity D, we compute ES(5) = ES(2) + T(D) = 26 + 2 = 28. For activity C, ES(5) = ES(3) + T(C) = 5 + 4 = 9. For the dummy, ES(5) = ES(4) + T(dummy) = 6 + 0 = 6. We identify the largest of the three, 28 days, and this becomes the ES(5). ES(6) and ES(7) are computed in the same manner and result in ES(7) of 49 days, which is the earliest we can expect to complete the installation.

The next step is the "backward pass," and it follows a similar logic. We begin with the last node, event 7. Since 49 days is the earliest we can complete the project, we set the latest time for this event equal to 49 days. We will call this LS(7). Now we wish to compute the latest time for each of the preceding events that will not delay our completion on day 49. Working backwards, if we need to reach node 7 on day 49, when do we need to be at node 6? Clearly we need to be at node 6 no later than on the 40th day. Therefore, the latest start (LS) of activity 6 must be 40. For node 5, we compute LS(5) = LS(6) − T(F) = 40 − 12 = 28. LS(4) = LS(5) − T(dummy) = 28 − 0 = 28. Node 3 is more complex (similar to node 5 in the forward pass). Node 3 has two arrows that trace backwards to it; therefore, we need to evaluate two paths. The two computations are: LS(3) = LS(5) − T(C) = 28 − 4 = 24 and LS(3) = LS(4) − T(E) = 28 − 1 = 27. In the backward pass, we must choose the smaller of the two; thus LS(3) = 24. Logically, consider what the consequences would be if event 3 were not achieved until sometime after day 24. It would delay the completion of the project, because of the time required by activities C, F, and G. Latest start times for nodes 2 and 1 are computed the same way. LS(1) will be 0 unless you have made an arithmetic error.

The critical path. The critical path consists of the activities associated with the longest path from the start of the project to its end. The critical activities must be completed on time or the project will be delayed; in other words, there is zero "slack" for these activities. Since we have computed all the earliest and latest start times, we can find the slack, LS-ES, for each node. The critical nodes will have zero slack, LS − ES = 0. An activity, defined by two nodes, is critical if the ES of the beginning node plus the activity time is equal to the LS of the ending node. For example, activity A is defined by node 1 to node 2. The ES(1) = 0, T(A) = 26 and LS(2) = 26, therefore activity A is critical because 0 + 26 = 26. Activity C is not critical since ES(3) + T(C) equals 9, which is less than 28 the value of LS(5). Indeed, activity C has nineteen days of slack. Those activities that connect the critical nodes will be critical activities. In figure 4-7, nodes 1, 2, 5, 6, and 7 are critical nodes. The associated activities A, D, F, and G are critical activities. There are no other paths connecting the critical nodes. However, consider an additional activity—H between nodes 1 and 5. Activity H is to fly in an installation expert who must be there before the equipment installation. If H takes only two days, then the activity is not critical even though it connects two critical nodes. If activity H were expected to take twenty-eight days, then it would be critical along with activities A and D.

Now that we have an estimate of our earliest completion date and have identified the critical activities, we can consider whether or not we need to finish sooner and, if so, which activities we must expedite. If management requires the new equipment in operation forty days from now, then we will focus our speedup efforts on activities A, D, F, and G. Since we have a great deal of slack in activities B (24 − 5 = 19 days), C (28 − 9 = 19 days), and E (28 − 6 = 22 days), we need not be very concerned that our expediting will lead to another path becoming critical. In other projects, however, we must be concerned about near critical paths—that is, those with little slack.

Using the PERT Network

The PERT network is not an inflexible, unalterable schedule. It is a dynamic tool that allows new networks to be formulated as changes occur in the schedule because of a lack of resources or in order to utilize available resources more effectively. The planner who understands this flexibility may find that rearranging activities or moving resources to the most critical areas can significantly reduce the total time required.

Key Concepts

Intrinsic/Extrinsic Forecasting Methods

Components of Variation

Exponential Smoothing

Mean Absolute Deviation (MAD)

Aggregate Planning

Master Schedule

Material Requirements Planning

Indented Bill of Materials

Capacity Requirements Planning

Job Shop Scheduling Rules

Gantt Chart

Progress Control

PERT/CPM

Independent/Dependent Demand

References

Chase, Richard B., and Aquilano, Nicholas J. *Production and Operations Management.* 4th ed. Homewood, IL: Richard D. Irwin, 1985.

Goldratt, Eliyahu, and Cox, J. *The Goal.* Revised ed. Croton-on-Hudson, NY: North River Press, 1986.

Meredith, Jack R., and Mantel, Samuel J., Jr. *Project Management.* New York: John Wiley & Sons, 1985.

Makridakis, Spyros, and Wheelwright, Steven C. *Forecasting Methods and Applications.* 2d ed. Santa Barbara, CA: John Wiley and Sons, 1983.

Silver, Edward A., and Peterson, Rein. *Decision Systems for Inventory Management and Production Planning.* New York: John Wiley and Sons, 1985.

Vollmann, Thomas E. "OPT as an Enhancement to MRP II." *Production and Inventory Management.* (2d quarter 1986): 38–47.

Vollmann, Thomas E., Berry, William L., and Whybark, D. Clay. *Manufacturing Planning and Control Systems.* 2d ed. Homewood, IL: Richard D. Irwin, 1988.

Discussion Questions

1. What are the five basic steps in the forecasting process?
2. How does external market demand differ from internal dependent demand? Why are the differences important?
3. Identify three general types of forecasting models and discuss how they differ.
4. Identify four components that may be found in a set of time series data. Why are these influences important to a forecaster?
5. How can you measure whether or not your forecasting model is doing a good job?
6. What is the manager attempting to accomplish by doing aggregate planning?
7. What trade-offs are the focus of the aggregate planning process?
8. Discuss the consequences the following errors would have on the MRP example of a picture frame in this chapter.
    a. Your inventory records says you have 100 units of Part No. 10141101 in the chapter example, but in truth there are only 80 units.
    b. The bill of materials calls for 2 ounces of white antique stain for each frame, but in reality you need 3 ounces.
9. What types of problems justify the use of PERT? Why is PERT particularly helpful in these situations?
10. How do split lots and lap scheduling speed some jobs through the shop?

Problems

1. Given the historical data below, use simple exponential smoothing to forecast sales for July. Use an alpha of .1 and assume that the smoothed forecast for January was 1,100 units.

t	Month	Actual Demand (A_t)	Smoothed Forecast (SF_t)
1	January	1,150	1,100 (initial smoothed forecast)
2	February	1,075	_____
3	March	1,230	_____
4	April	1,020	_____
5	May	1,185	_____
6	June	1,045	_____
7	July		_____

2. Given the data on the four jobs—A, B, C, and D—sequence them into work center 1 based on FCFS, SOT, and critical-ratio priority rules. Which rule gives the smallest average lateness per four jobs? Per late jobs only? Today is Tuesday. The current day is available to schedule as are the days on which a job is received. Work is scheduled Monday through Friday.

Job	Total Work per Job	Work Remaining on Each Job	Date Received	Due Date
A	3 Days	2 Days	Yesterday	Friday
B	2 Days	2 Days	Today	Wednesday
C	5 Days	4 Days	Last Thursday	Next Tuesday
D	1 Day	1 Day	Today	Next Monday

3. Compute the following for the PERT diagram below (assuming that the activity times provided are the expected times):

   a. The early start times for each event (ES)

   b. The late start times for each event (LS)

   c. The critical path

   d. The slack times for each event.

   e. Now assume that the project has begun and the times represent weeks. Six weeks have passed and task 1-3 was completed on time, task 1-4 is on schedule, but task 1-2 was delayed by three weeks and has just been finished. What impact does this delay have on the plan? Does the additional analysis required suggest to you the value of having a computer program to update the PERT analysis during the execution of a plan?

112 Fundamentals of Production/Operations Management

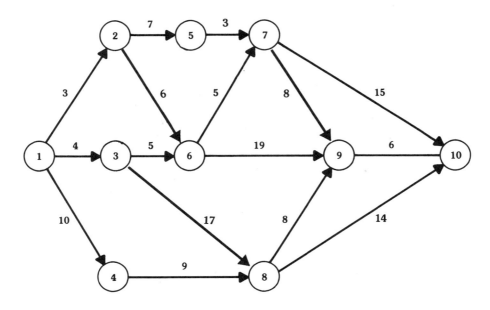

4. Develop the MRP time-phased inventory records for items A, B, C, and D based on the B/M, MPS, and inventory file information provided.

Indented Bill of Materials

Level	Part No.	Quantity per Parent
0	A	no parent
1	B	2 each
2	D	3 each
1	C	1 each
2	D	2 each

Master Production Schedule

Item	Wk. 1	Wk. 2	Wk. 3	Wk. 4
A	0	55	225	200
Others	No independent demand for items B, C, or D			

Inventory Status File

Item	Lot Size	On Hand	On Order	Lead Time
A	200	95 units	200 units due in Wk. 3	1 Wk.
B	L4L*	10	0	2
C	L4L	20	0	1
D	L4L	1200	0	1

*L4L = lot for lot

CHAPTER

5

Purchasing/Materials Management

All organizations (banks, computer manufacturers, hospitals, steel producers, airlines, government agencies, or universities) must have a continuous flow of materials, supplies, and services to support operations. The supply of these items typically is handled through the organization's purchasing department, which has the managerial responsibility of *providing, from outside suppliers, a smooth flow of materials, supplies, and services to support operations.*

Prior to 1940, most firms regarded the purchasing function as primarily a clerical activity. However, during World War II (1939–1945) a firm's success was not dependent on what it could sell, since demand was almost unlimited. Instead, the ability to obtain, from suppliers, the raw materials, supplies, and services needed to keep the production process operating was the key determinant of an organization's success. Because attention was given to the organization, policies, and procedures of the purchasing function, it emerged as a recognized managerial activity. During the 1950s and 1960s, purchasing continued to gain stature as the techniques for performing the function became more refined and as the supply of people trained and competent to make sound purchasing decisions increased. Many companies elevated the chief purchasing officer to top management status. Today, according to a 1988 study by the Center for Advanced Purchasing Studies, the chief purchasing officer in 297 major corporations carries the title of Director of Purchasing (38%), Vice President of Purchasing (23%), Manager of Purchasing (18%), or Vice President of Materials Management (9%). The salary of the head of purchasing often is in the $100,000 range, and substantially higher when bonuses are included.

In the early 1970s, firms faced two vexing problems: an international shortage of almost all the basic raw materials needed to support operations and the fastest rate of price increases since the end of World War II. The Middle East oil embargo during the summer of 1973 intensified both the shortages and the price escalation. These developments put the spotlight directly on companies' purchasing departments, because their performance in obtaining needed items from suppliers, at realistic prices, spelled the difference between success and failure. This emphasized again to top management the crucial role played by purchasing. Although the shortages lessened from 1974 to 1975 because of the worldwide recession, and the inflationary trend moderated in 1982, due to stringent government monetary and fiscal actions and a worldwide glut of crude oil, companies now recognize the importance of a capable, efficient purchasing function. Additionally, the purchasing department plays a key role in combating inflationary pressures by resisting unwarranted price increases.

As a result of this recognition of the impact of purchasing decisions on the long-term success of a firm (assuring a reliable supply of needed materials at a reasonable cost), many firms now are emphasizing strategic material planning. This activity attempts to forecast the long-term (five to twenty years) demand, supply, and price of those key raw materials needed to operate the firm based upon a variety of assumptions about the worldwide economic and political environment. If future problems can be spotted now, the firm can take action by, for example, substitution, backward vertical integration, or product line reduction to alleviate the difficulty before a crisis occurs.

Objectives of Purchasing/Materials Management

The main function of the purchasing department is to obtain the *right materials* (meeting quality requirements), in the *right quantity,* for delivery at the *right time* and *right place,* from the *right source* (a reliable supplier who will meet commitments in a timely fashion), with the *right service* (both before and after the sale), and at the *right price.* The purchasing decision maker might be likened to a juggler attempting to keep several balls in the air at the same time: The purchaser must achieve several goals—the seven "rights" just listed—simultaneously. It is not efficient to buy at the lowest price, if the goods delivered are unsatisfactory from a quality or performance standpoint or if they arrive two weeks behind schedule, causing a production slowdown or shutdown. The right price may be one that is much *higher* than normal if the item is needed immediately, preventing the buyer from adhering to the normal lead time. The purchasing decision maker attempts to balance out the often conflicting objectives and makes trade-offs to obtain the optimum mix of these seven rights.

A more specific statement of the overall goals of purchasing would include the following eight items. Purchasing should

1. **Provide an uninterrupted flow of materials, supplies, and services required to operate the organization.** Stock-outs (interruptions in supply)

of raw materials and production parts would shut down an operation and be extremely costly in terms of lost production, escalation of operating costs due to fixed costs, and inability to satisfy delivery promises to customers. For example, an automobile producer cannot complete a car without purchased tires; an airline cannot keep its planes flying without purchased fuel; and a hospital cannot perform surgery without purchased IV (intravenous) solutions.

2. **Minimize inventory investment and loss.** One way to assure an uninterrupted material flow is to keep large inventory banks. But inventory assets require using capital that could be invested elsewhere; the cost of carrying inventory may be 24 to 36 percent of value per year. If purchasing can support operations with an inventory investment of $10 million instead of $20 million, at an annual inventory carrying cost of 30 percent, the $10 million reduction in inventory represents a saving of $3 million. Just-in-time purchasing systems, which have as their objective the selection of suppliers who will deliver a small quantity of purchased items of the specified quality precisely on schedule, enable an organization to substantially reduce inventory dollars.

3. **Maintain adequate quality standards.** To produce the desired product or service, a certain level of quality is required for each material input. Otherwise, the end product or service will not meet expectations or will result in higher-than-acceptable production costs. For example, if poor-quality computer storage discs are supplied to data processors, the data-input operation will be inefficient, and much of the work will have to be redone, increasing the total wage costs of the organization.

4. **Find or develop competent suppliers.** In the final analysis, the success of the purchasing department depends on its skill in locating or developing suppliers, analyzing their capabilities, and then selecting the appropriate source. Only if suppliers who are both responsive and responsible are selected will the firm obtain the items it needs at the lowest ultimate cost. For example, if a complex computer system is purchased from a supplier who later goes out of business and is not able to perform the long-term maintenance, modification, and updating of the system, the initial favorable price turns out to be extremely high because of the supplier's inability to make good on the original commitment.

5. **Standardize, where possible, the items bought.** From an overall company viewpoint, the best item possible for the intended application should be bought. If purchasing can buy a quantity of one item to do the job that two or three different items previously did, the organization may gain efficiency advantages through a lower initial price resulting from a quantity discount, lower total inventory investment (without lowering service levels), reduced personnel training and maintenance costs in the use of equipment, and increased competition.

6. **Maintain and improve the organization's competitive position.** An organization will be competitive only if it can control purchasing costs to protect profit margins; these costs are the largest single element in the operation of many organizations. Additionally, product design and manufacturing methods must change to keep pace with changing technology and production environments; the purchasing department can inform product design and manufacturing engineering about new products available and changes likely to occur in production technology. Finally, the purchasing department is responsible for assuring the smooth flow of materials necessary to produce goods and provide services as required to meet delivery commitments to customers; in the long run, the success of any organization depends upon its ability to create and maintain customers.

7. **Achieve harmonious, productive working relationships with other departments within the organization.** Purchasing actions cannot be effectively accomplished solely by the efforts of the purchasing department; cooperation with several other departments and individuals within the firm is vital to success. For example, the departments requesting materials and the production control department must provide timely information on material requirements if purchasing is to have sufficient lead time to locate competent vendors and make advantageous purchase agreements. Engineering and production must be willing to consider the possible economic advantages of using substitute materials and different vendors. Purchasing must work closely with quality control in determining inspection procedures for incoming materials, in communicating to vendors the changes needed if quality problems are found, and assisting in evaluating the performance of current suppliers. To take advantage of payment discounts and to maintain good, long-term vendor relations, accounting must pay vendors on time. If there is a problem with the flow of information concerning payment to vendors, purchasing must correct the problem; the supplier deals directly with purchasing, not with accounting, receiving, or incoming inspection, and expects to be paid on schedule.

8. **Accomplish the purchasing objectives at the lowest possible level of administrative costs.** It takes resources to operate the purchasing department—salaries, telephone and postage expenses, supplies, travel costs, and accompanying overhead. If purchasing procedures are not efficient, purchasing administrative costs will be excessive. Because the objectives of purchasing should be achieved as efficiently and economically as possible, the purchasing manager continually must review the operation to assure that it is cost effective. If the firm is not realizing its purchasing objectives due to inadequate analysis and planning, perhaps additional personnel are needed. But the firm should be continually alert to possible improvements in purchasing methods, procedures, and techniques. Perhaps unneeded steps in processing purchasing paperwork could be eliminated; perhaps the computer could be used to make the storage and recall of necessary purchasing data more efficient.

Importance of the Purchasing Function

The key objectives of any organization are to provide a good or service needed by a customer and to do so effectively and efficiently in order to return adequate long-term rewards (profits) to the owners. The purchasing function plays an important role in achieving these key objectives.

Total Dollars Involved

Purchasing is the largest single dollar-control area with which most managers must deal. Obviously, the percentage of the sales or income dollar paid out to suppliers will vary greatly from industry to industry. For example, in a hospital or bank, purchasing dollars as a percentage of operating income will be less than 25 percent since these industries are labor intensive rather than material intensive. But in the manufacturing sector, material dollars typically account for well over half the sales dollar. When an automobile producer sells a new car to a dealer for $10,000, it already has spent more than $5,000 (more than 50 percent) to buy the steel, tires, glass, paint, fabric, aluminum, copper, and electronic components necessary to build that car. When a soft-drink producer sells $1,000 of packaged beverages to the supermarket, close to $750 already has been paid to vendors for the liquid sugar, carbonation, flavoring, bottles, caps, and cardboard containers necessary to produce the end product.

Table 5-1, which uses data collected by the U.S. Bureau of the Census for its *Annual Survey of Manufactures,* presents aggregate data for the entire U.S. manufacturing sector, broken down by type of industry. These figures show that, in the average manufacturing firm, materials account for 56 percent of the sales dollar; if expenditures for capital equipment are included, the figure goes up to 60 percent. This is one-and-a-half times the remaining 40 percent available to pay salaries, wages, other operating expenses, taxes, and dividends. In 1985, the 60 percent total purchase/sales ratio was about three times the 19 percent spent for all wages, salaries, and fringe benefits.

The material/sales ratio varies dramatically among industries. For example, in standard industrial classification (SIC) 38, "Instruments and Related Products," it is only 34 percent; but this industry includes firms making such items as the auto-pilot used on large commercial aircraft, which requires a higher percentage of engineering, quality control, and direct assembly labor. On the other hand, in SIC 20, "Food and Kindred Products," the material/sales ratio is 65 percent, almost twice as large. This category includes commercial bread bakeries and beverage producers whose production process is material intensive and requires a minimum amount of labor cost due to highly mechanized and automated manufacturing processes.

Table 5-1 shows that the average material/sales ratio in manufacturing has moved up from 53 percent in 1971 to 56 percent in 1985 because manufacturing processes have become more material and less labor intensive. The total purchase/sales ratio went from 56 to 60 percent in this same time period. Any function of the firm that accounts for the use of over half the firm's receipts certainly deserves a great deal of managerial attention.

Table 5-1
Cost of materials—Value of Industry shipments ratios for manufacturing firms, 1985

Standard industrial code	Industry	Cost of materials (millions)[a]	Capital expenditures, new (millions)[b]	Total material and capital expenditures (millions)	Value of industry shipments (millions)[c]	Material sales ratio	Total purchase sales ratio
20	Food and kindred products	197,275	7,049	204,324	301,562	65	68
21	Tobacco products	6,626	669	7,295	18,507	36	39
22	Textile mill products	32,258	1,863	34,121	53,277	61	64
23	Apparel and other textile products	29,130	697	29,827	56,993	51	52
24	Lumber and wood products	33,169	1,664	34,833	54,185	61	64
25	Furniture and fixtures	14,764	763	15,527	31,294	47	50
26	Paper and allied products	53,039	6,276	59,315	93,414	57	64
27	Printing and publishing	39,104	4,715	43,819	111,885	35	39
28	Chemicals, allied products	101,696	8,269	109,965	197,311	52	56
29	Petroleum and coal products	161,291	3,438	164,729	179,135	90	92
30	Rubber, miscellaneous plastics products	35,754	3,430	39,184	71,324	50	55
31	Leather, leather products	4,444	103	4,547	8,567	52	53
32	Stone, clay, glass products	26,179	2,780	28,959	55,064	48	53
33	Primary metal industries	70,603	4,755	75,358	110,301	64	68
34	Fabricated metal products	70,490	4,346	74,836	139,580	51	54
35	Machinery, except electric	102,831	8,323	111,154	215,080	48	52
36	Electric, electronic equipment	83,079	10,471	93,550	192,732	43	49
37	Transportation equipment	180,856	10,377	191,233	301,386	60	64
38	Instruments, related products	20,982	2,581	23,563	61,008	34	39
39	Miscellaneous manufacturing	12,442	667	13,109	26,527	47	49

	(1971)	356,016	20,940	376,956	53	56
	(1972)	407,418	24,072	431,490	54	57
	(1973)	478,169	26,978	505,147	55	58
	(1974)	581,580	35,696	617,276	57	61
	(1975)	597,327	37,262	634,589	57	61
	(1976)	681,194	40,545	721,739	57	61
All operating manufacturing	(1977)	782,417	47,459	829,876	58	61
establishments	(1978)	877,424	55,209	932,633	58	61
	(1979)	999,157	61,533	1,060,690	58	61
	(1980)	1,093,567	70,112	1,163,679	59	63
	(1981)	1,193,969	78,632	1,272,601	59	63
	(1982)	1,130,143	74,562	1,204,705	58	61
	(1983)	1,170,238	61,931	1,232,169	57	60
	(1984)	1,288,414	75,186	1,363,600	57	61
	(1985)	1,276,013	83,237	1,359,250	56	60

[a]Refers to direct charges actually paid or payable for items consumed or put into production during the year, including freight charges and other direct charges incurred by the establishment in acquiring these materials. Manufacturers included the cost of materials or fuel consumed regardless of whether these items were purchased by the individual establishment from other companies, transferred to it from other establishments of the same company, or withdrawn from inventory. It excludes the cost of services used, such as advertising, insurance, telephone, etc., and research, developmental, and consulting services of other establishments. It also excludes materials, machinery, and equipment used in plant expansion or capitalized repairs which are chargeable to fixed assets accounts.

[b]Includes funds spent for permanent additions and major alterations to manufacturing establishments, and new machinery and equipment used for replacement purposes and additions to plant capacity if they are chargeable to a fixed asset account.

[c]The received or receivable net selling values, f.o.b. plant, after discounts and allowances, and excluding freight charges and excise taxes. However, where the products of an industry are customarily delivered by the manufacturing establishment, e.g., bakery products, the value of shipments is based on the delivered price of the goods.

Source: U.S. Bureau of the Census, 1985 Annual Survey of Manufactures (Washington, D.C.: U.S. Government Printing Office), Statistics for Industry Groups and Industries, M85(AS)-1, pp. 1–8, 1–9, and Appendix.

Profit-Leverage Effect

If, through better purchasing, a firm saves $100,000 in the prices paid to vendors for needed materials, supplies, and services, that $100,000 savings goes directly to the bottom-line (before-tax) account on its profit-and-loss statement. If that same firm sells an additional $100,000 of product, the contribution to profit, assuming a 5 percent before-tax profit margin, would be only $5,000. Clearly, purchase dollars are high powered.

Perhaps an example, using a hypothetical manufacturer, will illustrate this:

- Gross sales $1,000,000
- Purchases (assuming purchases account for 50% of the sales dollar) 500,000
- Profit (assuming a before-tax profit margin of 5%) 50,000

Now, assume this firm was able to reduce its overall purchase cost by 10 percent through better management of the function. This would be a $50,000 additional contribution to before-tax profits. To increase before-tax profits by $50,000 solely through increased sales would require an additional $1,000,000, or a doubling, of sales.

This is not to suggest that it would be easy to reduce overall purchase costs by 10 percent. In a firm that has given major attention to the purchasing function over the years, it would be difficult, and perhaps impossible, to do. But in a firm that has neglected purchasing, it would be a realistic objective. Because of the profit-leverage effect of purchasing, large savings are possible compared to the effort necessary to increase sales by the much larger percentage necessary to generate the same effect on the profit-and-loss statement. Since, in many firms, the sales function already has received much more attention, purchasing may be the last untapped "profit producer."

Return-on-Assets Effect

Firms are increasingly more interested in return-on-assets (ROA) as a measure of performance. Figure 5-1 shows the standard ROA model, using the same figures as in the previous example and assuming, realistically, that inventory accounts for 30 percent of total assets. If purchase costs were reduced by 10 percent, the inventory asset base also would be reduced by 10 percent. The numbers in the boxes show the initial figures used in arriving at the 10 percent ROA performance. The numbers below each box are the figures resulting from a 10 percent overall purchase price reduction, and the end product is a new ROA of 20.6 percent. This is a highly feasible objective for many firms.

Effect on Efficiency

The effectiveness of the purchasing function shows up in other operating results. If the purchasing department selects a vendor who fails to deliver raw materials

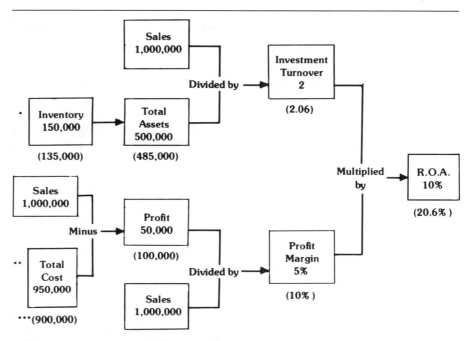

*Inventory is approximately 30 percent of total assets.
**Purchases account for half of total sales, or $500,000.
***(Figures in parentheses assume a 10 percent reduction in purchase costs.)

Figure 5-1. Return-on-Assets Factors

or parts that measure up to the agreed-upon quality standards, a higher scrap rate or costly rework, requiring excessive direct labor expenditures, may result. If the supplier selected does not meet the agreed-upon delivery schedule, the delay may require a costly rescheduling of production, decreasing overall production efficiency or, in the worst case, shutting down the production line while fixed costs continue, even though there is no output.

Effect on Competitive Position

A firm cannot be competitive unless it can deliver end products or services to its customers when they are wanted and at a price the customer considers fair. If purchasing doesn't do its job, the firm will not have the required materials when needed and at a price that keeps end-product costs under control.

Some years ago, a major automobile producer decided to buy all its auto glass from one firm (a single source). Some months into the supply agreement, it appeared that the forthcoming labor-contract negotiations might result in a deadlock and a long strike. To protect itself, the auto company built up a 90-day glass stockpile, even though the inventory carrying costs were high, and it had problems finding the physical storage facilities for that much glass. As anticipated, there was a strike in the glass industry, but the union struck only the glass firm supplying that auto producer. The strike lasted 118 days, and the auto producer had to shut down its production lines for more than a month.

The auto company had a large net financial loss that year, since that sales loss dropped it below its break-even point. The president explained to the stockholders that the glass strike cost the company the sale of about 100,000 cars (a month's sales). Auto customers evidently were not willing to wait until the strike ended, and they went "across the street" to buy a car made by a competitor. The dealer can tell a customer, "Here's the car. Bring it back in a month, and we'll put the hubcaps on for you," and he'll make the sale. but it's difficult to convince the customer to take the car now and bring it back later for the windshield! Actually, the producer probably lost closer to 500,000 auto sales: If a customer bought another maker's car when he couldn't get the car he wanted and if he liked the different make, he probably returned to the new dealer to buy another car two or three years later, and then did so repeatedly.

Effect on Image

The actions of the purchasing department directly influence the public-relations image of a company. This is particularly true of a company making industrial products, because purchasing has many more outside contacts (with vendors and potential vendors) than the marketing department (which calls on only a limited number of customers). If actual and potential suppliers are not treated in a businesslike manner, they will form a poor opinion of the entire company and will communicate this to other firms. This poor image will adversely affect the purchasing firm's ability to get new business and to find new and better suppliers.

Training Ground

The purchasing professional, in performing his or her daily activities, interacts with all other areas of the organization. This provides a critical exposure to the needs and operation of the organization. The individual's ability and willingness to take risks and assume responsibility are scrutinized and evaluated when he or she makes decisions under pressure, in an environment of uncertainty and with potentially serious consequences. Many organizations include an assignment in the purchasing area as part of the formal job rotation plan for "fast-track" employees.

Information Source

The daily contacts of the buyer or purchasing manager provide a good deal of potentially useful information about the outside environment. What new products are being developed by competitors? What are the competitors' marketing strategies? What is the availability of new material? Is innovative technology being developed? What is the manufacturing strategy of competitors? Who are potential merger and acquisition candidates? What is the direction of the economy? Buyers are in a prime position to answer such questions and feed this intelligence to top corporate management, where it can be evaluated and used in developing and refining the organization's own objectives and strategies.

Organization of Purchasing/Materials Management

A proper organizational structure is necessary for effective performance. This enables the specialization, planning, coordination, communication, and control to make effective materials-acquisition decisions.

Centralization Versus Decentralization

If a firm purchases on a *decentralized* basis, each department manager will handle his or her own purchasing. The advantage to this approach is that the user knows what is needed better than anyone else. Also, it may be faster: When a department needs something, the manager simply picks up the phone and orders it.

But the advantages of *centralized purchasing* outweigh those of decentralized purchasing, and almost all but the smallest of firms are centralized. In centralized purchasing, a separate individual or department is given authority to make all purchases, except, perhaps, the very unusual buy, such as a new company aircraft. Centralized purchasing offers the following advantages:

1. It is easier to standardize the items bought if purchasing decisions go through one central control point.

2. It reduces administrative duplication. Instead of each department head writing a separate purchase order for light bulbs, the purchasing department writes only one order for the firm's total requirement.

3. By combining requirements from several departments, purchasing has the clout to go to a supplier and discuss an order quantity that is large enough to interest the vendor. Often the purchasing department can persuade the supplier to give concessions, such as faster delivery or a quantity discount. There also may be freight savings, because shipment now can be made in carload quantities.

4. In periods of materials shortage, one department does not compete with another department for the available supply and thus drive up the price.

5. It is administratively more efficient for the supplier, who does not need to call on several people within the company. Instead, the vendor makes a pitch to the purchasing manager.

6. It provides better control over purchase commitments. Since a large percentage of a firm's cash outflow goes for material purchases, a central control point is needed to monitor the aggregate commitment amount at any specific time. Also, purchasing decisions about placement of orders with vendors

are sensitive: Kickbacks and bribery are possible if orders are issued to unscrupulous suppliers. It is easier to prevent such illegal and unethical practices if all decisions on the flow of purchase commitments go through one central funnel; this means the spotlight can be focused on the purchasing department, because purchase decisions are not scattered throughout the various departments of the firm.

7. It enables the development of specialization and expertise in purchase decisions and uses time more efficiently. When a department head also tries to be a purchasing agent, the time spent on purchasing probably could be better used in managing the department. Additionally, the department manager will not spend enough time in purchasing to develop any real expertise. A full-time buyer, who can devote undivided attention to purchasing, rapidly develops expert knowledge of purchasing techniques, sources of supply, available and new materials and manufacturing processes, markets, and prices. This development of expertise is the primary reason almost all firms have centralized the purchasing function.

A variation of centralized purchasing often exists in the multiplant organization. Here, the firm operates several different producing divisions, which often make different products requiring a different mix of purchased items. The firm often uses a profit-center management-motivation-and-control technique, in which the division manager is totally responsible for running the division, acts as president of an independent firm, and is judged by profits made by this division. Since material purchases are the largest single controllable cost of running a division and have a direct effect on the efficiency and competitive position of the division, the profit-center division manager insists on having direct authority over purchasing. It would be difficult to hold the division manager responsible for results if the manager lacked decision-making power over the major expenditure area.

This realization has led some firms to adopt decentralized-centralized purchasing, in which the purchasing function is centralized on a division or plant basis but decentralized on a corporate basis. Often a corporate purchasing organization operates in a staff capacity and assists the division purchasing departments in those tasks that are handled more effectively on a corporate basis: (1) establishment of policies, procedures, and controls; (2) recruiting and training of personnel; (3) coordinating the purchase of common-use items, where more clout is needed; and (4) auditing purchasing performance. Figure 5-2 presents a simplified organizational chart for a firm organized on a profit-center basis.

In the 1980s, there has been a gradual movement toward greater centralization of purchasing in the multiplant organization in order to gain the volume-buying advantages that lead to greater assurance of supply and closer control of purchase prices. *The Purchasing Function: From Strategy to Image,* a study published in 1982 by the Machinery and Allied Products Institute, found that 50 percent of the firms considered had further centralized their purchasing during the past decade; 65 percent predicted even more centralization in the next ten years.

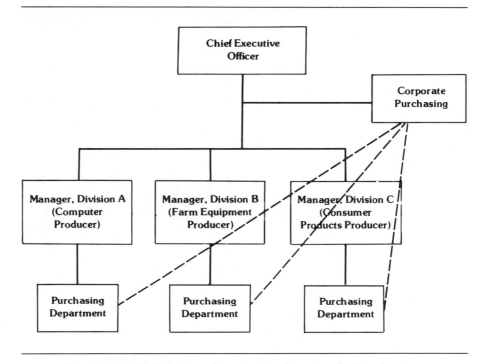

Figure 5-2. Multidivision Organization Structure for Purchasing

A 1988 study by the Center for Advanced Purchasing Studies, *Purchasing Organizational Relationships,* found that in 28 percent of the 297 large organizations, purchasing is centralized; all or most purchasing is done at one central location for the entire firm. In 13 percent of the firms it is decentralized; purchasing is done on a division or plant basis. But in 59 percent of the firms it is handled on a centralized-decentralized basis, in which some purchasing is done at corporate headquarters and purchasing also is done centrally at major operating divisions or plants. Evidently most organizations try to get the best of all possible worlds by mixing centralization and decentralization.

Changing Responsibilities

The 1988 study, *Purchasing Organizational Relationships,* also found that several new activity areas have been assigned to purchasing since 1980. Those activity areas newly assigned in at least 5 percent of the firms were personnel travel (14%), traffic/transportation (13%), countertrade/offset planning/execution (12%), strategic planning (9%), capital-equipment buys (7%), and providing economic forecasts/indicators (6%).

Several activity areas were indicated as ones in which purchasing has assumed an increased role or responsibility since 1980: strategic planning (in 43%

Several activity areas were indicated as ones in which purchasing has assumed an increased role or responsibility since 1980: strategic planning (in 43% of the firms), providing economic forecasts/indicators (41%), capital-equipment buys (37%), product development (31%), new-product evaluation (26%), traffic/transportation (23%), personnel travel (16%), countertrade/offset planning/execution (15%), and cash-flow planning (13%). Obviously, the purchasing function has assumed many increased responsibilities in the past decade, requiring more-talented, better-trained personnel to perform the function.

Materials Management

Some organizations have adopted the materials management organizational concept, whereby a single manager is responsible for planning, organizing, motivating, and controlling all those activities principally concerned with the flow of materials into an organization. Materials management views material flow as a system. Another way to look at materials management is to consider its major activities:

1. Anticipating material requirements
2. Sourcing and obtaining materials
3. Introducing materials into the organization
4. Monitoring the status of materials as a current asset

Figure 5-3 shows the specific functions that might be included in a materials management organization and their relations to other major functional areas of the firm. Not all eleven functions shown would have to report to the materials manager; production scheduling, in-plant materials movement, and incoming quality control often are excluded.

The materials management concept grew out of problems in the airframe industry during World War II. Production of an aircraft requires a large number of individual items, many of which are quite sophisticated and must meet stringent quality standards; these are procured from thousands of vendors located over a wide geographic area. Each item is vital to the total functioning of the end product. The objectives of materials management are solving materials problems from a total company viewpoint (optimize) by coordinating performance of the various materials functions; providing a communications network; and controlling materials flow. As the computer was introduced into organizations, it provided a further reason to adopt materials management: the materials functions have many common data needs and can share a common data base.

The single manager materials concept overcomes the shortcomings of the conventional organization, where the various materials functions are organizationally splintered. It recognizes (1) materials decisions as being additive and not independent of actions elsewhere, (2) the self-interest and potentially conflicting objectives of the individual materials functions, and (3) the need to concentrate authority and responsibility for materials decisions to avoid buck-passing. Materials management, in a formal organizational sense, is not needed in the small

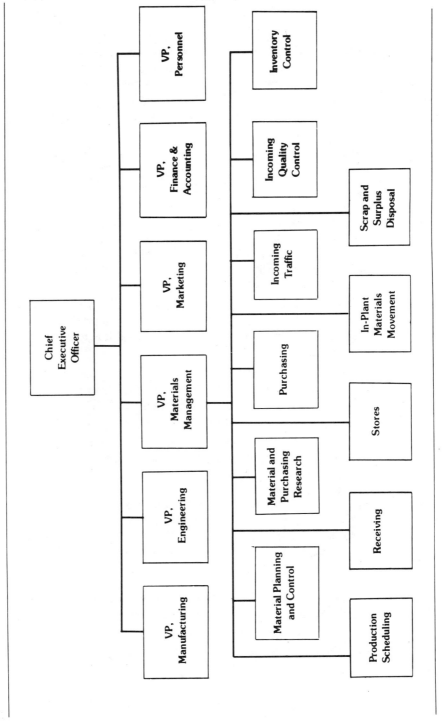

Figure 5-3. Organization Structure for Materials Management

organization where the chief executive (normally the owner) makes all the materials decisions and provides the needed coordination and control.

The 1988 *Purchasing Organizational Relationships* study found that 70 percent of the organizations used the materials-management concept (defined as an organization in which at least three of the following functions—purchasing, inventory, production scheduling and control, inbound traffic, warehousing and stores, incoming quality control) report to a single responsible individual. Materials management has become the typical form of organizations in recent years.

Purchasing Prerogatives

If the purchasing department is to meet the objectives of good purchasing, it must have four key prerogatives:

1. Right to select the supplier. Purchasing should be the expert in knowing who is capable of producing needed items and in analyzing vendor reliability. If someone else selects the supplier, purchasing then is in a sole-source situation and can do little to bargain for an advantageous purchase agreement.

2. Right to use whichever pricing method is appropriate and to determine the price and terms of the agreement. This is one of the main expertise areas of purchasing, which must have room to maneuver if it is to achieve the lowest possible price.

3. Right to question the specifications. Purchasing, which often can suggest substitute or alternate items that will do the same job, is responsible for bringing these items to the attention of the requisitioner. The user makes the final decision on accepting a substitute.

4. Right to control all contacts with potential suppliers. Communication with potential vendors must flow through purchasing. If users contact vendors directly, this encourages "backdoor selling," in which a potential supplier influences the specifications and creates a sole-source situation. Or, the requisitioner will make commitments to vendors that prevent purchasing from reaching agreements that will give the buying firm the lowest ultimate price. If vendor technical personnel need to talk directly with personnel in the buyer's firm, purchasing will arrange for such discussions and will monitor their outcome.

The above purchasing prerogatives should be established as matters of company policy and approved by the chief executive officer.

The Standard Purchasing System

The standard purchasing procedure consists of nine steps: (1) recognition of need, (2) description of need, (3) source selection, (4) price determination, (5) purchase-order preparation, (6) follow-up and expediting, (7) receipt and inspection of goods, (8) invoice clearance and payment, and (9) maintenance of records. Performance of these steps varies from company to company, depending on such factors as the status of purchasing within the total organization, competence of purchasing personnel, and the extent to which electronic data processing is used.

Good management dictates that the procedures and policies of purchasing be written out to assure that the firm follows an approach consistent with its particular needs, to assure consistency and fairness in its purchasing actions, to provide guidance to both buyers and requisitioners in how purchasing is to be handled, and to establish the authority of the purchasing department. A well-managed firm will have an established policy and procedure manual, which is the guidebook for those involved with purchasing. Policies should be established in areas such as authority to requisition, authority to purchase, use of competitive bids, maintenance of records, acceptance of gifts, use of local suppliers, disclosure of information to suppliers, purchasing for employees, charges for tooling, adherence to federal and state laws and regulations, and actions to be taken in the event of discrepancies between the purchase agreement and actual vendor performance.

The key managerial tool used to determine the allocation of time and attention of buying personnel and to establish purchasing strategy is ABC analysis. If a firm arranges any given year's purchase history by listing the one item on which the largest total dollar expenditures were made and then listing in descending dollar value all other items down to the item on which the smallest total dollar expenditures were made, it generally would look like this:

- A items—those 5 percent of the purchased items accounting for 75 percent of the total dollars spent

- B items—those 10 percent of the purchased items accounting for 15 percent of the total dollars spent

- C items—those 85 percent of the purchased items accounting for 10 percent of the total dollars spent

The A items primarily will consist of raw materials and production parts. The B items also will be raw materials and production parts, but the usage amounts and values will be less than for A items. The C items primarily will be maintenance, repair, and operating (MRO) supplies. A given firm may have only 15 items in the A category, 30 items in the B category, and 255 items in the C category, out of a total of 300 items. Since the average annual dollars spent on each A item is 10 times greater than for each B item and about 128 times greater than for each C item, the A item has the largest profit leverage, and this is where most of the time and effort of the purchasing department should be concentrated. A 1 percent saving in the purchase of an A item will produce greater profits than a 99 percent saving on one of the C items. Obviously a 1 percent saving will be more easily attained than a 99 percent saving, which is almost an impossibility. One approach that might be productive is to aggregate several of the individual C items into a family of items (such as all hand tools), thereby moving the family of items into the B category where purchasing can afford to spend more time and effort.

This same ABC analysis technique also applies to other areas of purchasing. Purchase orders segregated by dollar value approximate the ABC breakdown, since most purchasing paperwork is for small-dollar orders. To reduce the quantity and cost of paperwork, a firm should develop a simpler system for processing the small-value, C orders, which require less control since the dollar risk is much lower. If dollars spent with various suppliers are arranged from highest amount by vendor to lowest amount, it also normally will approximate the ABC breakdown. The suppliers with whom purchasing does the most business are those on whom the most attention should be spent, because purchasing has the most clout with them and should cultivate good relations with them.

All the routine data collection, processing, and recording functions involved in the nine steps of the standard purchasing procedure can be handled through a computer system. During the past twenty years, the computer has made substantial inroads into purchasing, resulting in three major benefits: (1) reduction of clerical, manual effort; (2) closer control over purchase actions resulting from more accurate and more timely decision-making data; and (3) better decisions, resulting from the better data base. Significant changes, beginning in the early 1980s, can be attributed to desktop, personal-computer systems. The low cost and ready availability of these small, stand-alone systems are making computerization an integral part of the purchasing function in both small and large organizations.

Recognition of Need

The purchasing process is triggered when someone within the organization recognizes that some material, supply, or service is needed and best can be obtained from sources outside the organization. Normally, a need is recognized by a user, such as production, which calculates its requirement for a particular production part based upon its next month's production schedule; or by marketing, which anticipates a need for a new advertising brochure; or by the personnel department, which requires an additional typewriter. This step normally is not performed by purchasing, except in the case of standard, inventory items where purchasing may be responsible for inventory management and resupplying when the stock on hand reaches a preset order point.

In the case of production parts, many firms now use a computerized materials-requirements-planning (MRP) system (discussed in chapter 4) to notify the purchasing department of parts needed, quantities, and need dates.

Description of Need

If purchasing is to fill a recognized need, the user must notify purchasing of the specific characteristics of that need. A simple, two-part form called the purchase requisition generally is used; the original is sent to purchasing, and the requisitioner retains the carbon copy. The information on the requisition should include date prepared; department preparing and a signature of an individual who can authorize purchase action; description of the item needed; quantity needed; place where delivery is needed; and the date needed. A specific date (month and day) should be indicated; "rush" or "as soon as possible" is not precise enough to guide purchasing. "Rush" may be interpreted by purchasing as a real emergency, and they may pay a higher price to obtain next-day delivery, even though the item really isn't needed for two weeks and could be purchased by normal means and at a much lower price.

The requisitioner need not indicate "suggested price" or "suggested vendor," as purchasing has the expertise to determine the right price and appropriate vendor. If purchasing needs help in locating a vendor, it can ask the requisitioner. Also, if the requisitioner feels obliged to indicate a suggested vendor and price, he or she probably will contact the vendor directly, opening up the possibility for backdoor selling. If, after submitting the requisition, the requisitioner hears nothing from purchasing, it can be assumed that the needed item will arrive by the date specified. If purchasing runs into lead-time problems, they will be discussed with the requisitioner.

If the item is a one-time, immediate-use purchase, the quantity decision is straightforward: Purchasing buys the entire quantity for delivery by the needed date. If the item is an MRO item that normally is maintained in inventory or is an item needed over an extended time period, either inventory control or purchasing will make an economic order quantity calculation, as discussed in chapter 6.

If the item is an A category raw material, purchasing may wish to "buy to the market," based upon purchasing's long-term forecast of the supply-and-demand factors. If the item is forecast to be in a market oversupply situation, purchasing may decide to buy only enough to meet immediate needs (called "hand-to-mouth buying") and wait for the price to fall before making additional purchases. If the item is forecast to be in increasingly short supply, purchasing may decide to buy a several-month supply now, in anticipation of a price increase, and put most of it in inventory for later use. Called "forward buying," this decision to buy more than the immediate need is based on data and a realistic estimate of the situation; it is not speculation, which is gambling on price changes when the firm does not have a foreseeable need for the item and is attempting to make a profit from the buying and selling of materials.

Two variations on the standard purchase requisition are the traveling requisition and the bill of materials. The traveling requisition is a cardboard form used when a particular item must be purchased frequently for a given department. The traveler contains a complete description of the item and is sent to purchasing when a resupply of the item is needed by the user, indicating quantity and date needed. Purchasing writes the purchase order; enters data on vendor, price, and order number on the traveler; and sends it back to the requisitioner, who files the card until a subsequent resupply is needed. As many as twenty-four to thirty-six purchases can be triggered by this traveler card. Use of the traveler eliminates the recopying of routine description data and substitutes for twenty-four to thirty-six individual purchase requisitions, saving paperwork and clerical time. It also provides a complete, cumulative purchase history and use record on one form.

A second variation, the bill of materials (B/M) discussed in chapter 2, is used by firms that make standard, manufactured items over relatively long periods of time; it is a quick way of notifying purchasing of production needs. A B/M for a toaster made by an appliance manufacturer would list the total number or quantity, including an appropriate scrap allowance, of parts or material to make one end unit. Production scheduling then merely notifies purchasing that it has scheduled 18,000 of that model into production next month. Purchasing then will "explode" the B/M (normally by a computerized system) by multiplying through by 18,000 to determine the total quantity of material needed to meet next month's production schedule. Comparison of these numbers with quantities in inventory will give purchasing the "open to buy" figures. The B/M system simplifies the requisitioning process when a large number of frequently needed line items is involved.

The description of the item to be bought is important, because purchasing must understand the requirements if it is to select the most appropriate supplier and clearly communicate quality needs to that vendor. Purchasing's objective is to buy the least expensive item with the attributes needed for the job or application in question. Incoming quality control then will determine whether the item actually received from the supplier meets the specification on the purchase order.

There are several ways quality may be described to purchasing and then by purchasing to the supplier. Each has its peculiar advantages and disadvantages.

Brand or Trade Name

Specifying a product by brand name is a quick means of describing quality, and it is easy to determine whether the right item was delivered. It also gives some assurance that the quality will be consistent over time. Therefore, this is useful in specifying the C category of item, where simple purchase decisions are sought. However, a prime reason manufacturers brand their products is to build up customer loyalty; this permits manufacturers to charge higher prices than those charged for similar, and equally good, unbranded products. The marketing of aspirin is a good example of the price advantage available to a vendor who establishes a brand name in the mind of the buyer.

Market Grade

Many raw materials, such as agricultural and mineral products, have an established grading system that can be used to specify quality. Lumber is a good example. Market grade is a quick and easy method of description if the established grading system classifies quality in sufficiently specific intervals to meet a firm's production needs.

Word Picture

This is a complete, written word picture of the characteristics the needed item must possess. Although these can be very exact, they are difficult to compose so that the vendor understands exactly what is requested.

Blueprint

This is a dimensional specification normally used in the purchase of production parts. It is the most exact type of description, but the buyer is responsible for any errors on the print. Blueprints are costly to prepare.

Sample

Why not give vendors samples and ask for duplicates? This is often done when purchasing repair parts, where age or use makes it difficult to locate the original manufacturer. Samples also frequently are used to describe printed matter, such as forms. Sometimes, however, the printer and the buyer disagree about whether the newly delivered printing complies with the sample, particularly when color is involved.

Performance Specification

When purchasing equipment from a vendor who is familiar with the purchaser's needs, it may be enough to tell the vendor what job the needed equipment must perform. For example, a commercial baker might specify a piece of bread-wrapping equipment by indicating the variations in loaf size it must be able to handle, the number of loaves to be wrapped per hour, and the various types of wrap (cellophane, plastic, waxed paper, or plain paper) the machine must use.

Source Selection

One key to good purchasing is the selection of responsible, cooperative suppliers. This is perhaps the most important step in the purchasing system, for all else depends on it. The care taken in selecting vendors will depend on the item involved and the dollar risk. Greater care will be taken in the purchase of a new item if it is hard to locate and crucial to the performance of the end product or if it is an A item in which the dollar risk from quality problems or delivery interruptions is high. In purchasing a routine, C-category item, purchasing cannot afford to spend much time, since the risk is small and the savings potential is low.

In some instances, a firm is faced with a make-or-buy decision. For example, instead of buying printed forms, we may decide to purchase the needed equipment and print our requirements in-house. Or, our existing print shop may have excess capacity, and we may decide to fill that capacity with our own needs. Another example would be the reusable hypodermic syringe and needles that are sterilized after use and returned to inventory in a hospital: Perhaps it would be more cost effective to buy disposables. Machined-parts requirements frequently can be made in-house on existing equipment, or they may be purchased from an outside vendor. The make-or-buy decision is based upon a combination of cost, quality, and delivery-service considerations. Purchasing also should provide much of the information for, and should participate in, the make-or-buy decision.

The purchase of a new A item will be handled in four steps, and the process may take several months, compared with selecting a supplier for a C item, on which purchasing may spend only five minutes.

Directory Stage

This is an attempt to make as long a list as possible of vendors considered capable of producing the needed item. The buyer wants several possible vendors on the list, since many will be eliminated later in the evaluation process. The buyer's past experience will be the starting point and probably will produce several vendor names. The buyer then may check with some purchasing counterparts in other purchasing departments, both inside and outside the company. Often, salespeople can provide good leads on available sources. Also, vendor directories list suppliers according to type of product; among these are the telephone book Yellow Pages, *Sweets Catalogs, McRae's Bluebook,* and the catalogs available for specific industries, such as suppliers to the chemical industry. Probably the most-used vendor directory is the *Thomas Register of American Manufacturers,* which claims to list all American manufacturers by type of product. The *Thomas Register* contains about 31,000 pages and lists more than 123,000 U. S. manufacturers, 50,000 products and services, and 102,000 brand names and trademarks. These directories, however, do not evaluate the quality or reliability of vendors. Also, buyers, by reading purchasing trade journals and journals in their own industry and by attending various trade shows, will gather general information about possible vendors.

In many firms, the purchasing department makes a concerted effort to find and develop minority vendors—that is, vendors in which at least half of the ownership and top management is by minority citizens such as Blacks, American Indians, Orientals, Eskimos, Aleuts, Puerto Ricans, or Chicanos. Some vendor directories, such as *Try Us '89,* list only minority vendors. Similar emphasis often is given to the use of small vendors (referred to in Public Law 95-507 as "disadvantaged"). Public Law 99-661, passed in 1986, requires that suppliers to the Department of Defense spend 5 percent of their purchase dollars on each contract with minority-owned suppliers. The conscious action by purchasing decision makers is a result of a combination of government pressures plus a realization that minority-owned firms and small businesses will only be part of the mainstream of American economic life if purchasing managers select them as suppliers to medium- and large-size buying firms.

Evaluation

Here the buyer gathers information to predict how well the supplier would perform if selected. Again, the amount of effort expended depends upon the importance of the item to be purchased. Obviously, the information the buyer gathers will be imperfect, and some of the vendors finally selected will not perform as predicted. The areas subject to evaluation are almost endless and will depend on the item to be bought. Some key areas to be evaluated are

1. **Reliability.** Will the vendor do what it says it will do?
2. **Quantity.** Can the vendor supply enough to meet our needs?
3. **Time element.** Can the vendor meet our delivery schedule?
4. **Service.** Will the vendor provide needed before-and-after-sale support?
5. **Quality and quality-control methods.** Will the vendor's quality be consistent and meet our requirements? Does the vendor use adequate quality-control methods?
6. **Research and development.** Is the vendor doing anything to improve its products and production process?
7. **Capacity.** If our requirements increase, can the vendor handle them?
8. **Financial capacity.** Is the vendor's financial situation adequate to assure it will be in business long enough to meet our requirements completely? Or will its internal financial situation force it to try to cut corners?
9. **Labor relations.** What has been the vendor's record of work stoppages? What is its future labor situation likely to be?
10. **Managerial ability.** Is the vendor's management competent and progressive?
11. **Warranties.** What types of guarantees are provided?
12. **Transportation facilities.** Does the vendor's transport situation match our needs?

The buyer has several possible means of gathering information to evaluate potential vendors and probably will use a combination of the following data sources to cross-check conclusions.

1. **Past experience.** If the buyer has done business with a particular vendor, the outcome of those agreements is a good indication of the future, unless there have been major changes in the vendor's management or operating situation. Certainly, if past dealings were unsatisfactory, the buyer will approach future dealings with that vendor very cautiously.
2. **Experience of others.** Through contacts with purchasing personnel in other firms, the buyer probably can find out how the vendor has performed on

purchase agreements. Purchasing people normally are quite willing to exchange vendor-performance information, if there is no discussion of prices.

3. **Obtain a sample.** This helps verify a vendor's quality capability. Unless the sample was obtained on a totally random basis, however, its utility is questionable. If the vendor-furnished sample is satisfactory, it merely indicates that the vendor is capable of producing a satisfactory item; it doesn't ensure that subsequent production quality will be as good as the sample, for the sample probably represents the vendor's best effort. But if the sample is unsatisfactory, that vendor can be eliminated.

4. **Salespeople's statements.** The buyer will talk with sales representatives and managerial personnel in the vendor firm, asking pertinent questions about the vendor's ability. This free information source should be used, but the buyer knows the vendor has a tendency to say whatever is likely to obtain a purchase order.

5. **Plant visit.** The best source of information about a new supplier is a visit to the vendor's plant for a firsthand look at the facilities and operating situation and a discussion with vendor personnel. The visit should be planned, and the buyer should know specifically what questions to ask and what data to obtain. After the visit, the buyer should make a complete record of information obtained for later evaluation and comparison. As part of the visit, the buyer should follow the product, starting with the vendor's purchasing department; if the vendor has a poor purchasing system, this will show up later in product quality, delivery, and/or cost. In many firms, the purchasing department periodically visits every A category vendor to note changes and to maintain close supplier contacts.

6. **Public data.** The business press, such as *The Wall Street Journal* and *Business Week,* often contains much useful data on medium-to-large vendors. The buyer may wish to consult *The Wall Street Journal Index* and the *Business Periodical Index* to locate such information. To evaluate a vendor's financial status, the buyer will get a Dun and Bradstreet Credit Report (subject to some error but containing useful information), a corporate annual report, and the Form 10-K and 10-Q reports filed with the Securities and Exchange Commission. In the case of a privately held firm, the buyer may insist on being furnished an audited financial statement.

Approved List

Based on the evaluation, many of the possible vendors probably will be eliminated for one reason or a combination of reasons. To encourage competition, the buyer should develop an approved list containing at least two firms; three or four would be even better. Being on the approved list does not mean that a vendor will receive an order; that depends on the prices and terms obtained.

Experience Rating

While technically this is not part of the source-selection process, good management dictates that current vendors should be evaluated as a basis for placing future business, dropping vendors, helping vendors improve, and improving the selection process. In many firms, this vendor-performance rating is based on intuition: The buyer simply rates each vendor's performance in categories of "excellent," "good," "needs improvement," or "unsatisfactory." But the intuitive method has two major weaknesses. First, the rating will be unduly influenced by the most recent happenings. If, for example, the vendor was late on this month's shipment, it probably will receive an unsatisfactory rating, even though performance was excellent in all other regards and this was the first time there were any delivery problems. Second, this method does not provide top management with any hard, factual evidence to support a decision to drop a vendor or place more business with that vendor.

As an alternative, some more sophisticated firms have developed a vendor point-rating system that systematically rates vendors on several factors, such as quality, price, and service, based on factual performance records maintained by purchasing and incoming quality control. The ratings are aggregated into a single-number overall rating that can be used to compare total performance among vendors. The individual factor ratings indicate where vendors can improve their performance. To establish such a system, the purchasing department must: (1) identify the important performance factors, (2) determine the relative weight of each factor, (3) assign points based on actual performance records, and (4) total the points. This is a more defensible and useful vendor-performance-evaluation approach. Those firms with a computerized purchasing data system can produce these rating reports easily as an almost-free by-product; such a system also can be maintained manually on the A items at a reasonable cost.

Determining Price

While price is only one aspect of the overall purchasing job, it is extremely important. Basically, the purchasing department exists to satisfy the firm's purchase requirements at a lower overall cost than could be accomplished through decentralized purchasing. The purchasing department must be alert to different pricing methods, know when each is appropriate, and skillfully arrive at the price to be paid.

Certain federal and state laws regulate pricing practices. If there is any question of possible violation, the firm's legal counsel should be consulted. The two most important such laws are the Sherman Anti-Trust and the Robinson-Patman acts. The Sherman Anti-Trust Act of 1890 states that any combination, conspiracy, or collusion with the intent of restricting trade in interstate commerce is illegal. This means that it is illegal for vendors to get together to set prices (price fixing) or determine the terms and conditions under which they will sell. It also means that buyers cannot get together to set the prices they will pay.

The Robinson-Patman Act (Federal Anti-Price Discrimination Act of 1936), known as the "one-price law," says that a vendor must sell the same item, in the same quantity, to all customers, at the same price. Some exceptions are permitted, such as a lower price (1) for a larger purchase quantity, providing the seller can cost-justify the lower price through cost-accounting data; (2) to move "distress" or obsolete merchandise; or (3) to meet the lower price of local competition in a particular geographic area. The act also states that it shall be illegal for a buyer knowingly to induce or accept a discriminatory price. The courts have been realistic in their interpretation of the law, however, holding that it is the buyer's job to get the best possible price for his or her company; as long as the buyer does not intentionally mislead the seller into giving a more favorable price than is available to other buyers of the same item, the buyer is not violating the law.

There are basically six methods the buyer can use in establishing price. Each is useful under certain circumstances.

List Price

Most suppliers periodically publish a catalog of the items they routinely sell; this normally is accompanied by a price list. The list price is not necessarily the only price the vendor will accept; it is the "asking" price. If the quantity is large enough to make the sale really attractive to the vendor, the buyer normally can obtain concessions, such as a lower selling price, larger trade-in allowance, better cash discount, or free service, such as equipment maintenance. But in the purchase of a C-category item, the buyer does not have the time to pursue a lower price, since a 10 or 20 percent price reduction is not significant. The buyer probably should pay the list price and use the time saved to do a better job of analyzing and purchasing the A items, where the real profit leverage exists.

Unpriced Purchase Order

Here the buyer sends out the purchase order (PO) complete in all respects, except that no price is shown. What this PO says, basically, is "ship the item as specified and send an invoice at the vendor's normally determined price." Unpriced POs should be used sparingly, for one of the key parameters in any purchase decision should be price, which should be determined prior to placing the order.

In two instances, use of an unpriced PO may be appropriate. In an emergency, such as an equipment breakdown, time may be of greater value than money, and the buyer may wish to get the vendor started immediately, even though price has not been determined. Second, in the purchase of routine, standard items—for example, a gross of No. 2 lead pencils—from a vendor with whom the company does other business, the buyer may decide merely to say "ship." If the price charged on the invoice is out of line, it will be challenged before payment.

Salesperson's Quotation

A salesperson may quote the buyer a price while in the buyer's office, and the buyer may accept by issuing a PO. Probably there will be no problem, although legally the salesperson presumably doesn't have agency authority, and the offer made by the salesperson legally does not commit the selling company *until* it has been accepted by an officer of that company. If the buyer wishes to accept a salesperson's offer and to know that the offer is legally binding, he or she should ask the salesperson to furnish a letter signed by an officer of the selling company stating that the salesperson possesses the authority of a sales agent.

Market Prices

The reported market prices for many raw-material items are listed regularly in many of the trade and business journals, such as *Iron Age* and *The Wall Street Journal*. Such market prices are the reported list prices at which commodities were offered for sale in the past. They are not offers to sell but indications of price levels. They may be used by purchasing as a general gauge of prices, although the astute buyer probably can obtain a better price.

Competitive Bids

This is the most effective means of obtaining a fair price for items bought; the forces of competition are used to assure that the price paid is barely enough to allow the seller to cover costs, plus make a minimum profit. Prospective vendors are sent a request-for-quotation form, which lists all aspects of the needed purchase (specifications, quantity, required date, terms, and conditions). These vendors are asked to respond with the minimum price at which each would be willing to supply this requirement. Each vendor knows that others also are being asked to bid and that the vendor with the lowest quote will get the order. Therefore, the vendor who wants the order should give the buyer an attractive quote. This places considerable pressure on the vendor.

For the bid process to work efficiently, several conditions must be present:

1. There must be at least two, and preferably several, qualified vendors.
2. The vendors must want the business; competitive bidding works best in a buyer's market.
3. The specifications must be clear so that bidders know precisely what they are bidding on and so the buyer easily can compare the quotes received from various bidders.
4. There must be honest bidding and no collusion among the bidders.

Negotiation

This most sophisticated and costly means of price determination is used for the purchase of large-dollar items where competitive bidding is not appropriate because one or more of the required conditions is absent. Negotiation requires that the buyer sit down across the table from a vendor; through discussion, they arrive at a common understanding of the essentials of a purchase/sale contract, such as delivery, specifications, warranty, prices, and terms. Because of the interrelation of these factors and many others, negotiation is a difficult art and requires the exercise of judgment and tact. Negotiation is an attempt to reach an agreement that allows both parties to realize their objectives. It is used most often when the buyer is in a sole-source situation; in that case, both parties know that a purchase contract will be issued, and their task is to define a set of terms and conditions acceptable to both. Because of the expense and time involved, true negotiation normally will not be used unless the dollar amount is quite large, probably $50,000 or more.

The buyer normally requests the vendor to present a proposal, accompanied by a cost breakdown detailing the following:

1. Direct material costs
2. Direct labor costs
3. Burden or overhead rates and costs
4. Tooling charges
5. Engineering charges
6. General, administrative, and selling costs
7. Profit

The buyer then analyzes these costs (or, if the vendor will not supply a cost breakdown, does a cost buildup, which is quite difficult) and determines areas of disagreement with the vendor's figures. These differences are called negotiation issues, and the purpose of the negotiation session is to resolve these issues in a manner satisfactory to both parties. Success in negotiation depends upon which party is best able to collect, classify, and analyze pertinent data. Some purchasing organizations have full-time price or cost analysts, whose sole job is to provide good data so the buyer can negotiate from a position of strength (knowledge).

Negotiation often is used to determine the price and terms on both capital-equipment purchases and the purchase of major raw materials over an extended time (long-term contract). In both of these situations, the vendor probably will be expending resources over a long future time (perhaps five or ten years) and faces many uncertainties that could cause production costs to accelerate greatly. To protect both the vendor's profit and the buyer's need for assured delivery, the vendor and buyer may need to talk out the various changes in the business environment that might occur and make reasonable provisions for handling each. Often the final, negotiated purchase contract will provide for a price escalation-deescalation clause as a protection for both parties.

Preparation of the Purchase Agreement

Actual preparation of the purchase order is the least important part of the purchase process; after decisions have been made on specifications, delivery dates, quantity, price, and conditions, PO preparation is largely a clerical process. In some firms, it is done by a computer *after* the pertinent information has been entered into the purchase data base. Because the PO has the status of a legal agreement, it requires a record of an offer (either a PO or a vendor quote) and the corresponding acceptance (a signed vendor acknowledgment copy responding to the PO or a PO accepting the vendor's offer). However, since it is unlikely that legal action to force performance would be taken, except in the case of very large dollar amounts, some firms have eliminated the use of the acknowledgment copy on all but large-dollar POs ($5,000 or over) to cut down on paperwork costs.

To reduce administrative costs in PO preparation, many variations can be used. Two examples are blanket orders and blank-check POs. Some firms write a PO with a vendor to cover the entire quantity of a given item for the next year. Terms and conditions are determined at that time. Since it is assured business, the vendor may be willing to give an attractive price and terms. Then, whenever the firm needs additional quantities, it simply sends a delivery "release" to the vendor, quoting the particular blanket-order agreement. The release may even be issued by someone other than purchasing, such as inventory control or the user.

With a blank-check PO, the vendor is sent a check along with the PO. When the merchandise is shipped, the vendor enters the amount due on the check and cashes it. This system has certain built-in safeguards: The check can be deposited only to the vendor's account; it must be presented for deposit within 60 days; and the check clearly is marked "Not good for an amount over $1,000." The risk to the buyer is small under these restrictions, and it reduces paperwork on those low-dollar purchases, which typically account for about 90 percent of the paperwork involved in purchasing. Also, it has other major advantages: It saves postage; the buyer can negotiate a larger cash discount in return for instant payment; and it requires complete shipment (no back orders allowed), which reduces the number of receiving reports, inventory entries, and payments. Since the vendor is receiving immediate payment for items shipped, there is a real incentive to ship the order complete.

Follow-up and Expediting

After a PO has been issued to a vendor, the buyer may wish to follow up or expedite the order. When the order is issued, an appropriate follow-up date is indicated. In some firms, purchasing has full-time follow-up and expediting personnel.

Follow-up is the routine tracking of an order to assure that the vendor will be able to meet delivery promises. If problems of quality or delivery develop, the buyer needs to know this as soon as possible so that appropriate action can be taken. Follow-up requiring frequent inquiries to the vendor on progress and possibly a visit to the vendor's facility will be done only on large-dollar or long lead-time buys.

Expediting is the application of pressure to get the vendor either to meet an original delivery promise or to deliver ahead of schedule. It may involve the threat of order cancellation or withdrawal of future business if the vendor cannot meet the agreement. Expediting should be necessary on only a small percentage of the POs issued; if the buyer has done a good job of analyzing vendor capabilities, only reliable vendors who will perform according to the purchase agreement will be selected. And if the firm has done an adequate job of planning its material requirements, it should not need to ask a vendor to move up the delivery date except in unusual situations. Of course, in times of scarcity, the expediting activity assumes greater importance. The use of MRP systems (see chapter 4) allows purchasing to make more timely decisions on where and when expediting is needed and whether vendor deliveries should be stretched out.

Receipt and Inspection

When goods arrive, a check (normally a simple count) must be made to verify that the quantity received is as ordered. In addition, if it is a production raw material or an item for which precise specifications have been supplied to the vendor, verification of the quality of the goods delivered must be made. Chapter 7 discusses the importance of incoming quality levels and the methods for verification. International competition and the use of concepts such as just-in-time manufacturing systems have intensified the need to ensure that purchased materials meet the requisitioner's quality and quantity specifications. In the medium- to large-size organization, there typically are separate receiving and incoming inspection departments. In the smaller organization, the purchasing department may handle receipt and inspection, although this compromises the checks and balances needed for adequate control.

Invoice Clearance and Payment

The vendor must receive payment for the delivery of satisfactory items. If cash discounts are available—for example, 2 percent cash discount if payment is made within 10 days, net amount due in 30 days—the paperwork flow must be handled expeditiously. A 2 percent/10, net 30 cash discount term amounts to a real annual interest rate of approximately 36 percent.

Payment will be made by accounts payable. Purchasing could handle the invoice clearance, but the clerical nature of this task dictates that it be done in accounts payable, provided it has the pertinent data for the task. Basically, the purchase order, the receiving report (showing quantities delivered), the incoming inspection report (verifying quality), and the vendor invoice are compared. If all documents agree or are not out of agreement by more than a set amount, such as either 10 dollars or 5 percent of PO value, the vendor is paid. If the documents do not agree, then the whole transaction goes back to the buyer for resolution.

Some companies with a computerized data system in purchasing use an invoiceless payment system: The PO goes into the computer on release, and the receiving report and incoming inspection data also go into the computer daily. The computer merely cycles through all POs each night; whenever it finds one in which the PO, receiving report, and inspection report all agree, it triggers a check to be written within a set number of days after the material was received. If the documents do not agree, then the whole transaction goes to purchasing. The advantage of this system is that the handling of the invoice is eliminated. This system also makes it more difficult for vendors to escalate prices after they receive the purchase order, for the PO is the action document that determines the price to be paid.

Maintenance of Records

Before the purchase transaction can be filed away and closed, the records of the purchasing department should be updated so they will be timely and accurate for future use. These records can be maintained in either a computerized or a manual data base. Numerous records might be kept for evaluation, review, and control purposes. The following are the four most important.

1. **PO Log.** Purchase orders are registered and controlled by serial number. A look at the log will identify any particular PO and show its status. When the order is closed, the log is updated to show completion.

2. **Vendor file.** Records should be kept on performance and evaluation of capability of those relatively few vendors with whom purchasing does the majority of business. These data permit a vendor-performance evaluation for later decisions.

3. **Commodity file.** A purchase-history file should be maintained, by commodity, on all major purchased commodities. It should indicate purchase date, vendor, quantity, price and terms, and the current order status.

4. **Contract file.** This shows all national contracts, blanket orders, and annual agreements that have been established, and performance under the contracts. For example, if the annual agreement commits the firm to purchase a total quantity over the next twelve months, the firm must know its current status. Also, a central reference point is needed to determine exactly what purchase items are under contract and should not be handled on an individual basis.

Current and Future Developments

Changes in the environment, the competitive marketplace, and technology, coupled with top management's growing awareness of the profit potential of effective purchasing and materials management, are causing several fundamental changes in purchasing. Additional changes, some predictable and some not currently identifiable, undoubtedly will occur, providing an exciting challenge to the professionals performing in this area. Seven of these developments are highlighted here.

Single Sourcing

Many items are available from several reliable sources; when a conscious decision is made to place *all* the requirement with only one vendor, this is called single sourcing. This gives the buyer the advantage of volume leverage, often resulting in a substantially lower ultimate purchase price. The potential problem is the risk of nondelivery caused by problems in the single-source supplier's plant or with the transportation system. For single sourcing to be effective, the buyer must do an extremely thorough job of analyzing the vendor's management and capabilities and of negotiating a complete contractual agreement, in which all contingencies are anticipated. Japanese industry has used this approach for years; indeed, it is a key element in the just-in-time production system (see chapters 4 and 6). U.S. manufacturers are incorporating single sourcing into their new systems for automobile production. For example, on the production of one of the new model cars, one exhaust-system manufacturer has been selected as a single source; truckload shipments of mufflers must arrive at the auto-assembly plant at regular intervals throughout each work shift.

Public Purchasing

Government purchases of goods and services are big business, deserving a major amount of attention by government administrators. The federal government buys about $380 billion worth of goods and services annually (about 80 percent of which is for national defense); state and local government purchases are over $535 billion each year. The total from all government sources is more than $900 billion annually. Government purchases were only $538 billion in 1980; thus, they have increased more than 70 percent during the 1980s.

An overall reduction of 10 percent in prices paid would result in annual savings for taxpayers of some $90 billion. Starting in 1978 in California with the passage of Proposition 13, often referred to as "the taxpayers' revolt," and followed by the 1983 recommendation of the President's Private Sector Survey on Cost Control task force (called the Grace Commission), much attention has been focused on improving the purchasing practices of governmental units. These taxpayer studies and actions underscore two points: Government buying does not differ basically from private-sector purchasing, and governmental units should follow the principles and practices of efficient purchasing outlined in this chapter in order to obtain maximum value for each public dollar spent.

Purchasing Transportation Services

The total transportation cost in the United States for movement of goods is estimated at nearly 7 percent of gross national product, or over $270 billion per year. A large share of that amount (perhaps half, or $135 billion) is payment for moving goods from a vendor's facility to the point where the buyer needs them. Depending on the type of goods, transportation may account for as much as 40 percent of the total cost of an item, particularly if it is of low value and bulky, such as construction materials. Before the 1980s, decisions about the mode of transport (air, rail, water, pipeline, or truck), routing, and tariff (price) were primarily clerical. In the past ten years, however, Congress has deregulated almost all modes of transportation, and the effects of deregulation have made decisions on carrier selection and pricing far more complex and important today.

The 1977 Air Cargo Act deregulated air cargo; the 1978 Airline Deregulation Act began the deregulation of passenger air transportation, permitting the entry of new airlines, routes, and ticket-price competition. The 1980 Motor Carrier Act relaxed the Interstate Commerce Commission regulation of trucking, allowing easier entry of new firms, new routes and schedules, and flexibility in setting rates. The 1980 Staggers Rail Act gave railroads greater freedom to set rates and to enter into long-term contracts with shippers; piggyback service was completely deregulated. The 1982 Bus Regulatory Reform Act removed all regulation of package express after 1985.

As a result of deregulation, many large organizations have separate transportation departments, often reporting to purchasing or to the materials manager. In the medium-size or smaller organization, where the number of traffic decisions does not warrant a full-time traffic specialist, the buyer or purchasing manager makes traffic decisions. In any event, the buying company is paying for transportation services. The transport decision maker must be able to make value analyses of alternatives, conduct cost and price analyses, negotiate with carriers, consolidate freight and obtain volume discounts, evaluate carrier performance, explore the possibility of using different transport modes, and develop compatible working relationships with selected carriers.

Electronic Data Interchange (EDI)

The use of the microcomputer in purchasing allows the purchasing data base to tie directly into a supplier's data base through the telecommunications system, using a computer modem. This helps both buyer and supplier obtain much more timely and accurate information, permitting paperwork reduction and better purchasing decisions. The cost of such direct data communication has decreased rapidly over the past few years, putting this technology within reach of almost all firms. With such communication links with suppliers, the buyer can quickly obtain price quotes, determine availability of items in a supplier's stock, transmit a PO, obtain follow-up information, provide information about changes in purchase requirements caused by schedule revisions, obtain service information, and send letters and memos. EDI rapidly is becoming the preferred way of doing business. A simple example is the use of facsimile-transmission (FAX) machines to transmit documents (e.g., purchase orders, change orders, and blueprints) over phone lines in a matter of minutes.

Foreign Purchasing

The amount of purchases U.S firms make from vendors outside North America has grown markedly in the 1980s. In the middle 1980s, U.S. buyers paid over $300 billion to foreign vendors each year. The reasons for specific foreign-sourcing decisions are many and varied and include lower overall costs from foreign sources; more consistent quality; unavailability of items, such as chrome ore, domestically; more predictable delivery schedules; advanced technology; and better technical service. In addition, when a sale of a U.S.–made product—for example, an aircraft or a computer—is made in a foreign country, the foreign buyer may demand that the U.S. firm spend a specific percentage (often 50 to 100 percent) of the selling price with suppliers in that country. This is called countertrade, and it has become a common practice for many firms. At least sixty-one countries, including Canada, Switzerland, and Israel, require countertrades. It is estimated that the value of world countertrade is over $150 billion per year, or about 8 percent of total world trade.

As the world grows smaller commercially, the purchasing department is becoming involved in sourcing and pricing with vendors all over the world. This brings new problems and opportunities that require a sophisticated degree of purchasing analysis and professionalism: The location and evaluation of foreign suppliers; extended lead times; expediting; currency fluctuations; payment methods; tariffs and duties; and legal, linguistic, and cultural differences are all concerns of the purchasing professional engaged in foreign transactions.

Purchase of Services

As firms move to reduce the size of their internal staffs, it becomes necessary to buy many services formerly performed in-house from outside service suppliers. Examples of services often bought outside are in areas such as advertising, architecture, auditing, cafeteria, computer programming, customs brokerage, household moves, insurance, interior decorating, janitorial, landscaping, legal, maintenance, payroll, personnel travel, protection and security, research, telephone, temporary help, transport, and waste removal.

While the techniques of service purchasing are very similar to those used in goods purchasing, the difficulties in evaluating vendor capabilities are greater (e.g., How do you evaluate in advance the capabilities of a law firm?). Also, since services cannot be inventoried, the importance of making good purchasing decisions is heightened. Anyone who has sat through a boring conference speech can attest to that! Modern purchasing departments are becoming more involved in service purchasing and are developing the analytical techniques needed to improve their decision making.

Purchasing/Materials Management Strategy

Over the past eighty years, the purchasing function has evolved from a clerical activity to one that uses complex processes to provide information for *effective decision making* by professional purchasing managers who perform the function in an asset-management context. This change has stimulated the development of strategies to maximize the effectiveness of purchasing/materials management and, thus, overall organizational effectiveness. A strategy looks at the long-term future (often from five to twenty years) rather than simply reacting to the current situation and requirements.

The five major categories of purchasing strategies are (1) assurance of supply, to meet future supply needs effectively and economically; (2) supply support, to maximize the likelihood that the considerable knowledge and capabilities of suppliers are made available to the buying organization; (3) environmental change, to anticipate and recognize shifts in the total environment (economic, organizational, people, legal, governmental, and systems) so they can be turned to the long-term advantage of the buying organization; (4) cost reduction, to reduce the total cost of acquisition and use—life cycle cost; and (5) competitive edge, to exploit market opportunities and organizational strengths. Among the more promising strategic opportunities are developing new supply sources (supplier development); buying an ownership interest in a supplier; foreign sourcing; single sourcing; promoting vertical integration by buying out a supplier; buyer-supplier data sharing; using the futures market (hedging); systems contracting; consignment buying; risk sharing with suppliers on new products or projects; make/buy; and supplier quality assurance or certification programs. Integrating some of these substrategies into a viable, overall purchasing strategy is a difficult task but one that is imperative for the survival of many of our current organizations into the twenty-first century.

Key Concepts

Material/sales ratio

Profit-leverage effect

Return-on-assets effect

Centralized purchasing

Materials management

Prerogatives of purchasing

ABC analysis

Supplier evaluation

Negotiation

Single sourcing

Services purchasing

Purchasing/materials-management strategy

References

Dobler, Donald W., Lee, Lamar, Jr., and Burt, David N. *Purchasing and Materials Management.* 4th ed. New York: McGraw-Hill, 1984.

Fearon, Harold E. *Purchasing Organizational Relationships.* Tempe, AZ: Center for Advanced Purchasing Studies/National Association of Purchasing Management, 1988.

Heinritz, Stuart F., Farrell, Paul V., and Smith, Clifton L. *Purchasing: Principles and Applications.* 7th ed. Englewood Cliffs, NJ: Prentice-Hall, 1986.

Leenders, Michiel R., and Blenkhorn, David L. *Reverse Marketing.* New York: The Free Press, 1988.

Leenders, Michiel R., Fearon, Harold E., and England, Wilbur B. *Purchasing and Materials Management.* 9th ed. Homewood, IL: Richard D. Irwin, 1989.

Shealy, Robert. "The Purchasing Job in Different Types of Businesses." *Journal of Purchasing and Materials Management.* (Winter 1985): 17–20.

Zenz, Gary J. *Purchasing and the Management of Materials.* 6th ed. New York: John Wiley & Sons, 1987.

Discussion Questions

1. "The purchasing function is not profit making but, rather, profit taking, since its job is to spend company funds." Is this statement correct or incorrect? Explain.
2. What is the overall price objective of purchasing?
3. "The most important part of the complete purchasing procedure is the writing of the PO, for this determines the agreement between seller and buyer." Do you agree or disagree with this statement? Explain.
4. What are the various means of price determination? Give an example of an item you would buy using each method.
5. Why have most organizations centralized the purchasing function?
6. Which of the eight objectives of purchasing is most important? Why?
7. Should an organization expend resources on strategic materials planning? Under what conditions?
8. Will the purchasing function become more or less centralized over the next five years?
9. Is foreign purchasing a viable alternative for most U.S. firms? What are the problems of foreign purchasing, and how can they be handled?

CHAPTER
6
Inventory Management

Every organization must manage inventories of some kind. These inventories may be raw material, parts, partly completed products, finished products, or simply office supplies. The management of raw materials is critical to the oil refiner. Partly completed components and purchased parts are important inventories for an assembler of finished products. Rapid turnover of finished goods is a cornerstone to the successful retailer. Having office supplies available when needed is important to the office manager. No one can ignore the challenges of inventory management.

The essence of inventory management can be summarized in three questions:

1. How much of a specific item should we make or buy at one time?
2. When should we make or buy a specific item to replenish our stocks?
3. How should we store our stocks until they are used?

This chapter considers these questions by discussing the functions of inventories, the costs and trade-offs involved in the use of inventories, and some of the decision-making tools and concepts used in inventory management.

The Functions of Inventories

Inventories contribute to the economy and efficiency of an organization in many ways, such as allowing economies of scale, improving customer service, and allowing greater flexibility in scheduling production.

Economies of Scale

In many instances, it is more economical to deal in large volumes. For example, if 55 gallons of paint will be needed during the next two months, it usually will cost less to buy one 55-gallon drum of paint than to buy 55 separate 1-gallon cans as they are needed. The savings result from quantity price discounts and reduced administrative costs of purchasing.

A similar situation arises in manufacturing when choosing the method of producing a product. If it is expensive to prepare (set up) equipment for a particular job, a manufacturer may decide to make a whole year's supply at one time instead of preparing the equipment several times during the year. For example, assume that the construction of a housing development consists of five homes. To build the homes, it is necessary to pour five concrete slabs. Since it is costly to get the required equipment to the construction site, it would be considerably cheaper to pour all the slabs at one time.

The purchasing and construction examples assume that the most economical quantities to buy or make are 55 gallons of paint and five concrete slabs, respectively. The purchased quantity is referred to as the economic order quantity (EOQ) and the manufactured lot as the economic lot size (ELS). Moreover, both quantities are referred to as cycle stocks, from the cyclic behavior of the inventory levels. When the 55 gallons of paint are received, the inventory goes up by 55 units. As the paint is used, the inventory declines until we have used all the paint. Assuming an ongoing need for paint, a new order for 55 gallons will arrive when the inventory balance reaches zero. Hence, the cycle stock goes from 55 units down to zero units and then back to 55 units over and over again.

Improving Customer Service

Inventories of finished goods allow customers to compress the time between their decision to purchase an item and the time at which they actually take delivery. Without inventories, the buyer would have to place an order and then wait while the item was produced. Compare purchasing an automobile off the showroom floor with ordering a car from the factory. Buying from the finished-good inventory on the showroom floor means possession in a matter of hours. The factory order may delay possession for weeks or months, or perhaps the sale will be canceled. The potential for lost sales is a major incentive to carry finished-goods inventories. This incentive is particularly strong when the manufacturing process takes a long time relative to the patience of the customer.

Smoothing Production with Seasonal Inventories

Many products have seasonal demand patterns. For example, snow skis are in great demand just prior to and during the winter months; conversely, water skis are in demand during the summer months. Some companies attempt to smooth out their production by manufacturing complementary products, such as snow and water skis, but this is not always a desirable or complete solution. Others will adjust their production to the demand pattern, but such an adjustment usually requires letting an excessive amount of equipment lie idle much of the year, as well as hiring and laying off employees.

To avoid the disruptive effects of seasonal demand, a company may choose an inventory solution. In this case, production is set at the level rate needed to meet the average annual demand. In the off seasons, production is greater than demand, and inventories are built up. During the peak demand months, production remains the same, which is lower than the demand, and the excess demand is supplied from finished-product inventories that were produced in advance.

Decoupling

Decoupling means to separate tasks or operations that normally are linked directly to one another. The earlier example of the automobile purchase illustrates a decoupling of the sales process from the manufacturing process. Decoupling is equally important within the manufacturing process. Visualize a three-step assembly line that prepares a mass mailing of company advertisements. The first operator addresses an envelope and passes it to a second operator. Operator 2 folds the advertisement, stuffs the envelope, and passes it to a third operator. Operator 3 stamps and sorts the envelope by zip code. If Operator 2 is faster than Operator 1, or if Operator 3 is faster than Operator 2, or if anyone has problems, the assembly operation bogs down. By placing work-in-process inventories between each operation, decoupling is achieved. Such inventories permit each operator to vary speed, have problems, or take breaks without disrupting the operations that precede or follow.

Stock-out Protection

When a customer goes to a store, a mechanic goes to a material stockroom, or a clerk goes to an office-supply stockroom, each expects to obtain specific items. To be out of stock risks lost sales, production stoppage, or a slowdown in office procedures. To reduce these risks, companies carry inventories called buffer stocks or safety stocks, which are designed to combat the problems caused by late deliveries of resupply orders and unusually high usage rates by customers, mechanics, or office personnel.

Economics of Inventory Management

The management of inventory focuses on the appropriate achievement of decoupling, buffering, production smoothing, and desired service levels at the least cost. Certain costs are involved in obtaining and carrying inventories. These costs must be minimized if the firm is to achieve economically the various functions of inventories. These costs, which must be justified by the benefits from decoupling and production smoothing, include ordering costs, setup costs, and carrying costs.

Ordering Costs

Every time a company purchases raw materials, parts, or supplies, costs are incurred. The previous chapter discussed the preparation of a purchase order, follow-up and expediting tasks, invoice clearance and payment procedures, as well as the record-keeping requirements of purchasing. Each of these activities requires employee time, which represents a cost. Even before the purchasing cycle begins, costs are incurred. The stock-keeper and users of purchased items must expend time and effort to determine what materials to requisition. This effort may consist of checking inventory records or stock bins to determine if more material is needed. In other cases, production scheduling effort results in a bill of materials that initiates the purchasing cycle. Each of these activities is a component of the ordering cost.

For a cost element to be considered part of the ordering cost, it must, first of all, be a relevant cost: If the order didn't exist, then the cost would not occur. And, second, the cost is *not* a function of the size of the order.

For example, the time and the corresponding wages required to process an order are relevant costs if that time (wages) could be saved or used elsewhere if the order were not processed. On the other hand, if the person processing orders is paid for eight hours and is busy for only four, adding two hours of ordering processing to the person's job will not increase the company's costs. This assumes that the idle time will not be put to any other use. In this case, the order processing does not incur a cost (at least in the short run). To the extent that additional order processing leads to more personnel and wages, these costs become relevant.

The second characteristic of ordering costs stresses that the cost element remains substantially the same regardless of the size of the order. For example, it will cost about the same amount to process an order for 1 ton of steel as for 2 tons, 10 tons, or 100 tons.

Setup Costs

Every time a manufacturer shifts from producing one product to another, certain changeover costs occur. These include removing leftover material from the previous production run, readjusting or modifying the work stations, assigning new work crews, and testing the new setup to assure that it performs properly. These costs are subject to the same two criteria as ordering costs. They must be relevant costs that (1) vary with the number of setups, but (2) not with the number of units that will be produced after the setup has been made. For example, it may take a mechanic two hours to obtain, attach, and adjust the appropriate jigs and fixtures on a machine for a particular job. This setup time is required whether 1 unit or 1,000 units are to be produced. Moreover, the mechanic may be working on overtime, so the time spent on the setup is clearly a relevant cost.

Inventory Carrying Costs

There are two categories of carrying costs: (1) those that are proportional to the value of the inventory and (2) those that are proportional to the physical characteristics of the inventory. In either case, the costs of carrying inventory vary with the amount stocked.

Costs that vary with the dollar value in inventory are

1. Cost of capital tied up in stocks
2. Insurance premiums on inventories
3. Property taxes on inventories
4. Obsolescence, deterioration, and damage to stocks
5. Pilferage

Carrying costs that are proportional to the physical characteristics of the commodity are

1. Storage space
2. Storage labor

These costs will increase as the amount stocked increases if space costs actually change with the storage required and if handling actually increases. These relationships are not always clear cut. For example, if excess warehouse space is available, then moderate increases in inventory will occupy only space that has little or no alternative use. In this case, the storage-space costs do not increase. If the space is rented on the basis of space actually used, however, then a storage-space cost is relevant. Similarly, if larger inventories lead to more rehandling and more time spent performing physical inventories, then the additional labor costs of carrying inventory are relevant.

Managing the Economic Trade-offs

To minimize inventory costs, it is necessary to find the order quantity or production run that spreads the ordering or setup costs over as many units as possible without incurring excessive carrying costs. The larger the order quantity, the lower the ordering cost per unit. The larger order quantity, however, leads to higher average and peak inventories. The higher average inventory results in high costs due to the dollar value in stock. The peak inventories can be particularly significant (and costly) if storage space is limited.

Finding the best balance between ordering and carrying costs requires a great deal of data collection. The data then can be analyzed and appropriate decisions made. Because data collection and analysis can be expensive, the firm should attempt to reduce the size of that task. One approach is to direct attention to those inventory items that have most significant value in dollars and are, therefore, the most important inventory items.

The next several sections consider the variety of techniques used to determine when and how much to order under different operating conditions. We consider the conditions of constant demand, the single-period order-quantity problem, the discrete batch pattern associated with materials-requirements planning, and the repetitive manufacturing environment associated with just-in-time. We begin with the economic order quantity approach applied to the relatively constant demand we see for finished goods, such as bath soap in a retail outlet.

Economic Order Quantity Model

The economic order quantity (EOQ) model determines the number of units to purchase that will minimize the combined costs of ordering and carrying the inventory. To use the EOQ model, certain assumptions must be met.

1. The annual usage of the item is known and constant, or at least very close to constant, over the entire period.
2. Material, when received, comes in all at once.
3. The order-cost factor includes all those relevant costs incurred when an order is placed, and these costs are not influenced by the size of the order.
4. The carrying-cost factor includes all the relevant costs that vary proportional to the size of the order.
5. No quantity discounts are considered.

The first two assumptions are reflected in figure 6-1. The representation of line AB as a straight line is consistent with constant usage. The vertical line BC shows that replenishment of stock is received in one shipment and enters stock immediately upon receipt. Minor deviations from these assumptions, as illustrated by lines CD and DE, do not seriously affect the model. Line FG shows the effect of delayed resupply. The result would be negative inventory (a stock-out) if reserves (safety stock) were not available. Line HI illustrates the consequences of above-average usage during the resupply cycle. These issues are discussed in more detail later in this chapter.

The Total Inventory Cost Equation

The basic inventory-cost equation combines the ordering or setup costs for a year (or some other time period) with the carrying costs based on the average inventory level. To be complete, purchase cost also is included.

The number of orders per year is merely the annual demand divided by the number of units in each order. The result is the number of times the ordering costs are incurred. The ordering cost(s) is a constant and does not vary with order quantity (Q), thus incorporating assumption 3.

The order quantity (Q) represents the cycle stock. If a zero safety stock is assumed, inventory will cycle from 0 units to Q units and back to 0 units. The

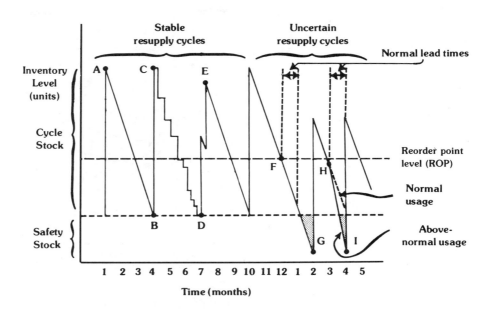

Figure 6-1. Inventory Levels over Time

assumption of uniform usage results in an average inventory of Q/2 units. This is the average inventory over the entire year, which is multiplied by the carrying cost per unit (IC) to get the annual carrying cost. As Q increases, the carrying cost increases, thus assumption 4 is incorporated into the following equation:

Total Cost = Ordering Costs + Carrying Costs + Purchase Cost

$$TC = \left(\frac{D}{Q}\right) S + IC \left(\frac{Q}{2}\right) + CD$$

where TC = total cost
D = annual demand (units)
S = ordering or setup cost
Q = order quantity (units)
I = carrying cost as a % of unit cost
C = item unit cost (purchase price)

$\frac{D}{Q}$ = number of orders per year

IC = carrying cost per unit per year

$\frac{Q}{2}$ = average inventory

EOQ Formula

Simple calculus is used to find the value of Q, which will minimize the total-cost equation. The resulting formula is:

156 Fundamentals of Production/Operations Management

Figure 6-2. Inventory Costs With and Without Quantity Discounts

$$EOQ = \sqrt{\frac{2DS}{IC}}$$

The EOQ quantity represents the optimum order size when the assumptions of the model are reasonably well met. One assumption that often is not met is that price is not affected by the order size. Another violation of the assumptions occurs when an order is received over a significant period of time. This situation will be considered later in this chapter in the discussion of economic lot sizes. The price issue is considered next.

EOQ with Discounts

Price discounts affect two components of the total-cost equation, the carrying cost and the purchase cost. Both costs are functions of the price. Price discounts lead to a family of cost curves, one curve for each price. Each curve applies to the range of order sizes for which the associated price is relevant. Figure 6-2 shows a contrast between the total-cost curve without discounts and the family of curves when there are three prices, based on two pricebreak points.

An iterative process is required to find the optimum order quantity when quantity discounts are available.

1. Compute the EOQ using the best price. If the result is large enough to obtain the best price, then this is the optimum, and the computation stops. If this EOQ falls below the relevant price break, go to the next step.

2. Compute the EOQ using the next best price. Check the result to see if it falls in the relevant range. If EOQ is below the relevant price break, redo this step at the next lower price.

3. Once an EOQ has been found that is consistent with the price obtainable at that order quantity, the final step can be taken. This step is required to determine if an increase to one of the break points offers enough savings to offset the increased carrying costs. Therefore, it is necessary to compute the total cost at the valid EOQ point and at the price breaks above the EOQ point. The decision is made to order the quantity with the lowest total cost. Figure 6-2 shows that EOQ(2) is in the relevant range but that the total cost at the second price break is lower and, therefore, is the optimum order quantity.

Economic Lot-Size (ELS) Formula

In the case of parts manufactured within the firm, the assumption of immediate, one-shipment replenishment often is unrealistic. The replenishment actually occurs over the period of the production run, which may be days or weeks. Figure 6-3 shows the basic pattern followed by the level of inventory on hand.

When the entire lot size is not delivered instantaneously, the peak inventory is lower. Specifically, it is lowered by the amount used during the time required to produce the lot. This period is equal to the lot size (100 units) divided by the production rate (50 units per week), or two weeks in this example. In figure 6-3, the usage during the production period is 10 units per week, or 20 units in total. Therefore, instead of 100 units (the lot size), the peak inventory is only 80 units. The average inventory carried is Q/2, or 40 units. Incorporating these changes into the total-cost equations and developing the optimum lot size (as done for EOQ) gives

$$TC = \frac{DS}{Q} + IC\left(1 - \frac{d}{p}\right)\frac{Q}{2}$$

$$ELS = \sqrt{\frac{2DS}{IC\left(1 - \frac{d}{p}\right)}}$$

where d = usage rate (units per time period)
p = production rate (units per time period)
D = annual demand
S = setup costs
IC = carrying cost per unit per year
Q = lot size
ELS = economic lot size

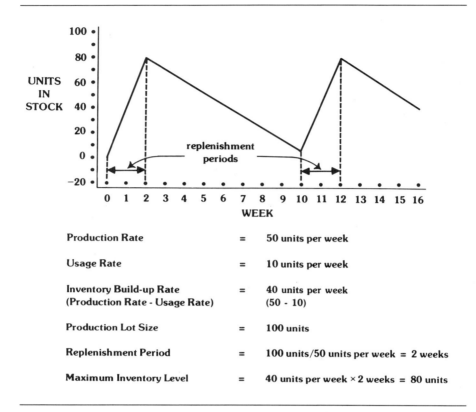

Figure 6-3. Inventory Levels with Replenishment Spread over Time

With the exception of the replenishment modification, all the assumptions of the EOQ formula still apply.

Periodic Review Model

It is sometimes more convenient to check inventory levels at regular intervals and order those items expected to run out before the next review is scheduled. By checking all inventory items or a class (for example, those items supplied by one vendor) at one time, the firm can combine all orders to a vendor and consolidate freight loads. Moreover, this approach does not require a perpetual inventory system—that is, one that keeps track of the inventory levels at all times. The other side of the coin reveals that more safety stock is required, and, if care is not taken, unbalanced work loads can be placed on inventory and purchasing personnel. Also, the review interval should reflect the economic order quantity. The desired interval for different items will vary, and this is in conflict with the consolidation advantages.

Assuming a review period of a month, the following procedure would apply:

1. Take a physical count of the items to be reviewed.
2. If the inventory balance of an item is less than a specified level, for example, (s) units, then order enough to raise the level to (S) units. Small (s) would be based on the demand over the review interval plus the normal lead time and the desired safety stock. Large (S) is the upper limit needed to cover the period between the current order and the next desired order review. If enough is on hand or on order, then do not place an order.

This approach results in unequal order quantities and requires more safety stock to obtain the same service level than would be needed if the EOQ model were used. However, simpler record keeping and consolidation advantages may make it desirable, particularly for class-C inventory items.

Sensitivity of EOQ and ELS

How accurate must the cost estimates and demand forecasts be? Figure 6-2 shows that the total-cost curve is quite flat in the area of the EOQ. This suggests that moderate departures from the EOQ will not be very costly. This observation is significant, considering how expensive it would be to develop extremely accurate estimates of all relevant costs. The insensitivity of the formulas permits the valid grouping of stock items and estimating the costs for groups as a whole. This approach, along with the ABC classification, can reduce substantially the cost of determining EOQ and ELS.

Safety Stocks and Uncertainty

If all the estimates and assumptions were realized in practice, then efficient inventory management would be relatively easy. But demand rarely is uniform and completely predictable, and stocks are not always replenished on time. The specific function of safety stocks is to reduce the risk of stock-outs due to unexpected demand, late resupply, or both. To set the level of safety stock, we must consider supply lead times, reorder points, and desired service levels.

Lead Times

Lead time refers to the time between the recognition of a need for and the receipt of the desired material. The purchasing lead time could consist of the requisition review time, the vendor-selection process, order preparation, mail-transit time, supplier-order-processing time, supplier-setup and manufacturing time, shipment time, receiving time, and the time to make the item available from stock. If the time to perform some or all of these elements varies, then some additional stock will be needed. This situation is illustrated in figure 6-1 by line FG. The order placed in month 12, when the inventory was at level F, was expected to arrive in month 1. The order was a month late, arriving in month 2. Had there not been any safety stock, the organization would have run out of material when the inventory level crossed the dashed line representing the amount of safety stock.

Reorder Points

The inventory level that triggers the resupply process is called the reorder point. If everything were certain, then the reorder point would equal the normal usage during the normal lead time. But because of uncertainties in both usage and lead time, the reorder point (ROP) is equal to the safety stock (S) plus the normal demand during normal lead time (DNLT).

$$ROP = S + DNLT$$

In figure 6-1, the ROP illustrates a reorder point based on a safety stock of 129 units and an average demand over normal lead time of 237 units, or an ROP of 366 units. This means that whenever the inventory level gets down to 366, an order for the economic order quantity should be placed. On the average, the order will be received just as the inventory reaches 129 units, the safety stock. (See figure 6-4.)

Service Level Policy

The inventory manager who is willing to have five stock-outs every 100 order cycles is expressing a 95 percent service level. Arriving at such a service-level policy requires judging the cost of such a stock-out.

The cost of a stock-out is difficult to define. Will the stock-out result in a lost sale or, worse, a customer lost forever? What is the cost of customer ill will? What are the costs of rescheduling production due to a stock-out? Once the stock-out cost has been estimated, then a safety-stock level can be set, based on the trade-off between the estimated stock-out costs and the inventory carrying costs.

Computation of Safety Stocks

Assume the inventory manager decided on a 90 percent service level instead of a "safer" 95 percent level. This decision now must be translated into a safety-stock level. First, data on the demand during the normal lead time are collected. Next, a frequency diagram is drawn from which the average demand during normal lead time can be determined. Then, the stock level required to service 90 percent of the demands experienced in the past can be identified. Figure 6-4 illustrates this procedure, which provides the safety stock necessary to reduce the risk of stock-outs caused by above-average usage, as shown in figure 6-1, line HI.

Figure 6-5 uses the historical data without any assumptions regarding the distribution pattern of the demand. Often there are not as much data as used

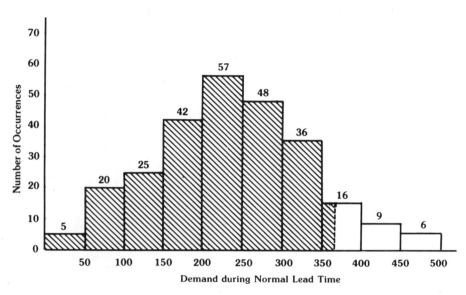

Figure 6-4. Safety Stock Determination Based on Historical Demand

in this example (264 different periods); with less data, much the same result can be accomplished by assuming a normal distribution and calculating the mean and the standard deviation. Using standard tables for the normal distribution tells the user the number of standard deviations above the mean that will include 90 percent of expected demand during normal lead time. For a 90 percent service level, the proper number of standard deviations would be 1.28. Computing the standard deviation of the sample of historical data would permit establishing the safety stock. Assume the standard deviation were 98 units; the safety stock then would be 1.28 × 98 units, or 125 units. The reorder point would be the sum of the average usage during the normal lead time (237 units) plus the safety stock (125 units), or 362 units in total. This result is similar to the 129 units of safety stock based on the frequency diagram.

The computations of safety stock are equally applicable to both risks due to variable usage rates (as illustrated) and risks due to variations in lead time. In the case of safety stock for variable lead time, the number of days (weeks) beyond normal lead time that must be covered to give a desired service level must be determined. This can be achieved by the frequency-diagram approach, or it can be based on the normal distribution.

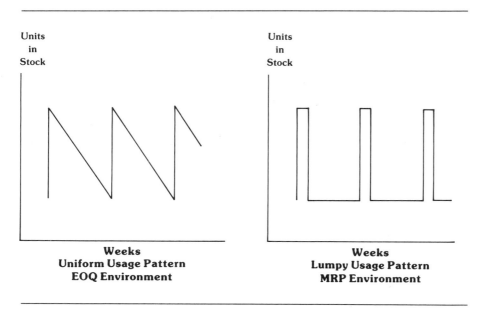

Figure 6-5. Contrast Between Uniform and Lumpy Demands on Inventory

A conservative policy would add the safety stock based on usage variations to the safety stock based on lead-time variations. Since it is unlikely that excessive usage will occur at the same time as delays in deliveries, this policy results in more safety stock than required by the stated service-level policy. Since lead time often is controlled to some degree—for example, by expediting and follow-up procedures—the lead time safety stocks might be reduced with less risk than the safety stocks due to demand fluctuations.

One-Time Order Quantities

In cases in which items quickly become obsolete, the need will not remain long enough to require a reordering strategy. Unlike the previous models, this situation requires determining the best size of a single order. Imagine the problem faced by the newspaper kiosk owner; the apparel buyer estimating the order size of a seasonal, high-fashion item; or the grocery-store produce buyer. Each of these people must estimate the market and buy to cover a period of time: for the newspaper carrier, it is the day's demand; for the apparel buyer, the season's demand; and for the produce buyer, the week's demand. The trade-off they face is between not ordering enough, thus losing sales, and ordering too much and having to throw the excess away or sell it at distress prices.

These situations lend themselves to classical marginal analysis. If the marginal profit (MP) of adding one more unit to the order is greater than the marginal loss (ML), then the order should be increased. The same logic applies in the uncertain case when one increases the order by one if the expected MP exceeds the expected ML. If P is the probability of selling the next unit, then the probability of not selling the next unit is 1-P. Therefore, the decision to add one to the order depends on whether or not

$$P(MP) > = (1-P)(ML)$$

which simplifies to:

$$P > = \frac{(ML)}{(MP + ML)}$$

If one knows what the profit is when a sale is made and what the loss is if the sale is not made, it is an easy matter to compute the ratio ML/(ML + MP), assuming MP and ML remain constant over the relevant sales volumes. The decision maker will increase the order size until the probability of selling the unit to be added is less than the computed ratio.

For example:

Sale Price = $5.00   Unit Cost = $3.00
Therefore:
MP = (5−3) = $2.00   ML = $3.00
Computed Ratio = 3/(2+3) = .60

nth Unit	Probability of Selling	
1	1.00	
2	.97	
3	.85	
4	.73	Optimum order size, since this is
5	.64	last item where P > = .60
6	.54	
7	.25	
8	.05	
9 or more	.00	

MRP and Inventory Management

Materials requirements planning has grown well beyond an inventory-planning tool to include priority planning and a means of coordinating the planning of organizational, financial, human, and productive facilities. In chapter 4 we discussed the planning role of MRP. In this chapter we focus on the sizing of orders and safety stock issues.

Readers might want to review the MRP section in chapter 4. In summary, customer demand is called independent demand, since it is not controlled by the firm. Either customer orders or forecast estimates of the demand serve as the basis for a master production schedule. Remember, the master production schedule represents our strategy for meeting the customer demand. MRP translated the master production schedule into gross requirements for lower-level components that we refer to as dependent demand. When MRP detects a negative projected balance or a balance below a safety stock level, it plans an order. The size of the planned order depends on a lot-sizing decision which we assumed as given in chapter 4. We now address this question.

Lot Sizing in a Materials-Requirements Planning Environment

The discrete batch approach common to many manufacturing firms does not meet the theoretical assumptions of steady production and usage rates required of the economic lot-sizing formulas. Still, the setup costs associated with each batch may require sizable lot sizes and the associated inventory carrying costs. Figure 6-5 shows the contrast between the uniform usage appropriate for EOQ and the lumpy demand pattern typical of the MRP environment.

The picture frame example used in chapter 4 illustrates the limitations of EOQ. The time-phased inventory record of the end item is reproduced in figure 6-6. If our annual demand is 2,340 (based on the average of 45 units per week in figure 6-6), the setup cost is $10 and our inventory carrying cost is $3 per unit per year, then our EOQ would be 125 units. This lot size has the same weakness as the 100-unit lot used in the example (the 100 may have been based on last year's demand of 1,500 units), the extra units stored from week 3 to week 5 involve carrying costs without saving any setups. An order quantity of 70 or 145 would involve a smaller combined cost of setups and carrying cost. If we converted the EOQ into the average number of weeks an order should cover, we would get 125/45 or essentially 3 weeks. This is called the period-order quantity, and in our example we would order 145 units covering the net requirements for weeks 3 through 5. In order of increasing complexity, the following approaches become less sensitive to the standard EOQ assumptions:

1. Period order quantity—converts the EOQ into the economic number of months to cover with each order

2. Part-period balancing—an incremental approach that adds additional months' requirements to an order until the carrying costs equals the ordering cost

3. Wagner-Whitin algorithm—an application of dynamic programming to inventory requirements over a specified planning period

Below the top level, the simple lot-for-lot approach is favored. This approach avoids the small residual stocks that are of little value, and, if it errs, it does so in the direction of low inventory.

PART NO. 10141101 10×14 Frame, White, Pine, White		Period				
		1	2	3	4	5
GROSS REQUIREMENTS	from MPS			100	50	75
ON ORDER						
PROJECTED ON-HAND BALANCE	80	80	80	−20* 80	30	−45 35
NET REQUIREMENTS				20		45
PLANNED ORDER RECEIPTS				100		100
PLANNED ORDER RELEASES			100		100	

PLANNED LEAD TIME = 1 Week   ORDER QUANTITY = 100 units

Estimate of Annual Demand = 52 wks per yr. × (100 + 50 + 75 units)/5 wks = 2,340
Setup cost = $10   *Carrying Cost* = $3/unit/yr.
EOQ = 125 units
*A negative projected on-hand balance triggers a planned order receipt, which in turn causes the balance to be adjusted.

Figure 6-6. Time-Phased Inventory Record

Safety Stock and Safety Lead Time in MRP

MRP advocates discourage the use of safety stocks for dependent demand items. One of the goals is to reduce inventory and fractional lots of safety stock that will not support a full production run. Safety stock can serve as a protection against variations in quantity—for example, scrap losses or short shipments. Safety lead time, in the sense of producing or bringing in a complete lot size early, is a hedge against timing problems, such as those caused by late deliveries or production delays. The Japanese approach would also discourage safety stock as well as safety time. The emphasis is on reducing the causes that lead to safety stocks, such as breakdowns, defective products, or production capacity expended on the wrong jobs due to invalid job priorities. If safety stock or safety lead times are used, those stocks should be made very clear to all so that priorities are not distorted. Generally, the firm should not be expediting a job to replace safety stock at the expense of efforts on jobs going to a customer.

Summary of MRP Benefits and Limitations

MRP makes a major contribution to the planning and acquisition of materials. In the short term, it tests the feasibility of the master production schedule when the component schedules and purchases are reviewed against available capacity and vendor lead times. MRP allows establishment of the valid priority of jobs, by highlighting which items should be expedited due to overdue situations and which items should be de-expedited due to decisions to delay orders. In the long term, MRP is useful in estimating capacity requirements through translating long-range market forecasts into specific capacity requirements.

The major limitations of MRP are associated with its demands for accurate data and extensive computer capacity. Since minimum inventory is one of the selling features of MRP, the system depends on the inventory records being very accurate (98 percent or better). Furthermore, if the bill of materials is not current and accurate, MRP will translate higher-level demand into incorrect lower-level requirements. This could result in work stoppages, quality problems, or wasted material. Therefore, it is imperative to maintain accurate stock-status records and closely manage engineering changes that affect the bill of materials. Many organizations have failed to achieve the accuracy levels required, with resulting failure of the MRP system. The volume of computations mandates the use of a computer, which brings many changes into organizations that are not computerized. Even with computer facilities, major changes in inventory and engineering procedures may be required.

Finally, MRP is not equally applicable to all organizations. Since it derives its value from coordinating the assembly of many components into a final product in batches, the technique applies best to assembly and batch manufacturing of multi-part products. On the other hand, fabricators often are dealing with one component, which negates MRP's strength, and process industries are less batch oriented, which devalues the replanning capability of MRP.

Inventory in Repetitive Manufacturing or the Pursuit of Stockless Operations

As production volume increases, we shift our strategies from a job-shop orientation and the discrete batches of an MRP environment toward repetitive manufacturing and the opportunity to apply just-in-time strategies. JIT is much more than an inventory system; in fact, it could be viewed as a systems approach to improved operations. However, even the narrow inventory reduction view of JIT will lead us to the greater breadth and power of JIT. Inventories can and have been relied on as insurance against stock-out risks, mistakes in scheduling, errors in demand forecasts, machine breakdowns, absent or inefficient personnel (managers included), and poor quality (ours or our vendors). In other words, many sins can be covered up with inventory. The success of Japanese manufacturers has forced U.S. firms to question their habits and seek better ways of doing business with less waste—less inventory, less setup time, less paperwork, less underemployment of people, less wasted space, and fewer dissatisfied customers. Common operations-management tools, including economic order quantities can guide us into the JIT world, if we let them.

We can use the concepts of EOQ and reorder points to direct our attack, once we accept the goal to reduce inventory to a minimum. If we can reduce setup and ordering costs, we can justify smaller lots. Methods analysis (chapter 3) identifies wasteful motions. Employee participation in small problem-solving groups improves motivation along with finding better procedures. Team building and practicing setup procedures improve skills on these nonrepetitive tasks. Group technology and cellular manufacturing organize work centers around similar products, so many of the products run on the same or very similar setups. The smaller lot sizes reduce our cycle stocks but not necessarily our safety stocks. The resulting reduction in our cycle stocks means increased exposure to stockouts due to the increased frequency of resupply. Therefore, we must look at the variables that affect lead times and usage rates that formerly were buffered with safety stock.

Relevant lead times are those of our vendors and those for each of our internal operations. The vendor lead times are addressed by the purchasing people in their supplier selection and development programs along with tools such as long-term contracts and electronic data interchanges. Internal lead times shrink somewhat because of shorter setup times; however, the real opportunity is reduced waiting time between operations. The smaller lot sizes reduce the total time from the beginning to the end of a job. If this happens for most jobs and we do not have many jobs waiting at each work center, then jobs will flow quickly through the plant. This means less work-in-process inventory and better customer service.

Shorter lead times also help with factors that cause variability in lead time. By reducing the lead time, we may be able to reduce our planning horizon. Remember from chapter 4 that forecasts are more accurate in the near future. The reduced error in our forecasts means less need for safety stock. Furthermore, short lead times tend to vary less and therefore safety stock can be reduced even more.

Further improvements in the stability of lead times can be achieved through dependable quality of products and preventive maintenance. JIT's emphasis on quality has important inventory implications. Total quality control, TQC, reduces the need for safety stock to buffer the effects of work delays and late shipments due to defective parts and materials from suppliers and internal manufacturing processes. Receiving and making quality parts speeds the product flow through the plant, reduces the need for extra people and machines to rework the mistakes or remove the waste from the good production. The faster flow further reduces the work-in-process inventory. Safety stock held in case of machine breakdowns or production of defects can be reduced by an effective preventive-maintenance program.

The pull system used in JIT facilitates simple shop floor control of work-in-process inventory. The kanban system of cards, or any of its variations, provides a means of authorizing production only when a user of the output calls for it. This user pull reduces or eliminates the tendency to produce units just to keep busy or merely to increase use of equipment. This reduces early production of work-in-process inventory. The number of kanban cards represents the amount of work-in-process stock between two work centers. When a card is removed from the system, the WIP is reduced. If the system continues to function smoothly, another card can be removed. This continues until a problem emerges in the flow. Then a team effort is directed to solve the problem that has been made visible by the removal of the obscuring inventory. This ongoing improvement cycle is integral to JIT. The team approach to solving problems illustrates the opportunities the JIT philosophy provides for using the whole employee. Regardless of the system use, some physical stocks will exist and will require storage and record keeping.

Physical Care of Inventories

This section discusses two of the major issues associated with the physical control and care of inventory—storage methods and record keeping.

Warehousing and Stock-keeping Objectives

The objective of warehousing (stock keeping) is to store stock-keeping units (SKUs) at minimum cost. This goal requires efficient use of space, elimination of unnecessary rehandling, protection of the goods, avoidance of obsolescence, and prompt delivery of the goods to users when requested.

Storage and Material Handling

Within the storage area, space is designated for each item so that it can be located when needed. Material handling involves moving items into storage and taking them out when they are needed for production. The different material storage methods have both advantages and disadvantages.

Containerized inventory can be mass stored on open floor space, one container stacked on another in rows. This provides dense storage (high space utilization) but results in a great deal of rehandling and possibly misplacing material behind stacks of inventory. Shelves or pallet racks can improve accessibility. In this case, every unit can be obtained directly, with lower rehandling cost and damage. Racks and shelves often require more space than mass storage to accommodate the same volume of material.

The methods of locating inventory can vary—from relying on people's memories to checking addresses maintained in computer files. Each SKU can be assigned a specific location (e.g., ½-hp. motors may be assigned to Aisle 12, Rack J, Shelf 3, Position B). Such addressing schemes provide precise locations. Unfortunately, they lead to low space utilization (half empty on the average) and problems in reorganization when inventory volume grows.

Random storage circumvents these space problems by storing items where there is space, not necessarily with similar goods. The challenge here is dealing with record-keeping errors and excessive order-picking costs. These are potential drawbacks to the random-locating approach, but the computer has helped significantly. For example, the computer can analyze order picking so that the stockkeeper is directed to find items in sequence of their position in the stockroom. One trip through the stockroom is required instead of a back-and-forth procedure. Computerization in stock keeping has been extended to automatic storage and retrieval systems that will take stock to a storage location, store the items, and update the computerized inventory locator file. Withdrawals from stock are similarly automated and driven by pick lists, which also can be computer generated.

Finally, the just-in-time philosophy has led to the concept of wall-to-wall inventory. This concept focuses on bringing raw material directly to the point of use in a plant. As a product flows through the plant, parts are added until completion. Minimum stocks are held on the factory floor. Formal stockrooms are reduced or eliminated. This contrasts sharply with the locked and controlled stockrooms used with many MRP systems as a means of assuring the necessary accuracy of inventory counts.

Record-keeping Requirements

The use of random storage procedures requires accurate records. The inventory manager must be able to specify the location and quantities available for any SKU. Records must be kept on shipments received and storage locations, withdrawals from stock, transfers of material between departments, shipments from finished goods, and write-offs necessitated by scrap, damage, or obsolescence.

Accurate records of inventory transactions are a necessity. Errors lead to wasted time looking for material, production shutdowns due to stock-outs, and inaccuracies in the MRP system, scheduling, and purchasing operations. The importance of inventory records justifies extensive efforts to detect and eliminate errors. The cost of physically counting every warehoused item one or more times per year is substantial, and errors are possible. Many firms are eliminating the annual physical inventory in favor of cycle counting.

Cycle counting has become an effective means of achieving record accuracy that far surpasses that of the traditional physical inventory procedure. Instead of devoting massive amounts of labor in an attempt to count everything during a plant shutdown period, cycle counting takes a more systematic approach on a day-to-day basis. First, the job is done by stockkeepers who are familiar with the material and can be held accountable for the accuracy of the records. Second, the counting of a specific item is proportional to its relative importance in the ABC sense (see chapter 5). That is, the high-dollar-volume items will be counted more often than slow-moving, low-cost items. High volume is associated with many record transactions and hence more errors. Frequent counts catch errors early, reducing the problems errors can cause and increasing the chances of finding and correcting the cause of the error. Prompt detection of human errors can be more easily traced, and often simple training or clarification of a misunderstood procedure eliminates any recurrence. The cost of counting can be reduced by planning. For example, cycle counting just before ordering or just before a schedule receipt minimizes the number of units and locations to be checked. Negative balances always indicate an error that must be corrected. By assigning specific people to manage a set of items and using cycle counting, these people will enjoy more responsibility and learn how to maintain the extremely accurate records needed by such systems as MRP.

Locked (closed) stockrooms reduce unauthorized withdrawals of materials. Record keeping is under the control of a trained stockkeeper. To reduce human errors, more recording tasks can be diverted to the computer. Computer-generated pick cards, prepunched with the quantity to be withdrawn, reduce the recording errors. Once the order is picked, the prepunched withdrawal card is submitted to the computer. Only certain exceptions such as partially filled orders will require stockkeeper inputs.

Key Concepts

Inventory Ordering Costs

Setup Costs

Inventory Carrying Costs

Economic Order Quantity (EOQ)

Cycle Stock

Safety Stock

Economic Lot Size (ELS)

Periodic Review Model

Reorder Points

Service Level Policy

Just-In-Time (JIT)

Cycle Counting

Stockless Operations

References

Chase, Richard B., and Aquilano, Nicholas J. *Production and Operations Management.* 4th ed. Homewood, IL: Richard D. Irwin, 1985.

Fogarty, Donald W., and Hoffmann, Thomas R. *Production and Inventory Management.* Cincinnati, OH: South-Western Publishing Co., 1983.

Hall, Robert W. *Zero Inventories.* Homewood, IL: Dow Jones-Irwin, 1983.

Schonberger, Richard J., and Knod, Edward M., Jr. *Operations Management: Serving the Customer.* 3d ed. Plano, TX: Business Publications, Inc., 1988.

Vollmann, Thomas E., Berry, William L., and Whybark, D. Clay. *Manufacturing Planning and Control Systems.* 2d ed. Homewood, IL: Richard D. Irwin, 1988.

Discussion Questions

1. What is meant by the decoupling function of inventories?
2. Discuss the cost trade-offs that are reflected in the EOQ and ELS formulas.
3. What happens to the ELS formula if p becomes very large relative to d? What if d = p? What real-world consequences might these outcomes have?

4. What are the assumptions of the traditional EOQ formula?
5. Describe the procedure for finding the best order quantity when price breaks are available.
6. Describe how the pursuit of minimum inventory is consistent with several just-in-time techniques or areas selected for improvement.
7. Why is the simple EOQ approach to lot sizing not appropriate in an MRP environment?
8. Under what circumstances is MRP most applicable, and what are some of the prerequisites of having a successful MRP system?
9. Discuss the pros and cons of different methods of storing goods.
10. Describe the concept of cycle counting, and indicate its advantages relative to traditional annual physical inventories.

Problems

1. Your company is offered the following price breaks on an electrical component of which it buys 1,000 per year.

Quantity	Price
0–200 pcs.	$12.50 each
201 & up	$10.00 each

   Your company has determined that it costs 10 percent of the purchase unit price to store an item for a year. Furthermore, your ordering costs amount to $15 per order. What is your best order quantity? Do not overlook the savings in overall purchase cost (the last term in the total-cost equation).

2. You are responsible for stocking the egg section of your grocery store once a week. Your supplier sells you the eggs for 60 cents per dozen. You price the eggs at 66 cents per dozen. At the end of the week you mark down whatever is left to 55 cents per dozen. This lower price has always cleared out the leftover inventory. Your past sales records support the following stable probability distribution of sales each week. What is your best stocking level each week? How would your decision change if you could get only 50 cents for the week-old eggs?

Demand (dozens)	Probability of Selling	Demand (dozens)	Probability of Selling
30	1.00	35	.57
31	.98	36	.37
32	.94	37	.19
33	.86	38	.07
34	.73	39	.01

3. Periodically you renegotiate a contract with your supplier of plastic beads for use in your injection-molding machines. You estimate that it cost you about $150 to negotiate and conclude the contract. Your company buys about 52,000 pounds of plastic per year at about $3.50 per pound. You use the plastic at a steady rate of 1,000 pounds per week. By agreement, your supplier will deliver a trailer load of 5,000 pounds a week until the order is completed. The last load may be a partial trailer load. It costs 90 cents to store a pound of plastic for one year. How much should you order, and what will be your annual inventory ordering and carrying costs? What would be the effect of an agreement to deliver at a rate of 2,000 pounds per week? What about an agreement to deliver reliably at a rate of 1,000 pounds per week?

CHAPTER 7
Quality Management

Product quality has become a major competitive factor in determining the survival and success of manufacturing and service firms. With the proliferation of goods and services available, customers are demanding manufactured items that work properly the first time and every time during the expected product life. Services, too, are feeling pressures from competitors that provide more accurate bank statements, faster delivery of documents, and friendlier, more efficient and more helpful service in face-to-face situations.

Many firms are learning that higher quality does not have to mean higher costs; in fact, often the opposite is true. Intense foreign competition—first in goods and now in some services—have caused managers to reexamine their quality priorities and policies in an attempt to eliminate the *hidden factories* that spend time and resources to correct product defects that should not have occurred at all.

Most important, managers are moving from the concept of quality control to the broader concept of quality management. Although testing and statistical control methods will continue to play a major role in any production process, quality is now becoming part of the strategic focus of successful companies. The management of quality reaches every aspect of the production function.

To better understand quality in the production of goods and services, we must determine what quality is and what it is not—what the relevant costs of quality are, and how quality is produced or controlled. Furthermore, we should appreciate the importance of quality in products as more than just an economic concept. Quality has strong legal and social implications as well. It is inconvenient to buy an electrical appliance that doesn't work, but if things such as automobiles or health care are of poor quality, lives may be lost.

Many people equate *quality* with luxurious goods or lavish services. Expensive sports cars, grand hotels, exclusive clubs and restaurants, fur coats, and precious jewelry are typical examples of *quality* products. In truth, each may have high or low quality relative to its price, just as simpler items have varying degrees of quality.

Product Quality

Much of the following discussion concerns manufactured goods, since many of the pertinent quality techniques have been developed within and for manufacturing. Service firms recognize, however, that quality is no less important to their success and that many of the tools developed for goods can be applied to services as well. The concepts and tools must be adapted, of course, to fit the different nature of services and the process of service delivery.

As this chapter unfolds, consider how each topic may be applied to a service business, such as a bank, hospital, university, or insurance company. *Products* become checking accounts, surgical operations, undergraduate courses, and insurance policies. *Defects* may be translated into "errrors"; *transportation* becomes "delivery of the service"; and so on. Not every concept will apply, but most will.

As noted in Chapter 1, many service firms produce a tangible product as well as a service. In a pizza parlor, for example, the quality of the food and the quality of the service can be separated; one can be excellent while the other is poor, and either can change from time to time. With firms that are more exclusively service oriented, defining the unit of output becomes difficult; legal counseling, consulting, teaching, and many government operations, such as parks and recreation or national defense, are examples. The closer the firm is to a pure service organization, the more difficult it is to define, measure, and control quality.

New methods are being developed, however, to measure quality characteristics and to identify countable errors in service industries. As these efforts continue, the establishment and use of quality-enhancement programs in service-oriented organizations are likely to increase as well.

The Meaning of Quality

To grasp the meaning of quality and its control, consider a business: Quality Doghouses, Inc. The basic product, a doghouse, is made from plywood and is spray painted. The deluxe model has a shingle roof, carpeting, and a chain that attaches to a clip next to a swinging door. The price of the deluxe model is twice the price of the standard model, but the deluxe model is not *necessarily* the *high-quality* model. Either model can be of high or low quality.

Quality Defined

Quality is a characteristic of a product, as is its size, shape, or composition. Specifically, it is a characteristic that determines a product's value in the market and how well it will perform the function for which it was designed. The quality of a product in general is expressed as a standard, and the quality of specific units of that product is measured in terms of the degree of conformance with the standard.

Thus, the definition of quality must include both the standard and conformance to the standard. Merely changing the standard does not change quality; quality must actually be built into the manufacture of a good or the provision of a service.

The standard may be set in a number of ways. First, customers may set standards by their past buying behavior; market research gives some idea of the quality level customers want and are willing to pay for. Second, top management may set a standard in terms of the policy or strategy the firm wants to implement; it can aim at the top, bottom, or middle of the quality market. Third, a design technician in the firm may set a tolerance that a certain part must meet if it is to fit properly with other parts. Ultimately, each of these standards must be translated into specific technical standards to guide the manufacture and assembly of the product.

These concepts can be illustrated with the doghouse example. The primary function of the doghouse is to protect the animal from the weather. To achieve this, the roof must not leak; this standard will be applied in a *leak test* as part of the manufacturing process. Another aspect of the doghouse is the finish. Runs in the paint will not affect the function of the doghouse, but they may affect its value in the market if the doghouse buyer considers it important. Another standard must be developed for the number and type of tolerable blemishes in the paint.

In manufacturing a product, the following fundamental elements of control must be applied to the quality dimensions of the product:

1. Measure the quality characteristic.
2. Compare actual results to the standard.
3. Take corrective action when the deviation between actual results and the standard exceeds tolerable limits.

Corrective action may consist of stopping the process, retraining workers, using different materials, or rejecting the day's production. In services, it may mean refunding money or returning to perform the service again.

Dimensions of Quality

Quality is not a single characteristic; it is multidimensional. Some organizations may separate some of these dimensions from their definition of quality, but they are related so closely that they should be included as part of the total quality concept.

1. **Functionality.** This refers to whether the product performs its function at the end of the manufacturing process or when it is first put to use. Functionality can be measured on a yes-or-no basis—either the light bulb works or it doesn't—or as a continuous measure—in terms of how many footcandles of light the bulb emits.
2. **Reliability.** How long will the product function under normal conditions? A product may function perfectly the first time but fail before completing its normal life span.
3. **Durability.** How well and how long will the product function under adverse conditions? Can the product withstand shock, vibration, heat, cold, dust, and other conditions that it reasonably might be expected to encounter?
4. **Esthetic characteristics.** This refers to the appearance of the product and is not necessarily related to its function. The smoothness of the surface, the symmetry of decorative designs, and the absence of chips, dents, or scratches illustrate this dimension.
5. **Safety.** Will the product perform its function without unnecessarily endangering the user? Electrical appliances should not produce electrical shocks during normal use; lawn-mower blades should stay attached to the spindle.

A high-quality doghouse cannot be produced unless all these aspects have been considered.

Total Quality Control

The quality-control function in an organization often is viewed as sort of a police department that checks outgoing products and gives tickets to offenders. A total quality program, however, must include much more than just an inspection function. Quality cannot be *inspected* into a product: It must be *designed* and *built* into the product. And quality control assures that this has been done.

There are several areas within the firm where quality (good or bad) can be introduced into the product.

Product Design

The end product probably will be no better than its design. Design engineers must consider not only the functionality of the early prototypes but also the ease with which the elements of the product can be produced in quantity and assembled into final units. The choices of screws versus rivets, tongue-and-groove versus miter joints, and braces or no braces determine whether the product will withstand the quality tests of the consumer. Designers may have to revise their basic design several times to fit the needs and constraints of later stages of development and manufacture.

Process Design

To manufacture the doghouse, certain machines, such as saws, sanders, spray painters, and hand tools, are needed. The choice of machines will affect the quality of output; more expensive saws may make a cleaner cut and give a closer fit of parts in final assembly.

The effect of other aspects of process design on quality is less obvious but nonetheless important. The layout employed, materials-handling and storage methods used, sequencing of operations, and even maintenance policies can influence the number of defective units produced.

Raw Materials

Generally, the better the quality of the raw materials, the better the quality of the finished product. Plywood, for example, comes in several grades, which indicate the smoothness of the surface. Cheaper grades of wood could be used, but to maintain the standard, much of this material would have to be filled, sanded, or discarded. Purchased parts, such as hinges or chains, also must meet specifications, even though the firm does not manufacture these items.

The problem of obtaining raw materials of proper quality can be subdivided into several steps. First, the proper material must be selected. Should it be plywood, particle board, or masonite? Second, the appropriate supplier must be selected. Third, incoming raw material receipts should be monitored to assure that the quality standard is met throughout the manufacturing period. Failure to consider any of these three steps may jeopardize the quality of the end product.

Employees

In addition to materials and equipment, the third major input category is people. To achieve the quality goals, employees must be trained properly in the quality aspects of the task they are to perform, and they must be motivated to produce at the level of desired quality. Selection and training policies should consider the level of quality that workers are expected to achieve. It is incorrect to assume that workers naturally will produce at the right quality level. And it is unwise, and often costly, to rely on inspection to police the employees' work.

Operation of the Production Process

The doghouse manufacturer might have the best design, the best equipment, the best raw materials, and the best employees, but if it fails to *manage* the quality function in its day-by-day operations, it may not produce an acceptable product. The maintenance policy for equipment may be sound but not implemented carefully. Housekeeping could be lax, resulting in damage to the product during manufacturing. Supervisory styles, communications, scheduling, stores control, wage and salary policies, and many other operating policies, rules, and procedures can determine whether the firm produces at or below its quality capability. Seemingly insignificant decisions such as the scheduling of coffee breaks often can have a pronounced impact on quality.

Packaging

Many firms incorrectly assume that their quality responsibilities end when the item comes off the assembly line. If it passes *final inspection,* then a quality product has been produced. The customer, however, does the *final* inspection. If a product fails to meet the customer's quality criteria when it is put to use, then it is a defective unit. Packaging is the first of several activities between the assembly line and the point of purchase that can influence the quality of the product.

If the doghouse is sent out with no packaging at all, it will end up with scratches, dents, missing parts, and a variety of other defects unacceptable to the customer. It could be put in a plastic bag to protect it from dirt or in a cardboard box to reduce the effects of rough handling. Ultimately, the firm could construct a packing crate more costly than the doghouse itself to assure that the item arrives in the same condition as it left the plant. Packaging that it is cost effective and commensurate with the characteristics of the product must be selected.

Transporting

Among the alternatives for shipping the doghouse to market are truck, air, rail, and boat. The type of transportation chosen will influence not only the costs but also the quality of the product. Air cargo is subject to extreme pressure and temperature. Rail and truck shipments may involve vibration and exposure to the weather, as well as several loading and unloading operations. Company-owned vehicles may be specifically adapted to the size and weight of the cargo, but cost effectiveness also must be considered.

Obviously, the packaging used and the transportation method chosen are interdependent. Items shipped by commercial carrier may need more protection, but air shipments should minimize the package-weight required. Whatever combination of packaging and transportation is chosen, the decision should be tempered by the effect on the quality of the product and should fit with the firm's overall quality policy.

Storage

An area often overlooked as a quality determinant is storage. The doghouses will be kept in warehouses, stockrooms, and other storage facilities for weeks, months, or years before they are sold. This product is fairly durable, but there are limits to how high it should be stacked, how far it can be dropped, and what environmental conditions it can withstand. A more delicate product might have severe restrictions on allowable temperature, humidity, dust, or light. Perishable products—those with a *shelf life*—should be rotated to assure freshness.

Packaging also is interdependent with storing: The more protective the packaging, the less likely the product is to deteriorate during storage. Also, packaging materials can be marked with storing instructions that help assure that the product will be in an acceptable condition when needed.

After all the effort that is put into the design and manufacture of a quality product, it is unfortunate to lose it through careless storage and handling.

A Total Quality Control Program

A total quality control (TQC) approach recognizes quality as a top business priority and coordinates all activities toward this goal. TQC makes quality a part of everyone's job and emphasizes prevention rather than detection and correction.

Many organizations are developing various TQC approaches, and most are demonstrating impressive records of success. Ford Motor Company is one example. According to Ford's executive director of quality assurance, quality is up dramatically over 1980 levels, as measured by defect rates and warranty costs, and surveys of customer satisfaction. The Ford approach to TQC is based on the following elements:

1. Employee awareness and commitment—Employees must understand the importance of quality and have the proper tools and information to achieve quality targets.

2. Teamwork—Managers in all areas promote communication and cooperation in an effort to enhance quality.

3. Quality designed into the product—The design can be mass produced to meet customer specifications and expectations.

4. Quality built into the product—The production process is managed day by day to assure that the desired quality level is maintained.

5. Quality monitored and customers served—An ongoing flow of information is maintained to assure quick response to problems and to prevent their recurrence.

6. Quality improvement in outside suppliers—By working more closely with carefully selected suppliers, the company is able to obtain high-quality raw materials and purchased parts.

In daily operations, these six elements guide decisions and actions that affect quality. Improved quality leads, in turn, to improved productivity, cost control, and profits.

Factors Affecting Quality

A total quality control (TQC) approach requires an understanding of the stages of production in which quality is affected: product design, process design, raw materials, and so on. If TQC is to lead to improved quality, however, managers also must understand the organizational factors that influence quality levels. Figure 7-1 is a useful conceptual framework for organizing these factors. Furthermore, it shows that inspection and testing do not improve the quality level. They can only catch some defects before products reach the customer and provide information to managers about problems that need correction.

Behavioral and Technical Factors Affecting Quality

The actual quality of the product (good or service) when it reaches the customer is determined by a multitude of factors involved in the creation and delivery of the output. Generally, these can be divided into behavioral factors (those that relate to the people in the process) and technical factors (the characteristics of the tools, equipment, materials, and processes).

Some behavioral factors, such as the amount of training an employee has received, will determine the potential for achieving high quality. A poorly trained employee simply is not as capable of high-quality work as a well-trained one. Similarly, technical factors, such as the capabilities of the equipment or the specifications of the raw material, determine the potential quality level of the process.

On the other hand, some behavioral and technical factors influence the quality levels in day-to-day operations. That is, they determine whether or not the potential quality level of the process is achieved. For example, employees may be properly trained and capable of doing high-quality work, but if they are poorly motivated due to inadequate rewards, they may fail to work up to their quality potential. Similarly, machines that are poorly maintained or materials that are handled improperly can introduce defects into a process that has been well designed but badly managed. If quality expectations are not being met, management must determine the reason by attempting to isolate the specific problem. Obviously, it would make no sense to try to increase employees' motivation toward higher quality if employees already are doing their best with the poor tools and materials with which they have to work. On the other hand, it is useless to invest in better equipment if employees lack the motivation to produce proper levels of quality.

Quality Programs

Many companies have established quality programs aimed more at the behavioral factors than at the technological factors affecting quality. These programs range from simple motivational efforts using posters, meetings, and perhaps incentives for quality improvement to elaborate programs intended to change the culture of the company with respect to quality. Some of the programs have met with limited success, but others have become so successful that they have developed a standard format applicable to a variety of companies in different industries.

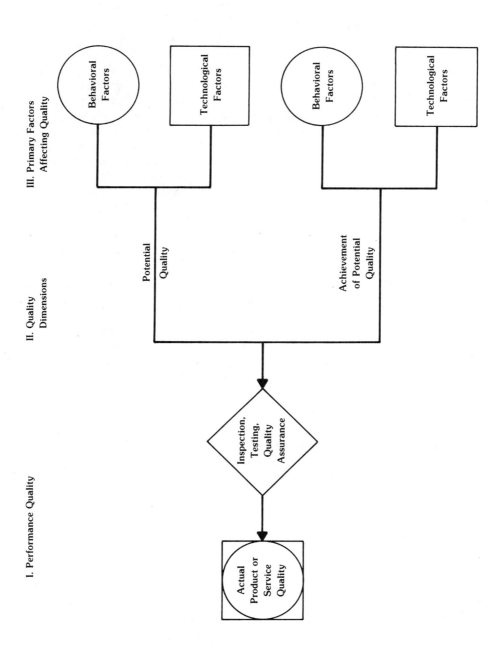

Figure 7-1. Behavioral and Technical Factors Affecting Quality

One example is *quality circles*, a technique developed in Japan in the 1950s. Some credit the quality circle approach with moving Japanese industry from the image of *cheap junk* to becoming one of the world's leading producers of high-quality, sophisticated electronic and mechanical products.

A quality circle is a group of workers who meet together weekly to discuss problems of quality, or other factors, and develop solutions. Employees who are close to the work on a daily basis often can find answers not apparent to engineers and analysts. If possible, solutions are implemented immediately, and the result is a higher-quality product and workers who feel they have made a positive contribution to that product.

Quality circles are no longer unique to Japan. American companies such as Westinghouse, Techtronics, Motorola, and many others have reported using them, with excellent results. Quality circles also have been successfully implemented in government operations such as the Naval Shipyard at Norfolk, Virginia. Based upon past results, the potential for quality improvement in products and services through the implementation of quality circles is enormous.

Another example is *Zero Defects,* which is applicable in service, office, and manufacturing operations. Designed primarily to raise the level of awareness of every employee to quality problems, this program promotes the goal of defect-free performance by isolating the cause of every error and tracing it to the source. If the root cause of defects can be identified and removed, then the goal of zero defects can be achieved.

Many adaptations of these ideas have been incorporated into quality programs for organizations of all types. Their success rate depends on many factors, but key among them is the degree to which the top management of the firm places quality in a high priority and supports efforts to make changes that will improve quality performance.

Quality Costs

Some managers state their objective as "producing the highest-quality product at the lowest possible cost," whereas others argue that higher quality costs more, so one must choose between the two. The crux of the argument lies in the differing definitions of quality. As stated earlier, quality is not the same as luxury. A Rolls Royce and a Volkswagen differ in many respects, but are they the same or different in quality? It may be difficult to decide which is the better value in terms of a quality/cost ratio.

It may be useful to differentiate between low quality and poor quality. A firm may choose to compete at the low end of the market for quality and price, but it cannot survive if it produces shoddy products that fail to give good value. For example, some airlines provide *no-frills* service by eliminating meals, preassigned seats, and other amenities in an effort to provide the lowest fare in the market. Yet they must still do proper maintenance on the aircraft and maintain an acceptable on-time record if they are to compete at any price. Similarly, disposable pens, cigarette lighters, and razors may be inexpensive, but they must perform their function well and meet the customer's expectation for reliability and durability.

The challenge in managing quality costs is similar to the challenge in many areas of operations management: Seek the lowest total cost of quality. To reach this goal, the operations manager must find the proper balance of four costs of quality (see exhibit 7-1).

Appraisal Costs

When raw materials are purchased and received, they normally are inspected and tested before being placed in inventory or released to production. Inspection of incoming materials requires inspection labor, test equipment, facilities space, and time to perform the tests. In some tests, part of the material must be destroyed before its quality can be properly checked. Test equipment must be maintained and periodically calibrated to assure accuracy. Finally, record keeping must be maintained to analyze quality histories on vendors and to perform quality audits.

Similarly, inspections and tests are performed at various stages in the process of manufacturing a product or producing a service. Sometimes these quality checks are performed by inspectors; often they are done by the worker doing the task. Inspections and tests throughout the process, including final inspection, incur more of the same costs described for incoming quality control. Together, these appraisal costs are incurred to determine whether the incoming material and the products produced meet quality standards.

Internal Failure Costs

If an unacceptable number of defects are found in incoming material or in a batch of partially completed units, the batch will be rejected. Rejected lots may be returned to the vendor, screened to eliminate defective items, reworked to correct defects, or disposed of as scrap. Rejected lots must somehow be replaced; either new material must be ordered, or employees will need to work overtime to catch up to production schedules. If items are being produced repetitively rather than in batches, quality problems may necessitate stopping the process to correct the cause of defects.

All this lost material and disruption to the production schedule incurs additional costs for the firm. Internal failures, by definition, never reach the customer, but internal failures raise the cost per unit of the good items that are sold.

In services, examples of internal failure include finding too much salt in the soup before it is served, or finding a misrouted package in time to correct the error and still deliver it on time. However, since services usually involve the customer in the process of producing the service, most failures are external rather than internal.

External Failure Costs

Inevitably, some defects pass final inspection, and other defects may be created in the operations of packaging, material handling, transporting, storing, display-

Exhibit 7-1

Costs of Quality

COSTS OF CONTROL		COSTS OF FAILURE	
Prevention	Appraisal	Internal Failure	External Failure
- Quality planning and administration - Process analysis and improvement - Design and development of quality information equipment - Quality training and work-force development - Product design verification - Systems development and management	- Test and inspection of purchased materials - Laboratory acceptance testing and other measurement services - In-process inspection and testing - Checking quality by direct labor - Test and inspection equipment and material; setup; maintenance - Quality audits - Field testing	- Scrap (labor + material) - Rework (labor + material) - Additional material-procurement costs - Disposal costs - Product and production engineering time spent on quality problems - Production disruption, downtime, and rescheduling	- Warranty costs - Complaints out of warranty - Service cost to correct defects - Product liability - Product recall - Product returns - Loss of reputation, sales, and profits

ing, installing, and other postproduction activities. Defects that reach the customer (industrial or consumer) are called external failures. The costs of servicing warranties and guarantees as well as servicing out of warranty can be substantial. If an item fails, it may require return, repair, or replacement. If serious defects, such as design flaws, are found, a product recall may be necessary. In some cases, an external failure can result in a costly lawsuit under product-liability laws. Finally, too many external failures begin to erode the company's reputation and consequently affect its sales and profits.

Whereas manufactured goods usually can be returned and corrected, often services cannot. Poor service in a restaurant or a late-delivered package cannot be redone. Recently a patient had an operation to remove a malfunctioning kidney. The surgeon made an error and removed the good kidney. Compensation through a malpractice suit is the only remedy.

Prevention Costs

Rather than emphasizing detection and correction of defects, many firms today are placing more effort on preventing defects. The quality management approach examines the design of the product or service, the process and equipment used, the capabilities of the work force, and the planning and administration of all information systems in an effort to eliminate the cause of defects. No system can be error free, but if quality carries a high priority for the firm, sufficient attention will be given to preproduction planning activities and day-by-day operations to effect significant increases in quality levels.

It takes time and costs money to carefully review a product design for defects in the design itself or for defects that easily might be introduced during its manufacture. Perhaps Ford Motor Company should have spent more time reviewing the design of the Pinto. Very likely, that is one of the reasons Ford now has the quality strategy described earlier.

Services, again, are subject to the same conditions. Many computer programmers and systems analysts have learned the hard way that additional time spent debugging the system prior to installation is less costly than dealing with errors after the system is implemented.

Minimum Total Quality Cost

It seems obvious that the way to reduce the costs of appraisal and failure is to prevent the defects and errors from being made. If causes of failure are reduced, less appraisal is needed and fewer corrections are required.

However, this is a classic cost trade-off problem, in which precise cost-benefit calculations for quality are difficult to obtain by traditional accounting systems. Most quality experts agree, however, that the total cost of quality is much higher than most executives would estimate and that far too little is spent on prevention rather than on appraisal or failure.

Conceptually, quality costs can be depicted as a cost-optimization problem (Figure 7-2). As more emphasis is placed on prevention activities, their costs

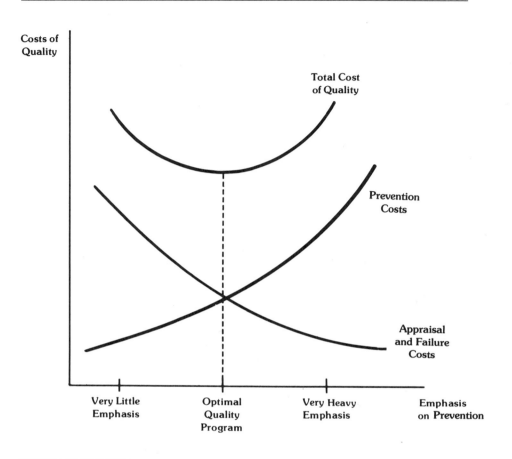

Figure 7-2. Quality-Cost Relationships

rise. Correspondingly, the need for appraisal is reduced and the number of internal and external failures falls so these three costs go down. Somewhere in between is the optimal quality program. Although these costs cannot yet be precisely measured, a firm is more likely to be to the left of optimal rather than to the right.

Toyota provides an example of this concept. In many of its assembly plants, a cord is hung above the line similar to the emergency cord on a train that signals the engineer to stop. If any production worker spots a quality or safety problem, the cord is pulled and the line immediately stops.

Since downtime costs hundreds of dollars per minute, this grabs the attention of supervisors, managers, and engineers who immediately converge on the line. The problem is corrected and the line restarted; but, more important, the cause of the problem is analyzed and eliminated if possible. No one wants it to happen again. If it is an operator error, that worker does not want everyone in the plant to know about the foul-up. If it is an equipment or material problem, the appropriate person will follow up to see if this type of error can be prevented in the future.

At first, U.S. auto executives discarded this idea as too costly. Yet they were tolerating vast numbers of internal and external failures. Warranty costs were high and, at times, acres of parking lots were filled with cars awaiting rework after they had failed final inspection. Recently, some U.S. automobile manufacturers have begun to experiment with this new approach to quality improvement.

Statistical Quality Control

As indicated, a total quality program involves much more than simply inspecting the product; yet applications of statistical quality control to inspection and testing can be the key to *ensuring* that the quality program meets its goals. In fact, many firms have dropped the term "quality control" in favor of a more descriptive term, such as quality assurance, quality evaluation, customer assurance, or product integrity.

Inspection and testing can be casual or sophisticated. Some items can be inspected visually by the worker or an inspector to assure that no parts are missing and that the product "looks okay." In other applications, such as in pharmaceuticals, elaborate tests are employed against rigid standards for purity, weight, and content. Inspection points sometimes are placed throughout the process to monitor progress at each stage of completion. In still other instances, only a final inspection is performed.

Some defects are dichotomous; that is, the item is either good or bad. For example, a light bulb either lights or doesn't, and a packet of washers contains the right number of units or it doesn't. This situation is referred to as quality by attributes.

In other instances, quality can be measured by some continuous gauge. A can of coffee rarely contains *exactly* 1 pound. An acceptable range for this measure might be 15.5 to 17.0 ounces; a container with less than 15.5 ounces or more than 17.0 ounces is considered a "defective" unit. Other examples would be in the diameter of a rod, the temperature of a mixture, or the percentage of fat in hamburger. Quality in these cases is measured by variables.

Inspection and testing are performed for two basic reasons: (1) to remove all or most of the defective items, which is done by 100 percent inspection or *screening*, and (2) to predict the number of defects present, in which a small sample of items is checked by acceptance sampling.

Screening

Screening is performed when the cost from a defect is relatively high and the cost of inspection is relatively low. Screening also is indicated when many defects are believed present.

Consider a simple test for an electronic part that goes into a TV set. The test costs an average of 80 cents per unit for the inspector's time, equipment, supplies, and overhead. If a bad part is assembled into the set, the set will not work and will be rejected by the final inspection at the end of the assembly line. Rejected sets then are examined by a technician who must find the problem, remove the bad part, and replace it with a good part. This procedure costs the company 20 dollars for each defective set.

If only 3 percent of the parts are defective, then 3 percent of the assembled TV sets will incur the 20 dollar repair cost, or an average of 60 cents per set. But inspecting every part increases the cost of each set by 80 cents. In this instance, the firm would not perform the test because it would be more economical to repair the sets after assembly. If however, 5 percent of the parts were bad, it would pay to do the inspection. The 80 cent inspection cost per unit would be lower than the average repair cost of 5 percent times 20 dollars, or 1 dollar per set. The indifference point is 4 percent, where the cost of inspection and the cost of repair would be the same.

The same analysis can be applied to defective items that reach the customer, but the costs usually are not as well defined. Defects that reach the customer cost the firm in return, repair, customer dissatisfaction, and, occasionally, lawsuits. These costs must be balanced against the costs of testing and inspection before the product is sold.

One hundred percent inspection or screening does not guarantee freedom from defects; no inspection is perfect. Items can be inspected three, four, or even ten times and still malfunction. The defect may not show up in the test. It may have been overlooked, or it may have been introduced between the time of inspection and use of the product.

Acceptance Sampling

Acceptance sampling applies statistical analysis to a small sample of items to predict the number of defects present. It can be divided into the major categories of batch sampling and process sampling.

Batch sampling by attributes. Suppose the electronic parts mentioned above were purchased from a supplier in lots of 1,000 units. If the batch contained 4 percent or fewer defects, the firm would want to accept it and use it in production. If the batch contained 5 percent or more defects, it would be best to reject it and either return it to the manufacturer or screen it before use. The challenge is to predict the number of defects in the batch through statistical analysis of a sample.

If a firm is sampling by attributes (the part is either good or bad), a sample is drawn, the number of defects in the sample is counted, and then the lot is accepted or rejected based upon the results of the sample.

A sample plan contains two elements: a sample size and an acceptance number. Charts and tables are available for determining the proper sample plan, but to use these effectively, the underlying theory of sampling must be understood.

	Accept	Reject
Good Lot	No Error	Type I Error (Alpha)
Bad Lot	Type II Error (Beta)	No Error

Figure 7-3. Sampling Errors

For example, take a sample of 50 units, with an acceptance number of two. This plan says to count the number of defects in the sample and accept the lot if there are zero, one, or two defects; three or more defects in the sample indicate the lot should be rejected. Sampling does not give perfect information; two types of errors can be made, as illustrated in figure 7-3.

In the example, a "good lot" is one with 4 percent or fewer defects; a "bad lot" is one with more than 4 percent defective items. With a sample of 50, it would be possible to get three or more defective items even though the lot contains less than 4 percent defective (less than 40 out of 1,000). The sample then would indicate rejection of the lot, which would be a Type I error. Usually, however, the sample would be correct, and the lot would be accepted.

With probability theory, the chance of accepting or rejecting a lot with a given percentage defective can be calculated. Calculating the probability of acceptance for each different lot percent defective produces an operating-characteristics curve like the one in figure 7-4.

The operating-characteristics curve indicates that lots with 2 percent defective items will be accepted 85 percent of the time; 15 percent of the time they will be rejected. This 15 percent is α (alpha) and often is called the *producer's risk,* because even though a good lot was produced, by chance it was rejected. Similarly, a lot with 7 percent defective would, with this sample plan, be accepted 20 percent of the time. This probability is labeled β (beta) and is called the *consumer's risk,* because the consumer runs a 20 percent chance of accepting this lot that really should be rejected.

A sample plan is set by choosing values for four variables. First is the specification, in terms of percent defective, of a really good lot, one that very often should be accepted. The percent defective specified is called the acceptable quality level (AQL), and the probability associated with "very often" is alpha.

190 Fundamentals of Production/Operations Management

Figure 7-4. Operating-Characteristics Curve

In this example, lots with an AQL of 2 percent will be accepted 85 percent of the time, but the plan will reject them 15 percent of the time. Next, a really bad lot, one that should be accepted infrequently, must be specified. The bad lot percent defective is called the lot tolerance percent defective (LTPD), and it is accepted with a probability of 20 percent (beta). These four coordinates define one, and only one, operating-characteristics curve that is associated with only one sample plan made up of a sample size and a given acceptance number.

To make fewer errors, or if the firm is willing to make more errors, a different sample plan must be used. The problem is one of balancing a Type I error (alpha) against a Type II error (beta) and then balancing the cost of these errors

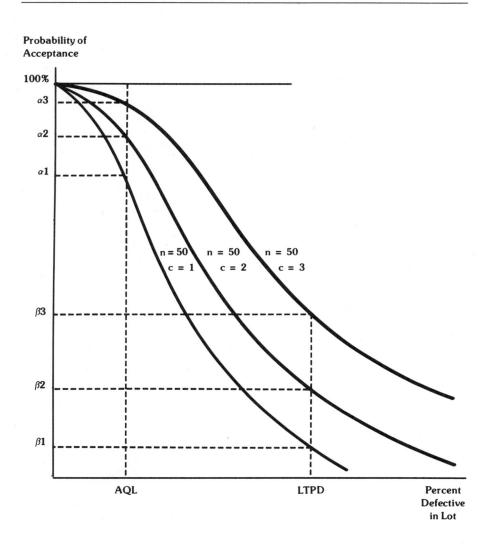

Figure 7-5. Effect of Changing the Acceptance Number

against the cost of sampling. Figure 7-5 illustrates the relationship of the acceptance number to the types of errors when the sample size remains the same. A *tighter* plan (n, sample size = 50; c, acceptance number = 1) will make more Type I errors but fewer Type II errors. Fewer lots of any percent defective will be accepted, meaning that more good lots will be rejected, but fewer bad ones will be accepted. A *looser* sample plan ($n = 50$; $c = 3$) would do the opposite.

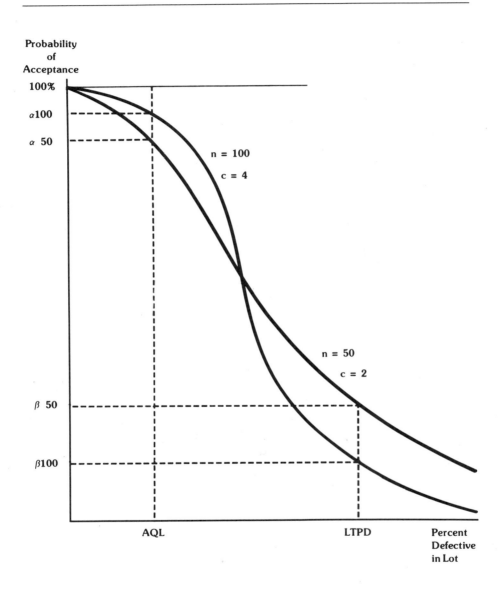

Figure 7-6. Effect of Changing the Sample Size

To make fewer errors of both types, the firm must go to a larger, more accurate sample. Figure 7-6 illustrates the effect of a larger sample size using the same relative acceptance number. The larger sample will lead to fewer errors but will be more costly.

The operating-characteristics curve illustrates the theory behind batch sampling for attributes. To find an appropriate sample plan, however, the decision maker needs only to set levels for the AQL, LTPD, alpha, and beta and use the charts established for this purpose.

Batch sampling by variables. If the quality characteristic being inspected, such as weight, temperature, or thickness, is measured on a continuous scale, tolerance limits must be set to distinguish good from bad items. For example, one type of automobile tire may be considered acceptable if it will last 25,000 miles, plus or minus 3,000 miles. A sample of several tires from the batch could be drawn and tested, and the average mileage in the sample would be used to estimate the percent of tires in the lot that would last 22,000 to 28,000 miles. The lot then would be accepted or rejected based upon that estimate.

Process sampling. If the item being tested is manufactured repetitively rather than in small batches, the problem involves monitoring the process to assure that quality standards are being met. Periodic random samples are taken and plotted on a chart to determine whether the process is "in control" and should continue or is "out of control" and requires corrective action.

Control charts used for this purpose have a line of central tendency (average) and both an upper and lower control limit. These limits generally are set at plus and minus three standard deviations from the mean.

A P-chart (figure 7-7) is used for process sampling by attributes. A random sample is taken from the process, and the percent defective is plotted. As long as the percentage of defects in the sample lies within the control limits, no action is taken. If the sample statistic exceeds either control limit, then the process should be brought back into control.

Process sampling by variables requires monitoring both the mean and the variance of the quality characteristic. The mean of the sample (average weight, for example) is plotted on an $\overline{X}$ ("x-bar") chart, illustrated in figure 7-8. Note that the fifth sample taken fell outside the lower control limit, indicating that the average weight of the units may be too light and that a machine adjustment is necessary. Below the $\overline{X}$-chart, the range of the sample is plotted to indicate the variance of the process. A sample outside of control limit on the R-chart would indicate that some units are too heavy and others too light, even though the average is still within acceptable limits.

Applications of Acceptance Sampling

Now we will apply the preceding concepts to the manufacture of the doghouse. Purchased materials—wood, roofing, and chains—would be sampled upon arrival. Each shipment, considered a batch, would be accepted or rejected based on the number of defective items in the sample. Rejected shipments could be returned to the supplier or screened before release to the shop. Some items, like pieces of lumber, could be sampled by attributes; others like the length of the chain, might be sampled by variables.

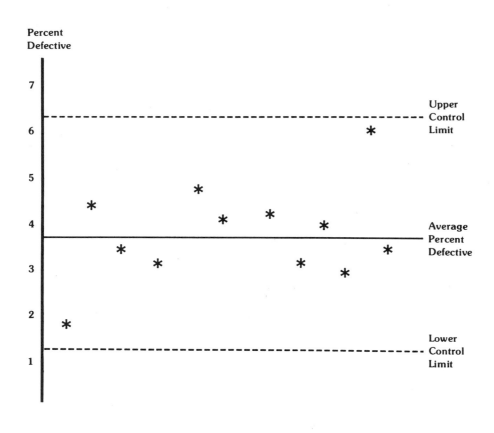

Figure 7-7. P-Chart

Within the manufacturing process, either batch or process sampling could be used. Labeling a day's production as a batch, the firm could accept or reject the total amount produced in a day. More likely, it would employ process sampling, using P-charts for attributes, such as missing pieces of trim, and $\overline{X}$ and R-charts for variables, such as the size of the door.

The degree of sophistication used—the size and frequency of the samples, as well as the nature of the test—would depend upon estimates and analysis of the relative costs involved.

Organization for Quality Control

The quality control department in the doghouse manufacturing firm needs the authority and autonomy to perform its job effectively. Because quality is a major

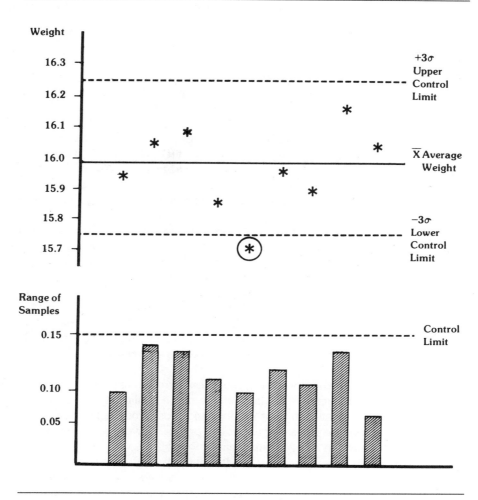

Figure 7-8. X̄ and R-Chart

company objective, it should not be downgraded by pressures from other company goals of efficiency, quantity, or timeliness of shipments.

When quality control rejects an incoming shipment of materials, adjustments may be necessary in the production schedule or worker assignments. A shop supervisor who has to wrestle with these problems might prefer to accept and use the unsatisfactory material rather than reschedule, even though the company as a whole might suffer.

It is important, therefore, that quality control be placed at a high position in the organizational structure, preferably reporting directly to the vice president of manufacturing or the plant manager. If the quality-control manager's decision is to be overridden, it should be done only by someone with the perspective to weigh all ramifications and with the responsibility of bearing the consequences.

The Growing Importance of Quality

Quality always has been an important factor in the production of goods and services, but recent developments have added emphasis and urgency. It is likely that the quality dimension of output will grow in relative importance as firms adjust to changing times.

Consumer advocacy, typified by the work of Ralph Nader, tells organizational leaders what consumers expect. They are tired of products that break, appliances that do not function, and services that are superficial and shoddy. Through both the marketplace and the media, united groups of citizens have found that even the largest organization can be influenced to change the quality of its output.

Consumers also are gaining more strength through new legislation and interpretations of existing legislation relating to product and service liability. Million-dollar lawsuits, which used to be rare, are becoming much more common. The cost of a defect should be weighted against the cost of quality-control efforts to prevent it. Product-liability suits have the effect of pushing up the cost of a defect. Rational decision makers within the firm respond by redoubling their efforts to assure that million-dollar liability defects do not leave the plant. Automobile recalls, food and drug prohibitions, malpractice suits, and scandals in financial institutions indicate that all forms of businesses, private and public, are feeling the pressures.

Increasing foreign and domestic competition merely intensifies the problem. Detroit automobile makers are painfully aware of the quality as well as the cost and style differences between their product and those from Japan or Europe. The U.S. Postal Service is losing business to private delivery services that can provide better service in some urban areas.

In response to these pressures and in anticipation of increasing emphasis in the future, some consumer-product firms have created a new corporate-level executive with the title of vice president of product integrity. The job involves not only monitoring the manufacture of many products but also working with designers, chemists, industrial engineers, and others who have an impact on the quality of the product. This executive conducts extensive environmental tests on all products and has the power to recall any item considered unsafe, unreliable, or unfair to the consumer.

Emphasis on quality is just one indicator of the recognition of its importance in the ever-changing production function.

Key Concepts

Definition of Quality

Dimensions of Quality

Sample Plan

Operating Characteristics Curve

Total Quality Control (TQC)

Behavioral and Technical Factors Affecting Quality

Quality Costs

Attributes/Variables

Batch Sampling

Type I/Type II Errors

Consumer's Risk/Producer's Risk

AQL/LTPD

Process Sampling

X-Bar and R-Chart

References

Crosby, Philip B. *Quality Is Free.* New York: McGraw-Hill, 1979.

Deming, W. Edwards. "Improvement of Quality and Productivity through Action by Management." *National Productivity Review* 1 (Winter, 1981–1982): 12–22.

Feigenbaum, Armand V. *Total Quality Control.* 3d ed. New York: McGraw-Hill, 1983.

Garvin, David A. "Quality on the Line." *Harvard Business Review* 61 (September–October 1983): 64–75.

Gitlow, Howard S., and Gitlow, Shelly J. *The Deming Guide to Quality and Competitive Position.* Englewood Cliffs, NJ: Prentice-Hall, 1987.

Grant, E. L., and Leavenworth, R. S. *Statistical Quality Control.* 5th ed. New York: McGraw-Hill, 1980.

Hostage, B. M. "Quality Control in a Service Business." *Harvard Business Review* 53 (July–August 1975): 98–106.

Juran, J. M. "International Significance of the QC Circle Movement." *Quality Progress* 13 (November 1980): 18–22.

Juran, J. M., and Gryna, F. M. *Quality Planning and Analysis.* 2d ed. New York: McGraw-Hill, 1980.

Leonard, Frank S., and Sasser, Earl. "The Incline of Quality." *Harvard Business Review* 60 (September–October 1982): 163–171.

Discussion Questions

1. An optimal quality-control policy balances opposing costs. What are the costs involved and the problems of finding the optimal balance in each of the following:

a. McDonald's hamburgers?
b. Grant County Blood Bank?
c. Southwestern Publishing Company—textbook division?
d. Gaines Petfood Division?
e. American Airlines—maintenance division?

2. Your company is planning to introduce a super-deluxe doghouse with lights, air conditioning, windows, and an automatic food and water dispenser. What quality problems would you anticipate?

3. You are the president of a company in a meeting with several of your department heads. The marketing vice president says that company salespeople have received customer complaints that the quality of the product is not up to that of competitors. Also attending the meeting are the following:
   a. Purchasing Manager—responsible for acquisition of all raw materials and supplies
   b. Personnel Manager—responsible for recruiting, selecting, and training all workers
   c. Plant Engineer—responsible for equipment installation, layout, maintenance, and repair
   d. Plant Supervisor—directs all eight lead workers who supervise production workers
   e. Quality-Control Manager—responsible for all incoming, in-process, and final testing and inspection

   What would you tell each of these department heads? Are there others who should be in this meeting? What additional information do you need?

4. Alice wants to take a random sample of the product her department is making to assess its quality. Because she is busy with other things, she decides that the easiest strategy is to take four samples: one the first thing in the morning, one before she goes to lunch, one when she returns from lunch, and one just before she goes home. What problems do you see with this plan?

5. A customer complained that the switch on the lawn edger your company produces is faulty. The salesperson explained that the switch is a purchased part; since your company does not manufacture it, you cannot control its quality. The customer, not satisfied with that answer, wrote a formal letter of complaint to you, the company president. What letter would you write in response?

6. Five dimensions of quality were discussed in this chapter. Do any or all of these dimensions apply to a service business, as a car wash or a pizza parlor? Explain.

7. Another dimension of quality that could be added to the list is "consistency," which refers to how well all units of a product conform to the standard. Is this dimension more or less important in service businesses than it is in manufactured products? Explain, using several examples.

8. Which is more important in affecting quality: technical factors or behavioral factors? Concisely explain the relationship between the two.

9. The various costs associated with quality tend to change as the environment changes. Which of these costs is likely to increase in the future, and which is likely to decline? What effect will this have on the optimal quality program?

10. If you were buying a bicycle and had a choice between one that cost $50 but fell apart at the end of one year, and a different model that cost $200 but lasted five to ten years, which one would you buy? Why? Which one is of the higher quality?

Glossary

ABC Analysis: Arrangement of activities—for example, total dollars spent for purchase of particular items—in descending dollar value, so that resources (time) can be allocated according to the relative importance of each activity.

Acceptable Quality Level (AQL): The percentage of defects in a lot that would be acceptable most of the time.

Acceptance Number: The maximum number of defects allowed in a sample for acceptance of a lot.

Acceptance Sampling: Inspection of a sample in order to predict the number of defects present in the entire lot. (*See* Batch Sampling and Process Sampling.)

Aggregate Planning: The broad, overall decisions that relate to the programming of resources for production over an established time horizon.

Alpha Error: In quality control, for a given sample plan, the percentage of times a good lot is rejected. (*See* Type I Error.)

Approved List: List of those vendors who have been evaluated and estimated to be capable of satisfactory performance.

Assembly Chart: A chart showing the components and subassemblies of a product and the sequence of assembly.

Attributes: In quality control, refers to dichotomous characteristics that make each unit either good or bad (defective).

Attributes Sampling: Quality sampling in which the characteristic is measured on a dichotomous basis, such as "good/bad."

Automated Batch Manufacturing Systems (ABMS): A system of several individual machines that process parts into finished units while carried through the system attached to pallets.

Batch Sampling: Inspection of a sample from a lot in order to accept or reject the entire lot.

Beta Error: In quality control, for a given sample plan, the percentage of times a bad lot is accepted. (*See* Type II Error.)

Bill of Materials: A list of all items and materials, including the quantities of each, that are required to produce one unit of a finished product.

Blank-Check Purchase Order: Purchase agreement in which vendor is sent a signed, blank check. (After shipment, the vendor enters amount due on the check and deposits it.)

Blanket Order: Purchase agreement with a vendor to provide the supply of an item for a fixed time period, normally one year.

Breakdown Repair: Maintenance work undertaken only after the equipment malfunctions or breaks down.

Break-Even Analysis: Determination of production volume where sales revenue equals the total of variable and fixed costs, or where costs from two processes intersect.

Break-Even Time: A model for evaluating research and development which determines the time for the operating profit for a product to cover all development costs.

Buffer Stock: *See* Decoupling Stock *and* Safety Stock.

Capacity Requirements Planning: A process that translates manufacturing plans into labor hours and machine processing hours required in each time period (e.g., one week) for the time covered by the planning process.

Carrying Costs: Those costs incurred because something is being stored and not currently used. (The cost is proportional to the number or quantity of the item stored. Typical carrying costs reflect the value of the space occupied by the stored item, the value of the funds tied up in the stock, and insurance costs to protect the stock).

Cash Discount: Discount, normally 2 percent, granted if payment is made to vendor within a limited time, normally ten days.

Cellular Layout: Arrangement of several machines into a cell or group to produce a family of related products.

Centralized Purchasing: System in which all purchase decisions must be made, and all purchase orders released, by the purchasing agent or department.

Competitive Bid: Offer to sell, at a price, made by a vendor.

Computer-Aided Design (CAD): A design technique in which the computer is used to instantaneously draw pictures on a television screen of what an engineer has designed.

Computer-Aided Manufacturing (CAM): Use of a preprogrammed tool path to provide direct numerical control in the operation of equipment.

Computer Information Exchange: Transmission of data between a firm's purchasing data base and a supplier's data base through a telecommunications system.

Computer Integrated Manufacturing (CIM): Integrating planning, scheduling, and production control with computer methods that link together automated manufacturing equipment.

Consumer's Risk: *See* Beta Error.

CPM: Acronym for the critical path method, a network modeling technique used to plan and control large-scale projects.

Cycle Counting: A method of checking inventory levels and records on a routine basis—for example, verifying 2 percent of all stock items each week, with some important items being checked more than once a year. (This approach avoids the disruptive effects of the annual "physical" inventory).

Cycle Stock: The active portion of inventory—that is, the quantity that is depleted, resupplied, depleted, and resupplied again and again. (Cycle stock does not include the quantity known as safety stock.)

Cyclical Component: Time-series variations that are periodic in nature, extending over a period of years.

Decoupling Stock: That inventory used to isolate sequential operations from one another so that they can be performed independently.

Dependent Demand: *See* Internal Demand.

Detailed Scheduling: Matching the job and resource flows required to meet the master schedule requirements on a time scale.

Durability: The ability of a product to function under adverse conditions.

Economic Lot Size: The number of units put into production to minimize the combined costs of setups and carrying inventory over a specified planning period, usually a year.

Economic Order Quantity: The number of units purchased at one time to minimize the combined costs of ordering material and storing the inventory over a specified planning period, usually a year.

Effectiveness: The degree to which the organization's goals or purposes are achieved.

Efficiency: The relative amount of resources and time consumed in the production of output.

Element: A subdivision of a task. (Elements are used in the analysis of work.)

Energy Management Program (EMP): A program designed to control and reduce energy requirements.

Escalation/Deescalation: Purchase contract clause in a long-term agreement which provides that price automatically increases or decreases if a specific economic change occurs (e.g., basic steel price increases).

Expediting: In purchasing, putting pressure on a vendor to assure that the original delivery promise is met or to get earlier delivery. (In production, it means changing the priority of a problem job so that it or other jobs may progress more smoothly through subsequent operations.)

Exponential Smoothing: A mathematical forecasting model that uses past forecasts and forecast errors to make a new forecast.

External Demand: Demand unrelated to the demands for other items produced by the firm; also called independent demand.

Extrinsic Models: Forecasting techniques that determine how variables external to the organization (e.g., new building permits issued) help predict variables internal to the organization (e.g., lumber sales).

Factory of the Future: The concept of a highly automated computer-controlled factory that can produce large or small lots efficiently and respond to changes quickly.

Fixed Path Equipment: Relatively inflexible equipment (conveyors, chutes, cranes, and hoists) that handles materials in large volume, normally in a continuous flow.

Fixed-Position Layout: Due to weight or bulk of the product being manufactured, the product remains in one position while workers, tools, and materials move to it.

Flow Diagram: Symbols connected by arrows on a floor plan to depict the flow of the work process.

Flow-Process Production: Continuous-flow manufacturing, where the output is not in discrete units. Petroleum refining is an example of flow-process production.

Follow-up of Purchase Order: Routine checking on the status of a purchase to determine whether the vendor will be able to meet the required delivery date.

Forecast Horizon: The time period over which the forecast is to be developed.

Foreign Purchasing: Purchase by U.S. firms of goods from vendors outside North America.

Fork Truck: Special mechanized truck fitted with a hoisting mechanism to transport and stack pallet loads.

Forward Buying: Purchase of a larger-than-normal quantity, due to anticipated shortage or price increase.

Functionality: The degree to which a product or service performs the function for which it was designed.

Group Layout: *See* Cellular Layout.

Group Technology: An approach to manufacturing that groups families of related products to gain planning and manufacturing economies.

Hand-to-Mouth Buying: Purchase of a smaller-than-normal quantity, due to anticipated market oversupply or price decrease.

Heuristic: A rule-of-thumb approach developed and utilized as a guide to solving problems and making decisions.

Independent Demand: *See* External Demand.

Intermittent Production: Producing in lot sizes larger than in a job shop but smaller than in repetitive production.

Internal Demand: Demand derived from or contingent upon the demand for an end product or other item; also called dependent demand.

Intrinsic Models: Forecasting techniques that use only the history of the variable to be projected; commonly called time-series models.

Job Shop: Produces output in small lot sizes or batches, such as a print shop.

Judgmental Models: Forecasting techniques that use expert opinion regarding anticipated happenings to predict future occurrences.

Just-in-Time (JIT) Inventory Systems: Scheduling of materials to arrive just as they are needed, to minimize inventory investment, reduce waste, and increase responsiveness.

Kanban: A card system originating in Japan for coordinating the flow of materials on the shop floor.

Layout: The arrangement of machines, equipment, materials handling, aisles, service areas, storage areas, and work stations within the facility.

Lead Time: The period (days, months) needed to replenish stocks once that need has been recognized.

Line Balancing: Arranging each step in the process within a product type layout to provide equal capacity so that material flow will be uninterrupted.

Loading: Assigning jobs to a work center, usually in terms of the labor content of the jobs relative to the labor capacity of the work center.

Lot Sizing: Determining the number of units to manufacture in one batch. (*See* Economic Lot Size.)

Lot Tolerance Percent Defective (LTPD): The percent of defects in a lot that would make it unacceptable most of the time.

Make or Buy: Consideration of cost, quality, and delivery time and reliability factors to determine whether a particular item should be made in-house or purchased from a vendor.

Mass Production: *See* Repetitive Production.

Master Schedule: A plan indicating the necessary timing and quantities of finished products or assemblies to be produced.

Material/Sales Ratio: Percentage of the sales dollar spent for materials, supplies, and services needed to build a product or create a service.

Materials Management: Organizational concept in which a single manager has authority and responsibility for all activities principally concerned with the flow of materials into an organization. (Purchasing, production planning and scheduling, incoming traffic, inventory control, receiving, and stores normally are included.)

Materials Requirements Planning: *See* MRP.

Methodology (of Transformation): Management principles and techniques, such as planning, forecasting, scheduling, and controlling, involved in transforming inputs into outputs.

Minority Vendor Program: Conscious action by the purchasing department to locate, develop, and buy from firms owned by minority citizens.

Modular Design: Design of products with easily detachable sections, or modules.

MRO: Maintenance, repair, and operating supplies (as distinguished from raw material or capital equipment).

MRP: Acronym for materials-requirements planning, a technique providing an integrated approach to scheduling.

Multiple-Activity Chart: Depicts against a time scale the respective activity of one or more persons operating one or more machines.

Negotiation: Arriving at an agreement on the essentials of a purchase contract, through discussion between buyer and seller.

Numerical Control (N/C) Machines: Equipment preprogrammed to follow a cycle of operations repetitively without human intervention.

Office Process Flow Chart: Depicts the chronological flow of multiple copies and accompanying operations in paperwork systems.

Operating Characteristics Curve: For each quality-control sample plan, the curve that shows the probability of acceptance of a lot relative to the percent defective in the lot.

Operation Chart: Uses symbols to depict how a worker uses each hand during the work cycle at an individual work station.

Operations Research: The use of quantitative tools—for example, simulation—to structure and analyze a problem in order to reach a mathematically optimal solution.

Ordering Costs: Those fixed costs associated with placing a purchase order, regardless of the dollars or number of units represented in the order.

P-Chart: Plots the percent defective (attributes) of samples taken from a continuous process.

Pallet Loads: Loads of materials placed upon a platform base to facilitate handling of multiple packages and heavy loads by means of mechanical handling equipment such as fork trucks or stacking cranes.

Performance Rating: Evaluation of the employee effort or pace against normal performance or normal pace (100 percent).

PERT: Acronym for the program evaluation and review technique; a network modeling technique used to plan and control large-scale projects.

Pilot Production Run: A trial run of a manufacturing or service process for a new product under simulated normal production conditions to determine any product defects or process inefficiencies that may still exist.

Plant Visit: Inspection and evaluation of a vendor's facility, normally done prior to purchase of the vendor's products.

Preventive Maintenance (PM): A program of scheduled maintenance designed to reduce the likelihood of equipment breakdown.

Process Chart: Use of standard symbols to chart the sequence, distance, and time involved in the flow of work.

Process Layout: Arrangement of work facilities based on grouping together similar types of equipment.

Process Sampling: Inspection of a sample from an ongoing process to see if corrective actions are needed.

Producer's Risk: *See* Alpha Error.

Product: The output of the production process including manufactured goods or services.

Product Layout: Arrangement of work and equipment so that material flows according to the progressive steps by which the product is made.

Product Life Cycle: The five steps through which a product passes during its life: introduction, growth, maturity, saturation, and decline.

Production Function: The process of transforming inputs (material, equipment, effort, energy) into outputs (goods and services).

Production Scheduling: Determination of the sequence and timing of production activities.

Productivity: The ratio of outputs to inputs—material, labor, capital, and energy. (Output-per-workhour often is used to measure productivity.)

Profit-Leverage Effect of Purchasing: A dollar saved by better purchasing has the same effect on profits as a sales increase of many (ten to twenty) times that amount.

Progress Control: Constant monitoring of jobs, as they pass through a facility, to assure that all manufacturing requirements are being met. Also called Shop Floor Control.

Project Production: Manufacture of items when only one or a very few complex units are produced. (Shipbuilding is an example of project production.)

Purchase Lead Time: Normal elapsed time from the date a need is recognized until the required item is received from a vendor.

Purchase Order: Legal document that spells out the quantity, quality, delivery date, price, and conditions of the purchase of items from a vendor.

Purchasing/Materials Management Strategy: Long-term (5 to 20 years) planning of purchase actions.

Quality: Characteristics of a product or service that determine its value in the marketplace and how well it performs the function for which it was designed.

Quality Circle: A group of workers who meet together weekly to discuss problems of quality, or other factors, and develop solutions.

R-Chart: Plots the range of a sample characteristic (variable) taken from a continuous process; *see also* X-bar Chart.

Random Component: Variations in time-series data that have no regular pattern or change over brief periods of time; also called irregular or noise influences.

Receipt and Inspection of Goods: Verification that quantity and quality of items received from a vendor agree with the purchase specifications.

Reliability: How long a product functions under normal conditions.

Reorder Point: Stock level that signals the inventory controller to start the reordering process because there is only enough stock to meet normal needs during the resupply lead time and still have the desired safety stock available.

Repetitive Production: Manufacturing of many units of the same product with a unit moving through each state of the process as that operation is completed—for example, an automobile assembly line.

Research and Development: Those activities principally concerned with investigation directed toward discovering new scientific knowledge (research) and translating this new knowledge into marketable goods and services (development).

Return-on-Assets: Measurement of the productivity of assets employed by a firm; computed by multiplying investment turnover times profit margin.

Robinson-Patman Act: Federal law requiring that a vendor charge all buyers the same price for the same item purchased in the same quantity.

Robot: Equipment that is computer controlled and designed to replace the human operator.

Route Sheet: Lists the sequence of operations necessary to start from material inputs (shown in the bill of materials) through production of the finished product.

Safety Stock: That inventory used to protect against running out of supplies because of late delivery from suppliers or unusually high usage during the resupply period.

Sample Plan: The number of units to be sampled from a lot, and the number of defects that determines acceptance or rejection.

Sample Size: The number of units sampled from a lot of material.

Sampling: *See* Work Sampling, Acceptance Sampling, Batch Sampling, *and* Process Sampling.

Screening: Inspection of *every* unit in a lot.

Seasonal Component: Time-series variations that are periodic and can be expected to recur regularly within a certain period, usually one year or less.

Seasonal Inventories: Items produced and stored to meet high demand in a later period.

Service: Something intangible that satisfies a customer's need in addition to or instead of providing that customer with a tangible product.

Service Level Policy: The policy that defines the percentage of time that an item will be in stock.

Setup Costs: Incurred when a system is rearranged to perform a different task—for example, changing a TV studio set in preparation for taping a different series. (The cost is independent of the number of times the new arrangement will be used.)

Sherman Anti-Trust Act: Makes illegal any combination, collusion, or conspiracy by sellers or buyers to set price or restrict trade.

Single Sourcing: Purchase of all requirements of a given item from only one vendor, even though several vendors could supply it.

Specifications: The detailed description of a product, usually including a list of measurable characteristics, the different parts or materials that go into a product, and often a detailed set of directions about how to assemble the unit or properly perform the service.

Stacking Crane: A device that lifts pallet loads vertically and horizontally for placement within very high storage rack areas.

Standardization: The process of establishing agreement on uniform identifications for certain characteristics of quality, design, performance, quantity, and service. (An agreed-upon uniform identification is called a standard.)

Statistical Quality Control (SQC): The use of probability theory and statistical principles to determine quality-sampling procedures.

Stock-keeping Unit (SKU): One unit of an item—for example, a given size or color—in a particular location.

Strategic Material Planning: Long-term forecast of demand, supply, and price of key raw materials to identify potential problems. Forecast results are used to formulate alternative action courses.

Technology (of Transformation): Scientific principles applied to convert inputs into outputs, such as the chemistry and physics involved in petroleum refining.

Therblig: A fundamental movement or action—for example, transport, load, grasp, or hold—used in constructing detailed motion charts for the analysis of hand movements.

Thomas Register of American Manufacturers: Widely used directory listing United States manufacturers by type of item produced.

Time-Series Models: *See* Intrinsic Models.

Time Standard: *See* standard time.

Time Study: Work measurement technique that normally uses a stopwatch to determine the time required to do a job. (The analyst then uses a performance rating, to allow for normal delays, to determine a standard time.)

Total Quality Control (TQC): An organizational approach to the strategic management of quality in all phases of the design and manufacturing process.

Transfer Machines: Provision for the automatic transfer of material between machines for continuous processing.

Transportation Deregulation: Removal of restrictions regarding service and rates for movement of goods by carriers.

Travel chart: Records the frequency of loads between departments, providing information for potential rearrangements.

Traveling Requisition: Used to notify purchasing of a need to purchase. (This form can be used for up to thirty-six buys, and it moves back and forth between requisitioner and purchasing without requiring repeated copying of routine information.)

Trend Component: The tendency of a variable to have a long-term increase or a long-term decrease.

Type I Error: Rejecting a lot that should have been accepted; also called an "alpha error" or "producer's risk."

Type II Error: Accepting a lot that should have been rejected; also called a "beta error" or "consumer's risk."

Value Analysis: The organized and systematic study of every element of cost in a material, part, or service to ensure that it fulfills its function at the lowest total cost.

Variable: In quality control, a characteristic measured on a continuous scale, such as temperature, length, or color.

Variables Sampling: Quality sampling in which the characteristic is measured on a continuous scale such as length, temperature, or weight.

Varied Path Equipment: Flexible equipment (such as a forklift truck) that normally handles equipment in lots.

Vendor: An outside supplier of raw materials, supplies, or services needed in the operation of an organization.

Vendor Directory: Volume that lists vendors and their addresses, arranged by product.

Vendor Point Rating System: Method of evaluating vendor performance in which points are assigned to how well the vendor performed on several factors, such as quality, delivery, and price.

Work Design: Systematic approach to finding the most effective and efficient method of doing a job; also known as methods study or motion study.

Work Measurement: Determination of how long it should take a qualified and trained employee working at a normal pace to do a specific task or operation, with due allowances for fatigue and personal and unavoidable delays; also known as time study.

Work Sampling: The application of probability theory involving random observations to determine the time distribution within a given work activity.

Work Study: Analyzing the people, equipment, materials, and product requirements to determine the most efficient methods and flow of work for a new or existing process.

X-bar Chart: Plots the mean of a characteristic (variable) for a sample taken from a continuous process; *see also* R-Chart.

Index

ABC analysis, 129–30
Acceptable quality level (AQL), 189–190
Aggregate planning, 93–95
Air Cargo Act, 145
Airline Deregulation Act, 145
American Express, 70
American Production and Inventory Control Society (APICS), 25
American Society for Quality Control (ASQC), 25
American Society of Mechanical Engineers (ASME), 72
Annual Survey of Manufacturers, 117
Assembly chart, 74, 75
Assembly lines, early, 10
Automated batch manufacturing systems (ABMS), 68

Babbage, Charles, 10
Backdoor selling, 131
Batch sampling, 188–93
Bic Pen Corporation, 33
Bids, competitive, 139

Bill of materials (B/M), 43–45
  materials requirements planning and, 95, 97, 98
  purchasing department and, 132
Booz, Allen, and Hamilton, 105
Break-even analysis, facilities location and, 58
Break-Even Time, 46–48
Buffer stocks, 151
Bus Regulatory Reform Act, 145

Capacity requirements planning (CRP), 101
Capital equipment, 15
Carrying costs, 153
Causal models of forecasting, 91
Cellular layout, 64
Center for Advanced Purchasing Studies, 113, 125
Centralized vs. decentralized purchasing, 123–25
Commodity file, 143
Computer-aided design (CAD), 11, 39, 69

213

Computer-aided manufacturing (CAM), 11, 68–69
Computer applications, 11–12
Computer-integrated manufacturing (CIM), 12
Consumer-opinion surveys, 87
Consumer's risk, 189
Contract file, 143
Contribution to profit, 22
Conversion process, 7
Coors beer, 33
CPM (Critical path method). *See* PERT/CPM
Creative Output, Inc., 104
Cycle stock, 154–55

Decentralized purchasing, centralized vs., 123–25
Decoupling, 151
Delphi technique, 87
Dodge, H. F., 11

Economic lot size (ELS), 150, 157–59
Economic order quantity (EOQ), 150
  formula, 155–56
  inventory-cost equation, 154–55
  periodic review model, and, 158–58
  sensitivity of, 159
  with discounts, 156–57
Effectiveness as a goal, 21
Efficiency as a goal, 21
Electronic Data Interchange (EDI), 145
Energy management, 70
Environment, business, 8
Environmental responsibility, 23
Equipment
  acquisition of, 5
  capital, 15
  facilities layout and, 68–69
Exploding, 43, 97
Extrinsic models of forecasting, 91

Facilities layout, 15–16, 60
  analyzing, 65–67
  cost comparisons of, 64–65
  data needed for planning, 67–68
  energy management and, 70
  equipment and, 68–69
  maintenance operations and, 69–70
  manufacturing layout, 62–65
  materials handling and, 67
  objectives of, 61
  service layout, 65
Facilities location, 15
  break-even analysis of, 58
  factors that affect, 54–56
  simulation model for, 58–59
  transportation method of linear programming for, 59–60
  weighted factor analysis of, 56–58
Factories, early, 10
Federal Anti-Price Discrimination Act of 1936, 137–38
Finite loading, 101
Firestone Tire and Rubber Company, 41
Fixed-position layout, 63–64
Flow diagrams, 74–75
Flow-process production, 19
Ford, Henry, 10
Ford Motor Company, 179, 185
Forecasting, 16
  assessing methods of, 91–92
  demand and objectives, 85–86
  evaluating methods of, 92
  extrinsic models of, 91
  intrinsic models of, 87–90
  judgmental methods of, 87
  methods of, 86–87, 89–91
  selecting a method of, 86
Foreign purchasing, 145–46
Forward buying, 131

Gantt charts, 103–4
General Motors, 5, 56
Gilbreth, Frank and Lillian, 10, 77
Gillette, 33
Goldratt, Eliyahu, 104
Government purchasing, 144
Graphical methods and aggregate planning, 94
Group/cellular layout, 63

Hand-to-mouth buying, 131
Harris, F. W., 10
Heuristic decision rules and aggregate planning, 94
Hewlett Packard, 46–48

Infinite loading, 101
Inputs, acquisition of, 5, 7
Intermittent production, 19
Intrinsic models of forecasting, 87, 89–90
Inventory management, 17
  costs, 151–54
  economic lot size, 150, 157–59
  economic order quantity, 150, 154–59
  functions of, 149–51
  just-in-time strategies and, 166–68
  materials requirements planning and, 163–66
  record-keeping requirements, 169–70
  safety stocks and uncertainty, 159–63
  storage and material handling, 168–69
  warehousing (stock keeping), 168
Inventory status file, 95, 97, 99–101
Invoice clearance and payment, 142–43

Job-shop production, 18
Judgmental methods of forecasting, 87
Jungle, The (Sinclair), 10
Just-in-Time (JIT) inventory systems, 11, 104, 166–68

Layout. *See* Facilities layout
Line balancing, 66
List price, 138
Location. *See* Facilities location
Lockheed Aircraft Corporation, 105
Lot tolerance percent defective (LTPD), 190

Machinery and Allied Products Institute, 124

McRae's Bluebook, 134
Maintenance operations, 69–70
Manufacturing
  layout, 62–64
  types of, 18–19
Marketing layout, 65
Market prices, 139
Market research, product design and, 39–40
Market surveys, 87
Mass production, early, 10
Master production schedule, 95, 97
Material, acquisition of, 5
Material/sales ratio in manufacturing, 117–19
Materials-management concept, 126–128
Materials requirements planning (MRP), 11, 95, 97–101
  bill of materials and, 95, 97, 98
  inventory management and, 163–66
  inventory status file and, 95, 97, 99–101
  master production schedule and, 95, 97
  purchasing department and, 130
  safety stock and lead time in, 165
Mathematical programming and aggregate planning, 94
Mean absolute deviation (MAD), 92
Microprocessors, 11
Minicomputers, 11
Minority vendors, 134
Modular design, 38–39
Motor Carrier Act, 145
Multiple-activity chart, 76, 77

National Association of Purchasing Management (NAPM), 25
Negotiation of price, 139–40
Netting process, 97
Numerical-control (N/C) machines, 68

Office layout, 65
Operation chart, 65, 77, 78
Operations research (OR), 11
Ordering costs, 152

Outputs, 8

Periodic review model, 158–59
Personnel, acquisition of, 5, 7
PERT/CPM
   analysis, 105–6
   background of, 105
   critical path, 108–9
   determining earliest and latest event times, 107–8
   network diagramming, 106–7
Pilot production run, 41–42
Planning for production, 16, 92–95
Polaroid camera, 31–32
Pricing
   laws that determine, 137–38
   methods buyer can use in establishing, 138–40
Process chart symbols, 72, 73, 74
Process layout, 62–63, 66
Process sampling, 193
Producer's risk, 189
Product
   availability, 33
   definition of, 3
   description, 42–45
   design and development, 14, 29–51
   level of, 32
   life cycle, 30–32
   line, 32–33
   research and development, 34–36, 45–49
   specifications, 43
   strategy, 32–33
   testing, 41
Product design
   computer-aided design, 39
   impact of resources on, 40–41
   market research and, 39–40
   materials for, 36
   modular design, 38–39
   pilot production run, 41–42
   standardization, 37–38
   testing of products, 41
   value analysis/value engineering, 36–37
Product/line layout, 63, 66
Production
   function, 5–8
   planning, 16, 92–95
   scheduling, 16, 95–105
Production/operations management (POM)
   careers in, 23–26
   definition of, 1
   functions of, 14–18
   future of, 12–14
   goals of, 21–23
   history of, 9–12
   merging of other business functions with, 8–9
   reasons for studying, 4–5
   type of organizations covered by, 3
Productivity as a goal, 22
Profit-leverage effect, 120
Program evaluation and review technique. *See* PERT/CPM
Progress control, 104–5
Project production, 19
Purchase agreement, preparation of the, 140–41
Purchase order
   log, 143
   unpriced, 138
Purchasing Function: From Strategy to Image, The, 124
Purchasing managers
   role of, 7, 17
   titles and salaries for, 113
Purchasing/materials management, 17
   ABC analysis, 129–30
   bill of materials and, 132
   centralized vs. decentralized, 123–25
   changing responsibilities of, 125–26
   competitive position and, 121–22
   describing quality, 132–33
   determining price, 137–40
   efficiency and, 120–21
   follow-up and expediting orders, 141–42
   future, of, 143–47
   image and, 122
   importance of, 117–23
   as an information source, 122–23
   invoice clearance and payment, 142–43

maintenance of records, 143
material/sales ratio in manufacturing, 117–19
materials-management concept, 126–28
materials requirements planning and, 130
objectives of, 114–16
prerogatives of, 128
profit-leverage effect, 120
receipt and inspection of orders, 142
recognition of purchasing needs, 130
requisition for, 130–33
return-on-assets effect, 120, 121
selecting vendors, 133–37
steps for the standard purchasing system, 128–30
strategy, 146–47
as a training ground, 122
Purchasing Organizational Relationships, 125, 128

Quality
batch sampling and, 188–93
circles, 182
control, 17–18
costs, 182–87
definition of, 174–75
dimension of, 175–76
employees and, 177
factors that affect, 179–82
importance of, 196
organization needed for quality control, 194–96
packaging and, 178
process design and, 177
process sampling and, 193
product, 174
product design and, 176
production process and, 177–78
raw materials and, 177
screening and, 187–88
storage and, 178–79
total quality control program, 179
transportation and, 178
Quality, describing
by blueprint, 133
by brand or trade name, 132
by market grade, 132
by performance specification, 133
by sample, 133
by word picture, 133
Quotation, salesperson's, 138–39

Radio Shack, 33
Recalls, product, 41
Recordkeeping, 143
inventory and requirements for, 169–70
Reorder points, 160
Repetitive production, 18–19
Requisition for purchasing, 130–33
Research and development (R&D), product, 34–36
evaluating, 45–49
Resources, product design and impact of a company's, 40–41
Responsiveness as a goal, 22–23
Return-on-assets (ROA) effect, 120, 121
Robinson-Patman Act, 137–38
Romig, H. G., 11
Route sheet, 45, 46
Running sum of the forecast errors (RSFE), 92

Safety stocks, 151
computation of, 160–62
lead times and, 159–60
materials requirements planning and, 165
one-time order quantities and, 162–63
reorder points and, 160
service level policy and, 160
Scheduling production, 16, 95–105
capacity requirements planning, 101
development of detailed schedules, 103–4
master schedule, 95, 97
materials requirements planning, 95, 97–101
progress control/shop-floor control, 104–5
sequencing jobs, 101–3
Screening, 187–88

Service layout, 65
Services
  designing, 42
  purchasing of, 146
  types of, 19–21
Setup costs, 152
Sherman Anti-Trust Act, 137
Shewhart, W. A., 11
Shop-floor control, 104–5
Sinclair, Upton, 10
Single sourcing, 144
Small Parts, Inc., 5
Smith, Adam, 10
Spreadsheets and aggregate planning, 94
Staggers Rail Act, 145
Standardization, 37–38
Stopwatch time study, 79–81
Storage and material handling, 168–69
Storage layout, 65
Sweets Catalogs, 134

Taylor, Frederick W., 10
Testing, product, 41
Therbligs, 77
Thomas Register of American Manufacturers, 134
Time-and-motion study, 81–82
Time-series models of forecasting, 87–90
Total quality control (TQC) program, 179
Transformation, technology vs. methodology, 7
Transportation method of linear programming, 59–60
Transportation services, purchasing, 144–45

Traveling requisition, 131–32
Try Us '89, 134

Unit cost, 22
U.S. Bureau of the Census, 117
U.S. Navy Special Projects Office, 105

Value analysis/value engineering (VA/VE), 36–37
Vendors, 133
  directories for selecting, 134
  establishing an approved list of, 136, 143
  evaluating, 135–36
  experience ratings for, 137
  minorities as, 134

Waiting-line theory, 11
Warehousing (stock keeping), 168
Wealth of Nations, The (Smith), 10
Weighted factor analysis, 56–58
Work design and measurement, 16
Work measurement, 77, 79–82
Work sampling, 82
Work study, 70–75
Work-study charts, 72–75

Yard layout, 65
Young, John, 48

Zero Defects, 182